15 —

MOVING
TARGETS

MOVING TARGETS

WOMEN, MURDER AND REPRESENTATION

Edited by Helen Birch

UNIVERSITY OF CALIFORNIA PRESS

Berkeley • Los Angeles

University of California Press
Berkeley and Los Angeles, California

Originally Published by Virago Press Limited

Copyright © in each contribution held by the author 1993

Published 1994 by The University of California Press

Library of Congress Cataloging-in-Publication Data

Moving targets : women, murder and representation / edited by Helen
Birch.
     p.   cm.
   Includes bibliographical references and index.
   ISBN 0-520-08573-6 (alk. paper).—ISBN 0-520-08576-0 (pbk. :
alk. paper)
   1. Women murderers.   2. Sex discrimination in criminal justice
administration.   3. Feminist theory.   I. Birch, Helen.
   HV6046.M65   1994
   364.1'523'082—dc20   93-25139
                                                             CIP

Printed in the United States of America
9 8 7 6 5 4 3 2 1

The paper used in this publication meets the minimum requirements
of American National Standard for Information Sciences—Permanence
of Paper for Printed Library Materials, ANSI Z39.48–1984. ⊚

Contents

Acknowledgements

For support and stimulation thanks to Susan and Leo Castillejo, Lorraine Gamman, Stella Kane, Suzanne Moore, my Mum and Dad, Liz Murray and Briar Wood.

Thanks especially to John Lyttle, who shared my obsessions and made me laugh when I needed it most. This book is for him.

Introduction

Helen Birch

Glancing through the British press over the last couple of years, a casual observer might be forgiven for thinking that something very strange had happened to the female of the species. Suddenly, the newspapers were full of reports of women killing spouses, lovers and each other with a variety of weapons and in a number of different circumstances; feature articles, drawing together quite disparate cases, inquired whether the traditionally passive, gentler sex was indeed becoming more violent.

Yet women do not often kill. In England and Wales, only about 14 per cent of suspects in homicides recorded between 1983 and 1990 were women. Of these, the vast majority were domestic homicides, in which a woman kills her husband or lover, followed not far behind by the killing of children.[1] Nor do the numbers appear to be increasing. So why this sudden surge of interest?

In recent years, the rampaging female has become a new cliché of Hollywood cinema, stabbing and shooting her way to notoriety in a range of popular films from *Thelma and Louise* to *The Hand That Rocks the Cradle*, *Basic Instinct* and *Single White Female*. That the real-life dramas of women who kill rarely resemble those of their celluloid contemporaries is a moot point; as audiences become more image-literate and the recessionary 1990s force the news media to grab readers with a shocking headline or a startling image, the always shifting boundaries between fact and fiction, reality and representation, have in some cases become so blurred as to be almost indistinguishable. And precisely because she is relatively rare, the woman killer presents a far more dramatic spectacle than her male counterpart. Male violence is, after all, old news.

Another, more prosaic reason is that women's groups, galvanized by the rising numbers of women reporting domestic violence to police (the number of cases reported to the Metropolitan Police in 1992 was up 46 per cent) and seeking sanctuary from violent partners in refuges, have forced the issue of why women kill on to the political agenda. While the arguments about motive continue to rage, the different sentences meted out to women who kill, and the legal arguments used to defend their actions, raise a number of questions pertinent to all women.

In February 1990, thirty-six-year-old Sara Thornton was convicted of murdering her husband Malcolm, an ex-policeman. She had stabbed him in the stomach as he lay in an alcoholic stupor at their home in Warwickshire. Thornton had been repeatedly battered by her husband during their ten-month marriage. Once, he knocked her unconscious and threatened to kill both her and her ten-year-old daughter. On other occasions he had punched her in the eye and on the back of the head, broken an ashtray over her hand and threatened to throw her through a plate-glass window. On the night of 14 June 1989, she and Malcolm had a furious row. Malcolm told her to leave and take her daughter Luise, or Luise would be 'dead meat'. She ran into the kitchen to find his truncheon to defend herself, found a knife instead and sharpened it. When her husband passed out, she plunged the knife into his stomach. She then called an ambulance, but Malcolm Thornton died four hours later in hospital.

At her trial, Sara Thornton's lawyers submitted a plea of diminished responsibility: that she was suffering from some abnormality of mind at the time of the killing which substantially impaired her responsibility for her actions. The jury disagreed, and Thornton was sent to jail for life.

In July 1991, she appealed against her sentence and again lost. This time her lawyers pleaded provocation, defined as 'a sudden and temporary loss of control'. Two days later, Joseph McGrail walked free from the courtroom with a two-year suspended sentence after successfully pleading that he had been provoked into punching his 'nagging' common-law wife to death. Passing sentence, Mr Justice Popplewell said that the woman he had killed would 'try the patience of a saint'. On hearing the news, Sara Thornton immediately began a hunger strike which lasted several weeks.

The stark differences in the way these two cases were treated in the courts prompted fierce debate among women's groups and women's refuge organizations, and in legal and political circles. (Lorraine Radford discusses these issues in depth in Chapter 7 of this book.) The appeal verdict, coming within a few weeks of the British release of Ridley Scott's rape-revenge movie *Thelma and Louise*, sent the press into a feeding frenzy, its appetite whetted by what appeared to be an increasing number of sensational new cases. The stories of Christine Dryland, an army major's wife who ran over and killed her husband's lover, thirty-four-year-old Marika Sparfeld, in her car, and twenty-one-year-old Michelle Taylor, convicted, with her younger sister Lisa, of the murder of her lover's wife – a particularly vicious killing in which the victim was stabbed fifty-four times – made the front pages of the tabloids, prompting one to state that 'spurned women make the most violent revenge killers', linking the case to a tradition of scorned women killers going back to Ruth Ellis, who was hanged for killing her lover in 1955.[2] For feminists, though, there was also some cause for celebration: Pamela Sainsbury received a probationary sentence for killing her abusive husband; June Scotland and Amelia Rossiter, both convicted of the murder of their violent spouses, were freed on appeal.

The story of Susan Christie, a private in the Ulster

Defence Regiment, however, was less salutary. When she began her affair with Captain Duncan McAllister, an older, married man, she was still a virgin. The affair lasted several months until, in November 1990, she suspected that she was pregnant and said she had suffered a miscarriage. Shortly afterwards, she invited his wife Penny McAllister out for a walk in the woods, and cut her throat with a butcher's boning knife. At her trial in June 1992, Lord Justice Kelly, responding to the jury's majority verdict of not guilty of murder, sentenced twenty-three-year-old Christie to five years in prison on the grounds that she had been subject to an 'overwhelming emotion' and was suffering from pre-menstrual tension. Legal experts believe she could be released within eighteen months.[3]

The contrast between the leniency shown towards Susan Christie and the severity of Sara Thornton's sentence presents a number of difficult questions for feminists. On one level, it indicates how the judicial system, reflecting the attitudes of society as a whole, often punishes women who step beyond the bounds of acceptable female behaviour, while demonstrating a chivalric, paternal attitude to those whose acts of violence can apparently be explained by reference to their hormones (biology) or emotions (irrationality). When, as in the case of Sara Thornton, a woman's violence appears as a response to anger, her refusal to be a victim (particularly where she kills a man), the full weight of the law is brought to bear. But in cases where diminished responsibility, a kind of temporary madness induced by anything from PMT to the experience of systematic abuse, can be shown to account for her actions, the issue of a woman's moral agency, her responsibility, disappears. She killed because she was out of control.

The diminished responsibility defence is a problematic one for women, many of whom cherish, along with the more conservative elements of society, the notion that women are inherently more peaceable than men, life-givers rather than life-takers. For them, the fact of a

4

woman engaged in an act of violence begs the search for a motive – if a woman kills, it must be out of desperation or fear, even when, as in the case of Michelle and Lisa Taylor, the violence used seems disproportionate or misplaced. While it is true that when women kill, they usually just want the victim out of the way and do not resort to the kind of frenzied attack typical of the male sexual murder, the idea that women are capable of extreme violence is anathema to most of us. Meanwhile, in courtrooms and newspapers throughout the Western world, women who kill are divided into two camps: bad – wicked or inhuman; or mad – not like 'ordinary' women. The extreme defines the norm.

But the concept of diminished responsibility obviously plays an important role in allowing certain evidence to be presented in court which might otherwise be deemed irrelevant. An explanation of the effects of a history of domestic violence on a woman, for example, is of course crucial to our understanding of why she did what she did. And while there may well have been mitigating circumstances in the case of Susan Christie, her representation as a victim (she was 'driven' to kill Penny McAllister by dint of her emotional state and her biological predestination) denies her any agency at all in what was a particularly brutal, calculated killing. If we really want women to be treated equally in the courts, in the workplace and in the home, we have to distinguish between the contexts that help to explain our gendered responses to particular events and which can lend a logic to extreme acts of violence, and those which, as the feminist criminologist Frances Heidensohn has put it, are so easily 'turned into moral fables about the lives of the women involved'[4] and, by extension, those of all women. Because women have traditionally internalized their feelings of anger or injustice, does this mean we have to pathologize those who do not?

It is one of the purposes of this book to explore some of

these issues – of agency, legal discourses and the way the counterpointing of women and murder in fact and fiction so often marks the limits of socially acceptable femininity. The female serial killer (which Candice Skrapec discusses in Chapter 10 of this book), for example, disrupts some of our most sacred ideas about women. The case of Aileen 'Lee' Wuornos, a prostitute who confessed to shooting and killing seven men in 'self-defence' in 1990, and is now on death row in Florida, has excited considerable controversy. Some women, quick to place Wuornos as yet another victim of the oppressive patriarchy, argue that her abusive childhood drove her into prostitution, which then became a significant factor in the crimes. One more aggressive trick was enough to drive her over the edge: she wanted to turn the tables. Law enforcement agencies, on the other hand, caught out by the spectacle of a gun-toting female murderer, have dubbed her 'America's first woman serial killer' and argue that she is self-conscious about what being a serial killer means; in other words, murdering men was her way of courting celebrity. It is somewhere between moving targets like these that the stories of and about women who kill begin to make sense.

An eye for an eye

The case of the
Papin sisters

Nicole Ward Jouve

On the evening of 2 February 1933, in the quiet rural French town of Le Mans, a Monsieur Lancelin, a well-to-do retired solicitor, was annoyed. His wife and daughter, who were supposed to join him at a relative's for dinner, were late. He tried to phone home: no reply. He became worried, went to his house: the door was locked from the inside; nobody answered when he rang. Yet the maids at least must be home: a dim light shone in their attic window. M. Lancelin went to the police. A policeman climbed through a window at the back of the house. And the horror began. Madame Lancelin and her daughter, a young woman, lay across the landing. They had been murdered, were battered and slashed. Most horrible of all, their eyes had been torn from their sockets: so vile had been the fury of their assailant.

He must have been a mad burglar, a vicious and sadistic monster. And what about the maids, two young women who lived in the house, who had shown no sign of life, had failed to answer the door . . . ? They also . . . The policemen rushed upstairs to the attic bedroom. It was locked from the inside. They smashed the door open. The maids, the two sisters, Christine and Léa Papin, lay in each other's arms, in bed. They were clean, if dishevelled; they wore only pink dressing-gowns. Next to the bed was a hammer soiled with blood. They had killed their mistresses, they said.

*   *   *

In the second volume of her autobiography, Simone de Beauvoir has produced a good account of the reaction of the French intelligentsia. The case immediately attracted a great deal of attention. The trial, which took place in September, was attended by forty Paris journalists, reporting for a fascinated readership:

> The tragedy of the Papin sisters was immediately
> intelligible to us. In Rouen [where Simone de Beauvoir
> was teaching at the time] as in Le Mans, perhaps even
> among the mothers of my own pupils, there certainly
> were some of those women who subtract the price of
> a broken plate from their maids' wages, who put on
> white gloves to track down motes of dust that have
> been left on the furniture: in our eyes, they deserved
> death, a hundred times over. With their waved hair
> and white collars, how good Christine and Léa seemed,
> on the old photograph which the papers published!
> How could they have become the haggard furies
> which the snapshots taken after the drama offered to
> public indignation? What was responsible was the
> orphanage in which they had been put as children,
> the way they had been weaned, the whole hideous
> system devised by so-called good people and which
> produces madmen, murderers and monsters. The horror
> of society's grinding-machine could only be exposed by
> a corresponding, exemplary horror. The two sisters had
> made themselves the instrument and martyrs of a dark
> justice. The papers told us that they loved each other,
> and we dreamt of their nights' caresses and hatred, in
> the desert of their attic.[1]

Simone de Beauvoir goes on to explain that she and Sartre ('we') had been bewildered by the defence's plea of paranoid delirium, and then convinced by it. It had meant that the murders were not a gesture of freedom, more one of blind terror. They were 'loath to believe this' and continued 'dimly to admire' the sisters. But when the psychiatrists for the prosecution declared them sane, they were 'indignant'; and so incensed by the complacency of the bourgeois members of the jury who sentenced the elder sister to death despite the fact that it was now evident that she was insane that they came to see society as worse than the sisters, 'tarnished' as their crime might have been by insanity. Since the victims were 'bourgeoises', the murderers had been made into 'scapegoats', so that 'so-called civilised society', which was no more enlightened than 'so-called primitive societies', could continue on its repressive path.

The passage is filled with a strange irony. Strange, because while the tone suggests that the writer is mocking the rigidity of young idealistic Parisian intellectuals such as Sartre and herself and some of their philosopher friends, nothing further is said to show that their wish that the sisters had killed lucidly – as existential heroes before the letter, as it were – was patronizing, or that other readings of the case might have been tenable. The mature Simone, who wrote this passage, seems unaltered in her hatred of petty-bourgeois employers and mother figures, or in her dislike of the 'grinding-machine' that produces murderers, then makes them into 'scapegoats'. What is noteworthy here, however, is that when you replace the passage inside the chorus of actions and representations that the case of the Papin sisters attracted in 1933, its sense of easy recognition strikes an unusual chord: the crimes were immediately 'intelligible'; the young Jean-Paul and the young Simone had no trouble detecting the 'mystifications'. But everybody else thought the case was deeply mysterious. Reason was struck blind by the sisters, as if their plucking their mistresses' eyes had metaphorically put out the eyes of the interpreters.

Take Jacques Lacan's essay, based on the findings of the psychiatrist for the defence, Dr Logre, and published in 1933 in a Surrealist review:

> The two sisters, 28 and 21, have been for years in the household of these honourable bourgeois . . . It has been said that they were model servants, that people envied the Lancelins for having them; they were mystery-servants also, for if the masters seem to have been strangely lacking in human sympathy, nothing indicates that the servants' haughty indifference was simply a response to that lack; from one group to the other, 'nobody talked'. This silence, however, could not be empty, even if it was obscure in the eyes of the actors.
>
> One evening, 2 February, this darkness is materialized by a banal blowing of the fuses. It has been brought about by the clumsiness of the sisters, and the mistresses, who are not there, have already shown a quick temper on lesser occasions. What mood did the mother and daughter show when upon their return they disovered the slender disaster?[2]

Christine and Léa Papin had been about to do the ironing. The iron blew the fuses through no fault of their own. Mme Lancelin had been extremely annoyed when this had happened before. The iron had just been mended. And at that point, Mme Lancelin and her daughter, who had gone out shopping and were supposed to go straight from there to their dinner, turned up unexpectedly at the house. Found it in darkness . . . And . . .

And this is where the blinding, as well as the blindness, occurs. It is twofold (of course: there are two sisters; everything has, as Lacan points out in his article, a double dimension here). First, the motive: how can something as '*mince*' (Lacan: thin) as a damaged iron or blown fuses provoke such a savage and disproportionate murder? Second, the idea of metamorphosis: how can model servants turn into – as the sensational review *Détective* put it – 'enraged ewes'?

Let us note – interestingly – that Simone de Beauvoir owns that she and Sartre did find the second black or blind spot, the metamorphosis, puzzling: 'what good girls they seemed . . . how could they become the haggard furies . . . ?'. But Simone, speaking for once very much for herself – not saying 'we', as she does throughout most of the passage – has no trouble with motive. She has only to think of the mothers of some of her pupils, of her own anger at examples of domestic bourgeois tyranny, and it makes the case 'immediately intelligible' to her. Unlike the communist paper *L'Humanité*, she does not have to blacken the situation, imagine that a system of slavery existed in the Lancelin household. I do find this interesting: hers is a lone voice, and one that seems to arise from a gender experience – not just a female experience of domesticity, but identifying with the killers as daughters against the mothers. It is a point of entry which the male commentators of the period seem to be lacking.

Two famous journalists reporting on the case, the Tharaud brothers, on whose articles Lacan's paper was based, stressed the darkness at its core:

No photograph can give an idea of the mystery that enters [into the courtroom] with these two girls. Léa, the younger one, all in black, her hands inside the pockets of her coat, her eyes open, but you know not what they're seeing. Christine . . . remains motionless with a stiffness that seems corpse-like.

Her eyes are closed, and from 1 p.m., when the trial opens, to 3 a.m., when it closes, she will not open them once, not even to reply to the questions she is asked.[3]

One has her eyes open, but she does not see. The other has her eyes closed. The sisters physically embody the lack of rational vision from which the onlookers suffer. For, as one of the Tharaud brothers goes on to say, how do you reconcile the fact that everything that is said at the trial should evoke horror, but that, looking at the sisters, 'not once did I feel a horror corresponding to that act'? For them also, then, the darkness arises from the metamorphosis – but also from the lack of motive: how can such 'butchery' have taken place when the motive was 'nothing': *'un motif de rien'*, the episode of the iron?

Of course (you might say), women would understand the charge of domestic details better than men, and this is what Simone de Beauvoir is doing. So what? The real mystery, which is the mystery of madness – paranoid delirium, as Lacan calls it, and as even de Beauvoir accepts – remains intact, a matter for psychoanalytic explanation.

Yet the fascination of murder cases is that they do not stop at the crime itself, the perpetrators, the victims, the immediate surroundings. Every representation or explanation that is offered becomes part of it. Murders – partly because they touch chords we had rather not allow to vibrate in everyday circumstances, partly because they awake in us the desire for retributive violence (Lacan speaks of the gruesome literal appropriateness of the phrase 'an eye for an eye') – reveal things which nothing else reveals as clearly. The case of the Papin sisters is particularly significant in terms of gender.

It was the Surrealists Breton and Péret who, in a short, dramatic piece in their review *Le Surréalisme au service de la révolution*, launched the sisters as a literary phenomenon. Holding the notion of gender in mind, let us see how they tackle point two, metamorphosis: what mysterious alchemy changed model servants into 'enraged ewes'?

The Papin sisters were brought up in a convent in Le Mans. Then their mother placed them in a bourgeois home. For six years they bore observations, demands, insults, with the most perfect submissiveness. Fear,

weariness, humiliations, were slowly begetting hatred
inside them: hatred, the very sweet alcohol that secretly
consoles, for it promises to add physical strength to
violence one day. When the day came, Léa and Christine
Papin repaid evil in its own coin, a hot iron coin.
They literally massacred their mistresses, plucking out
their eyes, crushing their heads. Then they carefully
washed themselves and, freed, indifferent, went to
bed. Lightning had fallen, the wood was burnt, the sun
definitely put out.

They had come fully armed out of one of Maldoror's
songs . . .[4]

Maldoror is the satanic rebel and eponymous hero of
Lautréamont's poem *Les Chants de Maldoror*, one of the
Surrealists' favourite texts. The early, succinct details here
register the female gender of the sisters: the convent
education, the nun-like obedience, being in the mother's
power. The final image is of Athena, emerging fully
armed out of Zeus' head. Athena is a female goddess:
femaleness seems to be consistent. Let us reflect, however,
that the coming to power of Athena in the history of
Athens signifies the waning of mother-right. Athena is
born from a male god, without the intervention of any
woman. Did the crime emancipate the girls from their
mother, from all mothers? Furthermore, in this piece,
Maldoror, a male hero-poet, conceives violence, as his
creator, the male poet Lautréamont, conceived him. And
in the photographic montage designed to accompany the
article, the sisters 'before' look like proper young women.
'After', they do indeed look like young men. Indeed, the
montage graphically exemplifies – and perhaps contrives
– the metamorphosis. You cannot look at those two pairs of
faces, at the captions 'before' and 'after', without thinking
about the crime that separates them, that made the one into
the other. In the context of the Surrealists' article, Christine
in particular does rather look like . . . André Breton.

Does that mean that through the act of killing, women become men – that a nobler, a revolutionary, male and poetic self is thus born? Does this further imply that women as women cannot emancipate themselves, cannot kill? It certainly looks as if Breton and Péret, through this passage and through the montage, were recuperating what they saw as the poetic charge of the deed for themselves, young men such as themselves. They glorify the heroes, not heroines, who rebelled against the bourgeois order, got rid of the mothers. The transformation is effected through the image of hatred as a sweet alcohol, breeding violence and physical strength in the womb-like sisters. They are almost Pythonesses from whom the liberating, vengeful male god can at last be born.

The protagonist of Sartre's short story 'Erostrate', written in the mid 1930s, has either been reading Breton and Péret, or is of a like mind:

I have seen photographs of these two beautiful girls, the servants who killed and devastated their mistresses. I have seen their photographs 'before' and 'after'. 'Before', their faces swayed like tame flowers above their embroidered collars. They exhaled hygiene and a savoury honesty. A discreet pair of curling tongs had given their hair an identical wave. And, even more reassuring than their curled hair, their collars and their air of being at the photographer's, was their likeness as sisters, their so proper resemblance, that straightaway spoke of blood bonds and the natural roots of the family group. 'After', their faces shone like blazing fires. They had the bare necks of those about to be beheaded. Wrinkles everywhere, horrible wrinkles of fear and hatred, folds, holes in the flesh as if a beast with claws had gone round and round on their faces. And those eyes, always those large bottomless black eyes . . . Yet they did not look alike. Each bore in her own way the memory of their common crime.[5]

This is obviously a complicated passage, with several possible readings. It is fiction, spoken by an anarchist, out to commit an act of self-regarding terrorism. Erostrate is glorifying himself as criminal-to-be whilst and through glorifying the sisters. He is voicing his hatred of maidenly bourgeois propriety, but there is also a mixture of fascination and sadism there: he insists on the eyes, with the knowledge of what these women did to other women's eyes. He invents or adduces the decapitation motif: if anything, the sisters' necks are more bare in the 'before' than in the 'after' photograph; and it is as if he projected the hurt that the sisters inflicted on their victims on to the 'after' faces. I cannot see those holes and wrinkles he describes. Is the gloating, the fascination, meant to portray the mind of Erostrate? Only the mind of Erostrate? It seems evident to me that there are some recognizable Jean-Paul Sartre motifs here also: distaste for the ideology and the bourgeois order of the family. Distaste for neo-fascist theories, those that insist on blood bonds and sameness. The speaker's horror of the sisters' resemblance in the 'before' photograph conveys Sartre's individualism. The apparent gratuitousness of the deed introduces the Sartrean notion of freedom. Yet one thing is remarkable here. The gender of the sisters is visible only when they are being perceived as potential victims: when their *bien-pensant* look enables the speaker to voice his hatred of *bien-pensant* women – it is as if what had to be murdered was precisely this quality in the sisters, as if the 'after' women had killed the 'before' women. They are also perceived as female when their exposed necks, their belaboured faces, suggest decapitation or torture.

As killers, as sadists themselves, they are never seen.

It is, to say the least, worthy of note that male writers who are revolutionary in their lifestyle, discourses, poetic and fictional voices, are so conservative in their reading and writing of gender. Neither the specific class and familial reality of the maid in a domestic household,

15

nor her sexual position, nor indeed the particular history
and tragedy of the Papin sisters, bother them. Their
deed becomes an empty vessel. Their bodies and the
(hysterical?) inscriptions that can be read on their faces,
that can be imagined on the eyeless bodies of the victims,
become the bearer, the trace and the vacant container that
enable the male poet or terrorist protagonist to make
divine and murderous metaphor. The Breton and Péret
text evokes familiar Surrealist tropes, deflagration and
phosphorescence and sudden illumination ('lightning had
fallen'; 'their faces shone like blazing fires' in the Sartre),
black suns ('the sun was definitely put out'), Bataille's *The
Story of the Eye* with its displacements on to male genitals,
its reference to Dali and to the eye as a 'cannibalistic titbit'.
A 'phallic' tool ('the axe had fallen') replaces the servant's
bare hands and use of any domestic implement that was
to hand. The overall effect is very similar to what a conservative poet like Valéry might have achieved with his
'Pythie' whom the god Apollo possesses, through whose
writing and wordless contortions Divine Language is born.
It makes the sisters into the sufferers and recipients, not
the actors, of their deeds. And in the process, it raises
questions often raised elsewhere as to the use of women
(in particular of lower-class women), and the imaginary
use of women's bodies, by left-wing ideologies.

But perhaps one must turn to psychoanalysis for an
open exploration of the mysteries of the case, the nothing
motif, the metamorphosis of the sisters, the missing act?
Certainly this was what Lacan thought; what many since
have thought. Lacan's essay, written straight after the
publication of his thesis on *De la Psychose paranoïaque
dans ses rapports avec la personnalité,* [6] endorses the radical
findings of the psychiatrist for the defence, and fleshes
them out. It has been seen as seminal, the first formulation
of the mirror stage.

For Lacan, there was one powerful sister, Christine,
exerting her influence over the younger, more timid sister,

Léa. Both sisters harboured a homosexual tendency directed at each other. The fact that sister loved sister shows
that there was a strong element of narcissism in that love.
Each sister loved the being most like herself, the being
in the mirror. The 'sacrificial exigencies' of society were
integrated as sadism. A love–hate relationship was at
work, making the unattainable-because-tabooed sister into
a persecuting figure, just as President Schreber, whom
Freud analysed and found to be paranoid, had made God,
the loved father figure, into a persecutor. A glass obstacle,
the complaint of Narcissus, forever prevents the sufferers
from this particular psychosis from being liberated from
this love–hate relation to the persecuting figure. 'Between
themselves the sisters were unable to take the distance that
is needed to hurt one another. True Siamese souls, they
form a world forever closed.'

Lacan suggests that the sisters killed their mistresses
because they saw in them their own mirror-image, 'the
mirage of their own complaint. It is their own suffering
that they project and hate in that other couple of women',
and they pluck out their eyes 'as the Bacchae castrated'.
They kill their mistresses as they might kill each other
and themselves. Too close, too 'Siamese' to take the right
distance to hit at each other. And also female, therefore
castrated, they are punishing other women for their own
native mutilation.

A recent book by Francis Dupré, a Lacanian analyst,
admiringly develops Lacan's analysis and adds to it a
multiplicity of explanations. In particular, Dupré says,
the verdict of schizophrenia, offered by the psychiatrist
who examined Christine after her death sentence had
been commuted to life imprisonment, must be added
to that of paranoia. Dupré's book is called *La Solution
du passage à l'acte: Le double crime des soeurs Papin*. The
title itself suggests the answer: the deed, the murders,
which contemporary commentators saw as the mystery,
was itself the solution, the only solution, to the unbearable

pressures created by a paranoid state that was verging on schizophrenia. That the deed should be the solution means in a sense that it cannot be spoken, it cannot be understood in words. Dupré argues that it is at the opposite end of the spectrum to Freud's Schreber, for whom, on the contrary, verbal systems proliferated. With Christine and Léa, it is the deed that speaks. They themselves have nothing to say, nothing about their deed. When, under lengthy questioning, they produced varying and self-contradictory reports, Léa very much modelled herself on what she was told Christine had said. Their testimony, you could say, defies reason. For instance, Léa claimed that she had held one of Mme Lancelin's arms pinned down, her head back with another hand, and battered her with a pitcher. The judge: 'You had three hands then?' Léa: 'No, but I accomplished my foul deed just as I told you'. Christine also produced some extraordinary answers, then refused to speak. Muteness accompanies blindness. The act confirms Lacan: 'This silence could not be empty, even if it was obscure in the eyes of the actors'.

Some of what Lacan says and most of what Dupré says comes across as sympathetic, ingenious, convincing, or at least persuasive. I certainly have no psychoanalytic expertise or counter-expertise to offer. If, however, I read their texts as texts, still with the idea of gender in mind, I am struck by the concordance of what they say with the Surrealists or Sartre. Lacan was, after all, writing for the Surrealist review *Le Minotaure*; he was the Surrealists' friend. Perhaps, then, one should not be so surprised at the recurrence of explanations that make the sisters into non-actors (passive), non-speakers (silent), non-knowers (ignorant/innocent).

1. Passive: They are compared to the Bacchae, who in a state of frenzy, possessed by the spirit of a male god (Dionysos), murder a male god (Dionysos). Not only is it the male in them that kills, but the enigma that

bedevils them is that of female castration, a 'gaping wound'. It is their impotence, their frustration with their own inability to act out their desire for each other, that urges them.

2. Silent: Dupré's entire book is based on this: they cannot speak, they can only act.

3. Ignorant/innocent: Lacan presents them as unaware of their own desire, as realizing it only after the murders, when Christine, in a state of despair and madness in jail, throws herself on to her sister, screaming, 'Léa, say yes'. There is strong evidence, however, to suggest that the sisters were lovers, and that Christine, a country girl, was not as 'innocent' of the 'mystery of life' as Lacan says.

Not only, therefore, is there in the psychoanalytic accounts offered here the same assumptions as one sees everywhere else – designed, it seems, however unconsciously, to keep women in their place. Active/passive; speaker/silent; knowing/ignorant: the binarisms that Derrida, Cixous and Irigaray have pointed to as the hallmark of phallogocentrism, that keep 'women' permanently in the inferior position, are at work. The discourse of psychoanalysis may well be as culturally relative and questionable as every other one – all the more so as the explanations offered in some instances contradict or disregard the known facts.

Dupré's sense that an intuition of genius being at work here, the gaps or mistakes do not matter; his desire to demonstrate the brilliance of Lacan's article despite the fact that his own findings show that he seriously misread things, helps to perpetuate stereotypes which, in the detail, he questions. Why does Lacan do nothing with the fact that he mentions in passing: that the young women had a brutal alcoholic father, who had raped or seduced an older sister, who had had a major impact on Christine's life? In the light of former psychoanalyst Alice Miller's work on the major repercussions

of childhood abuse or trauma, and the abreactive quality
of much mental illness, we may now wonder how central
'the enigma of female castration' was. The sheer mention of
'castration', suggesting impotence of some sort, when discussing a deed of shocking violence requiring exceptional
physical strength, suggests that some unconscious motive
is at work. Every man's account that has been examined
so far seems to tend to one end: to guard against the
unacceptable idea that women have killed. Either the act,
or the sisters' gender, has to be suppressed. Why? Is it
fear? Upset at the destruction of comfortable or nice ideas
about women? Or not wanting to let them have access to
a terrifying form of power?

I began with Monsieur Lancelin: Monsieur Lancelin
being out of the house when the murders were committed,
kept out by the door which the maids deliberately bolted
before going to bed – out of kindness, perhaps, to spare
him the awful spectacle, or because they felt he had
nothing to do with any of it. That they should so markedly
have signified that Monsieur was excluded makes it all
the more ironic that so many men should have dealt with
the case. It seems as if, for the sisters, the men of the
powers that be – the police, the judiciary, the psychiatrists
– were made genderless by their institutional quality. It is
interesting that they were defended by a woman barrister,
and that the more telling bits of evidence about their
behaviour after their arrest came from female wardens.
Also, the only piece of genuine research into the life and
private history of the sisters was conducted by a woman,
Paulette Houdyer, who wrote a novel about them called
Le Diable dans la peau. Some of her findings contradict
what Lacan, for one, suggests. Like Simone de Beauvoir,
she has no sense that the case is unintelligible to the
lay mind. Since the book is written as an imaginative
biography, and is full of persuasive information, I shall
describe it as if it were fact – on the understanding that
in a case in which there were no witnesses, and about

which the perpetrators always refused to say what they knew, everything is faction.

Christine and Léa Papin were the daughters of country people, from the vicinity of Le Mans. The father, Gustave Papin, worked at a wood-saw and drank too much. The mother, Clémence, enjoyed the company of men. She was not the motherly type. She had to get married because the first daughter, Emilia, was on the way. When Christine, the second child, came along, she gave her to her sister-in-law, Gustave's elder sister Isabelle, to bring up. When, seven years later, Léa, the third daughter, was born, she gave her to a great-uncle to bring up. Christine is reported to have been happy at her Aunt Isabelle's, and to have imbibed from her a distrust of men. Isabelle had had a small inheritance left to her by an elderly employer, whose maid she had been. She enjoyed her independence. She had seen her own mother destroyed by too many pregnancies. She disapproved of Clémence's activities: a woman was all right as long as she kept away from men.

Christine's happiness with her aunt came to a brutal end when she was seven. Her father, Gustave, had seduced Emilia, her elder sister, who was ten or eleven. Houdyer claims that Emilia was not Gustave's daughter, that she loved her father and was willing. Be that as it may, Clémence reacted with (to me understandable) fury, but also with (as Houdyer presents it) vindictiveness. She divorced Gustave: he never reappeared, fought in the First World War, then married somebody else. He kept no contact with his daughters. Clémence put Emilia in a religious orphanage that was known for its harshness, the convent of Le Bon Pasteur in Le Mans. For good measure, she removed Christine from Isabelle's care (as Isabelle was Gustave's sister) and sent her also to Le Bon Pasteur. Baby Léa was entrusted to the great-uncle, and Clémence made a living as a maid, doing odd cleaning jobs.

The harshness of Le Bon Pasteur, where she spent eight years – between the ages of seven and fifteen, and where she learnt to be an excellent housekeeper and seamstress – was relieved for Christine by the protection and love of Emilia, whom she worshipped. At the end of the war, because she had lost all hope of getting her father back (according to Houdyer), Emilia became a nun. Clémence was furious: just when the girl could have started earning, could have been a help to her! Christine wanted to become a nun too. Clémence used her legal rights as a mother to forbid this and removed her from the convent, placing her as a maid. Christine was fifteen. From then on, she transferred all her love to her little sister Léa. Her aim in life became eventually to find a place where she could be with Léa, where Léa and she could be employed by the same people. She eventually found the Lancelin home, in which they had been employed for seven years when the tragedy occurred.

Still according to Houdyer – but this makes sense in terms of the other documents that have survived – Clémence loved Léa but not Christine. She tried to get the younger girl back in a variety of ways, and was to succeed much later, since Léa, after serving her ten-year sentence, went to live with her mother (Christine died of self-imposed malnutrition after a year in jail). But whilst at the Lancelins', Christine fought her mother for her sister's love, and won. Some time before the murders, when the Lancelins were away, the sisters went to see the town mayor, claiming that they were being persecuted, that their mother was the source of the persecution, and asking to have Léa emancipated from her mother's custody. The mayor thought they were disturbed, but nobody really took much notice of the episode. Mme Lancelin, however, had backed the sisters in their bid for emancipation. She had agreed to pay their wages directly to them, not to their mother. She sent Clémence packing if Clémence tried to see the girls. Clémence wrote strange letters, warning her daughters to beware of masters and priests, who take daughters away from mothers. As Dupré says, the Papin sisters were three, not two. The mother was the hidden third, also feeling persecuted. You might even claim they were four, if you think of Emilia in her convent, choosing the celestial Father, or husband. Certainly Christine and Léa showed no interest in men. They went to church; they saved money carefully. A medium had told Christine that in her next life she was to be her sister's husband. Their plan seems to have been to save enough to start a small business, then leave. And live together for ever.

It makes a lot of sense to see the disaster of the iron and the blown fuses in the context of the enormous passional domestic charge that had built up inside the Lancelin household. Mme Lancelin had come to occupy the position of the mother, the potential persecutor. Houdyer imagines that Christine and Léa were interrupted by their mistresses whilst they were making love. To the daughters of a man who had committed incest with their elder sister when she was a child, to women who believed that by keeping away from men they stood a chance to better themselves, to sisters who had found in each other's love all the compensation they needed for their disappeared father, their unloving and abandoning and dictatorial mother, their other lost sister, the words incest and homosexuality must have meant very little. They knew, though, that if they were caught in the act they stood to lose everything: their reputation as model servants, their chance of another job, each other . . . their mother had intruded yet again, was about to separate them yet again . . . 'I was black with anger,' Christine would say to one of her interrogators. It does not seem to me so difficult to understand why.

There is not the space here to comment fully on Houdyer's book, but it strikes me that whilst her documentation is impressive and her empathy makes her intuitive, some of her interpretations are open to doubt. Clémence the mother is presented in an unremittingly hostile light, when some of the details given make you feel sorry for her against the grain of the book. Was she more of a victim than a villain? And if she was so awful, why did Léa go back to live with her? More disturbingly, it is hard to swallow the idea that ten- or eleven-year-old Emilia was so happy to be seduced by her father. There is no evidence for this. One could read her entry into the convent as the refusal of men, and her sisters' equal refusal of men as the reaction of young women who have been thoroughly put c 'f at an early stage. I mentioned Alice Miller above. In the light of the work that she and feminists have done in recent years on incest and child abuse, the bias of Freud's theories about the daughter's seduction and all that followed from this bias, surely a reading different from Houdyer's is possible.[7]

I am struck, however, by the fact that when a woman writes about the case, it becomes intelligible, the act is written about as an act. Instead of 'female castration' you have *une histoire d'amour*, a love story.

This opens a can of worms, and I shall let the reader take a peep before I put the lid back on. Have I used the term 'gender' in the crassest possible way, arguing that when men write about the maids they see one thing; when women write they see another? Is it the case that each writer, man or woman, attempts to project the scenario that is most flattering, most agreeable, most self-aggrandizing to their own sex? Is there no truth, then – do men see women in a particular way, women see themselves in another, the two views being irreconcilable? Is it a question of power? Does sex determine a writer's gender-position?

Evidently not: if it were so, perhaps Houdyer would not have been so forgiving to Gustave, so merciless to Clémence. Simone de Beauvoir would not have sympathized so readily with the murder of the mistresses. And a writer like Genet would not have written *The Maids* (1946).

Genet the homosexual, the thief, does not deny the sisters their act. Of course, since this play is by Genet, act here assumes the meaning of acting, actor, acting out, as well as of deed. But instead of the *délire à deux*, the twin delirium, that Lacan found, Genet focuses the entire play on the build-up to the murder. All is there to be seen, and all is theatre. What is blind and unrealized in the sisters according to Lacan is conscious and acted out in the Genet.

There are two sisters, Claire and Solange. Claire is the powerful one, as Christine Papin was. The two sisters both love and hate Madame. They play in turns at being Madame, and at being each other: Claire is Madame while Solange is Claire. The mirror, in other words, is not only present to their consciousness, they play at entering it and coming out of it, they constantly play at being other. It enables them masochistically to enjoy being humiliated as the maid and sadistically humiliating the maid as Madame. It also enables them not to be so, since it is make-believe. It enables them to act out their hatred in pretend rebellion and vengeance against Madame, and to plot the murder of Madame. The acting out is magic – it gives them distance from and control over their situation. Solange is never humiliated as Solange, but as Claire. Claire, pretending as Madame to humiliate her sister, is humiliating somebody called Claire. And vice versa.

Furthermore, the sisters not only know that they love each other, they are lovers. 'Their eye is clear,' Genet says, 'for they masturbate every night.' No plucked nor blinded eyes here, no after-the-event discovery. Whereas Lacan claimed that it was only after the murder that Christine Papin cried out to her sister, 'with the eyes of passion that at last is no longer blind: "Say yes, Léa, say yes"'; whereas Lacan insists on female castration and blindness, on murders that are pure delirium, Bacchic possession, Genet creates lucidity, magic control, willpower. For in

25

the end, as Madame has escaped from the sisters, as she has failed to drink the poisoned cup prepared for her by the sisters, Claire, dressed up as Madame, drinks it: thereby making both her sister and herself into the murderers they wanted to be. For Solange will claim to have poisoned her sister, and be guillotined for the murder. Claire and Solange choose to die impersonating whom they are not. They become murderers through a double suicide. In that sense Genet is not far from Lacan's claim that the killing of the mistresses by the Papin sisters is an attack against themselves. But he is a very long way from Lacan in every other way: in the sisters' recognition and acting out of their homosexual and incestuous desire, in their magic control over their fate.

You might say: it's all very well to claim that Genet makes the sisters lucid, and actors, where the Surrealists or Sartre or Lacan make them into Pythonesses, male heroes, or Bacchae. But Genet is completely reinventing the case – his maids do not kill Madame, they choose poison, they are clever, arguably sane, not a bit naturalistically presented; whereas all the others are representing or discussing the real crime, the real sisters. Genet can do what he pleases, and you may like it better. We can see you coming a mile off. You're about to argue that Genet, because of his own homosexuality – because of his real, and chosen, and enduring marginality – is better able to imagine femininity, to conceive of the maids as murderers and female, than these other writers who, whatever their motives, either virilized the sisters or saw them as prompted to castrate out of their unconscious horror at their own castration. Genet's play may be an agreeable alternative to you, but what does it have to do with reality?

More than meets the eye, I would answer. I would indeed hold that Genet, because of his gender-position, was able to see things that none of the others could see. I would be tempted to add that it is precisely because there is so much theatre about his theatre that he puts his finger on truths the others were blind to.

His maids, for one, are, in terms of social and domestic power, infinitely more real than Lacan's or Breton's. Their talk is of sinks and spit and rubber gloves and putting on or dealing with Madame's clothes. It is of poverty versus wealth. It is of the strange female intimacy that the respective positions of maid and mistress generate – what was immediately clear to Simone de Beauvoir and to no one else. No slender disaster here, but an ongoing tragedy. His maids fail to kill Madame and are destroyed instead because in the real world maids do not kill their mistresses, and when the odd one does, it changes nothing to the system of mistress-ship or mastership: maids go on working and sleeping in cold attic bedrooms. The Papin sisters are recuperated as male revolutionary heroes by the Surrealists. The prosecution, presenting the Lancelin family's case, denies their humanity. Refusing the plea of insanity, the prosecution barrister said, 'they are not enraged dogs, they are snarling dogs'. Receptacles for a male god, or animals: women, never. And it seems to me that it is this denial of the Papin sisters' common humanity that Genet – among other things – dramatizes.

Genet insisted that the play was to be acted by men only: Madame, Claire and Solange must be played by male actors. Sartre saw this as Genet's dislike and refusal of the female sex:

> One might read this demand of Genet's as the expression
> of his pederastic taste for young boys; yet this is not the
> essential reason for it. The truth is that he wants from
> the start to *radicalize appearance*. No doubt an actress
> could play Solange: but the unreality will not be radical
> because she will not need to act being a woman. The
> softness of her flesh, the limp grace of her movements,
> the silvery sound of her voice will be *given*; they form
> the substance which she will fashion as she pleases

to make it appear as Solange. Genet wants to make
this female clay itself into an appearance, the result of
a comedy. It is not Solange who must be a theatrical
illusion, it is *Solange the woman*. To achieve this absolute
artificiality, nature must first be eliminated: through
the roughness of a breaking voice, the dry hardness of
male muscles, the bluish sheen of a nascent beard, the
degreased (streamlined), spiritualized female will appear
as man's invention, as a pale, gnawing shadow – which
cannot rise up to being on its own: the evanescent result
of an extreme, temporary contention, the impossible
dream men might have in a world deprived of women
. . . Everything must be so false it sets your teeth on
edge. But as a result, woman, since she is false, acquires
poetic density. Exfoliated from her matter, purified,
femininity becomes a heraldic sign, a cipher. As long
as it remained natural, the feminine blazon remained
glued to woman. Spiritualized, it becomes a category
of the imagination, an organizing schema of dreams:
everything can be 'woman': a flower, a beast, an inkpot.[8]

This is seductive, and it contains some truth, although
the unconscious misogyny is breathtaking: the female, all
softness and limp flesh, is redeemed here only by being
'degreased', spiritualized – equal to an inkpot, mind you,
neither the ink nor the pen – and made into a . . . cipher.
Passive, silent, ignorant, impotent, and now both a vessel
and nothing. Oh deary deary deary me. How familiar. No
wonder Simone de Beauvoir had a hard time.

I think that by stipulating male actors Genet is pointing
to the fact that the men who write – or wrote – about the
maids make – or made – them into men (rather as he
insists that there must be a white audience for his play
The Blacks). It is not that maleness or femaleness is this
or that particular bundle of qualities, as Sartre claims, but
that men have used the sisters as vehicles or receptacles,
and Genet is subverting the show. Perhaps, as Philippe

Lacoue-Labarthe suggests, 'masculinity imagines itself but poorly; it can only, at most, imagine itself by feminizing itself'. The Papin sisters' crime provided the Surrealists & Co. with something that nothing else provided – in particular an opportunity to feel good about the overthrow and destruction of the bourgeois mothers. Women had done it for them! Long live the Papin sisters! The matrix of the act, the empty socket, had been provided. All that was needed was to inhabit that space, put an eye in it. But in *The Maids*, although the three actors are men, there is no entry for men. The real sisters shadow Claire and Solange's performances, as a real black revolution is carried on in the wings while the blacks of the play by that name carry on their parodic rape and murder of a white girl by a black man for the benefit of a pretend white audience, or as the revolution rages and aborts while the women of the brothel-Balcony act out their clients' favourite fantasies. That Claire and Solange should fail to kill Madame and could only kill themselves, that they only achieve symbolic and make-believe emancipation, is a comment on the fact that the Papin sisters failed to kill mastery: that the whole case is a theatre, a decoy, that enabled the powers that be to carry on in the wings. And yet – for in Genet there is always a swing of the pendulum; sometimes the revolution succeeds and sometimes it fails – the maids' symbolic triumph is a powerful, an exclusively female one: even though the case never ceases to be represented by men . . .

But there are no men in the cast of the play. Madame has a lover, Monsieur, but Monsieur never appears. Monsieur does not matter, Monsieur has nothing to do with the tragedy that unfolds entirely among women – just as there was no Monsieur Lancelin.

The sisters have not finished generating representations. There have been films, other plays . . . there is a strange dynamic at work here that continues to vex interpreters. What emerges strikingly from the material considered here is the refusal of the act, the denial of the 'eye', the 'I' of the sisters by all commentators identifying with a 'male' position. I think this is through fear of the potency of the act, fear of potential female power. Certainly, such a case makes manifest the importance as well as the trickiness of the concept of gender. There can be no 'truth' that does not take it into account. 'My crime is great enough for me to speak the truth,' Christine said. The question of truth, it seems, is shot through with the question of gender. What is at stake in the interpretations seems almost more important than the interpretations themselves.

Through their account of the case, everyone expressed what it mattered to them to express. De Beauvoir showed that murder can be understood as a revolt against injustice. The Surrealists saw the deed as a Romantic rebellion against a bourgeois order that stank. Sartre saw it as fierce individualism, freedom from the glueyness not just of existence but of femininity. Lacan saw it as an attack against the self in the mirror, and hatred for female mutilation. Houdyer saw it as the extremity of passion; Genet as the individual's power to control his or her fate through symbolic words and deeds.

Whoever creates shadows brings forth a world. It seems to me that ultimately, for men and women alike, it is the nobility of the world called into being that matters. Genet's gift of tragic grandeur to his Solange and his Claire, however remote in point of fact they may be from the Papin sisters, makes him, for me, far superior to anyone else. His recognition that the sisters were somehow himself ennobled the man who was capable of such openness:

> Sacred or not, these maids are monsters, as we are
> ourselves also when we dream of being this or that. I
> cannot say what theatre is, I know what I won't allow
> it to be: the description of daily gestures seen from

the outside. I go to the theatre so that I can see myself, on stage . . . such as I could not – or would not dare – see myself or dream myself, and yet such as I know myself to be.[9]

'Pride is faith in the idea that God had, when he made us,' Karen Blixen wrote. 'The barbarian loves his own pride, and hates, or disbelieves in, the pride of others.'[10] Only the civilized being is able to love the pride of his or her adversaries, his or her servants or bosses, his or her lover. Startlingly, of all the men who wrote about the Papin sisters, only Genet the outcast, Genet the thief, was civilized.

If looks could kill

*Myra Hindley and
the iconography of evil*

Helen Birch

There's a photograph of Myra Hindley, taken at the time of
her arrest in 1965 and reproduced in the numerous articles
and books written about the Moors Murders, which has
become synonymous with the idea of feminine evil. In it
a young woman with dyed blonde hair and dark, hooded
eyes stares blankly from beneath a heavy fringe. More
than a quarter of a century after Myra Hindley took
part in the murders of five children with her lover Ian
Brady, that photograph continues to stare from the pages
of newspapers, books and magazines, triggering fierce
controversy, even among those too young to remember
the original case. The name of Ian Brady, meanwhile, rarely
hits the headlines.

Like the image of the Medusa, this photograph has
acquired the attributes of myth, the stony gaze of Britain's
longest-serving woman prisoner striking terror, mingled
with fascination, in those who look upon it. At once
atavistic – drawing its power from potent symbols of
wicked women from the Medusa to seventeenth-century
witches – and portentous – what kind of violent acts might
women be capable of? – that image has become symbolic
of the threat of femininity unleashed from its traditional
bonds of goodness, tenderness, nurturance. It strikes at the
heart of our fears about unruly women, about criminality,
and about the way gender is constructed.

Over the last twenty-seven years, the image of Myra

Hindley and the bizarre grip it holds over the public imagination has become detached from its subject, the woman who committed a series of terrible crimes all those years ago. For what Myra Hindley has come to represent, the symbolic weight she carries, exceeds the crimes of two individuals at a particular place and time. Why, more than any other criminal this century, has Myra Hindley been singled out for vilification? What is it about the case that is so unique? One answer to this, it seems to me, is the fact of her gender. There is an implicit assumption that for a woman to be involved in killing children is somehow worse, more ineffable than it is for a man.

Between 1965 and 1967, around the same time as Brady and Hindley were arrested and convicted, thirty-nine-year-old Raymond Morris abducted, sexually assaulted and killed three young girls. He was tried and convicted in 1968, but his name was quickly forgotten. Nor is Hindley the only woman to have killed children. In Chapter 8 of this book, Allison Morris and Ania Wilczynski note that between 1982 and 1989, 'almost half of the child killings attributed to parents . . . were committed by mothers'.[1] In 1971 Carol Hanson was convicted, with her husband, of the murder of a child. She had also colluded in the sexual abuse of several others. Yet she has been the target of little public opprobrium. And although since Ian Brady and Myra Hindley went to prison their crimes have been equalled, if not surpassed, by those of Peter Sutcliffe and Dennis Nilsen,[2] the case of the Moors Murders has become a kind of Gothic soap opera (with all the elements of fear, melodrama and histrionics the term implies), and its leading lady a monster beyond compare.

Like most people living in Britain, I was always dimly aware of Myra Hindley – or rather, of the brooding presence of that photograph. When I was still at the age when my reading matter was selected from the volumes on the parental bookshelf, I read Emlyn Williams's bestselling fictional account of the murders, *Beyond Belief.* I remember being terrified – not so much by the revelation that people could do this kind of thing to others (like most girls, early on I had absorbed the sense of sexual vulnerability my gender conferred on me) – but by what I can now call its excess: the use of apocalyptic metaphor, the congruence of grimy backstreets, moors swathed in mist and the totemic battle Williams conjures between the forces of good and evil. (In this particular psychodrama, Myra Hindley was the innocent, the slave, and Ian Brady the corrupter, the master.) Later, as I began to recognize my own experience of being female in the structural analysis of patriarchy advanced by feminism, I began to wonder what lay behind this iconic image of a woman killer, and what it revealed about the ways we look at women.

I was also struck by the deafening silence from feminists on the subject of Myra Hindley. On one level, of course, this is understandable. She was not a battered wife who hit back, a victim who took action to protect herself or her children. Quite the reverse. There is no easy way to appropriate her actions for the purpose of advancing the cause of women. Why, indeed, should we want to? But the fact remains that Hindley's notoriety is endemic in her femininity, and this has resonances for all women.

Many images of women are overdetermined. They may, like the fantasy women who populate the pages of glossy magazines, bear little resemblance to 'real' women, or to their lives; yet in a system of signification which is so often dominated by a male point of view, they carry a significance, a series of messages – about ideals of beauty, status, desirability, power – which exceed their literal meaning. Often – in advertising, for example – images might be used precisely to convey such a message; at other times, their use in a particular context is unconscious. Either way, we cannot escape them: the relationship between images and the real is a complex process of give and take. To examine, as I will here, how the image of Myra Hindley has been used to convey the horror of femininity perverted from its 'natural' course is not to say that this process is deliberate, conspiratorial (though in some instances it may well be); but that it has – coincidentally, even unconsciously – come to stand in for some of our most paradoxical 'common-sense' ideas about women: that on the one hand, to be a woman is to be passive and innocent (Myra Hindley was just the dupe of Ian Brady); while on the other, her agency must be explained by reference to her duplicity, her taintedness (Myra Hindley as imbued with evil, manipulative, devious). Her acts rightly invoke our moral repugnance; but the meaning of her image hovers somewhere on the no-man's-land between those two poles.

Crime and punishment

At 6 a.m. on 7 October 1965, police received an emergency telephone call from David Smith, Myra Hindley's brother-in-law. When Smith arrived at the police station in Hyde, Manchester, he told how, the previous evening, Hindley had asked him to come to the house she shared with Ian Brady to collect some miniature bottles of wine. When he got there he said he heard screams coming from the living-room, and Hindley shouted to him to come and help. He watched, horrified, as Brady hacked 'a young lad, about seventeen years old' with a hatchet until the boy lay face down on the floor. Brady then strangled him. The boy was seventeen-year-old Edward Evans. Afterwards, according to Smith, Brady said to Hindley, 'It's the messiest yet'.

Although Smith – who appeared as chief prosecution witness at the trial, held at Chester Assizes in April 1966 – testified that he was unsure if Hindley had been in the room the whole time the murder was taking place, he recalled that afterwards, Brady had turned to Hindley and instructed her to start clearing up the mess. Once the three of them had mopped the blood from the walls and floor and carried the body upstairs, Smith left the house, promising to return the next day and help dispose of the body. Instead, his call to the police led to Brady's arrest.[3]

During their investigations, the police found a note in Brady's handwriting detailing the disposal plan for Evans's body. In a locker at Manchester railway station, they recovered two suitcases containing books about sado-masochism, two tape-recorders, photographs of a nude girl in various poses, of Hindley and Brady having sex, and of Hindley on the Yorkshire moors, along with a number of audiotapes. One of these, played to a stunned courtroom at the trial, was a harrowing, seventeen-minute record of a young girl's terror as she was tied, gagged and photographed naked. Both Brady's and Hindley's voices could be heard on the tape, along with music: the hit single 'The Little Drummer Boy' by Ray Coniff and his orchestra, and the Christmas song 'Jolly St Nicholas'.

The body of the girl in the photographs, ten-year-old Lesley Ann Downey, who had disappeared from a fair-ground on Boxing Day 1964, was found the next day in a shallow grave at Hollin Brown Knoll on Saddleworth moor. She had been sexually assaulted and strangled. A few days afterwards, on 21 October 1965, the badly decomposed body of twelve-year-old John Kilbride, who had been missing since November 1963, was discovered a few hundred yards away. Pathologists were unable to establish the cause of death. Police had located the graves with the help of snapshots, taken by Brady, of Hindley posing on the graves. Two more children – sixteen-year-old Pauline Reade and twelve-year-old Keith Bennett – whom police suspected Brady and Hindley had also killed, were not found.

Five days after Brady's arrest, twenty-two-year-old Myra Hindley was charged with the murders of Edward Evans and Lesley Ann Downey and with harbouring Ian Brady knowing he had killed John Kilbride. Twenty-seven-year-old Brady was charged with all three murders. Both pleaded not guilty. At the trial, faced with the damning evidence of the tapes and Smith's testimony, Brady and Hindley tried to implicate Smith in the killing of Evans, saying that he and Brady had planned to go out and 'roll a queer' that night, and things had got out of hand. They also insisted that Lesley Ann Downey had left their house alive in the company of Smith. Both were found guilty as charged. In 1986 Hindley made a full confession of her involvement, with Brady, in the murders of Pauline Reade and Keith Bennett. She also admitted that Smith was in no way involved in any of the crimes.

The progress of romance

Like so many aspects of this case, the facts about Hindley's relationship with Brady are few. In the absence of any coherent explanation from either Brady or Hindley of why they committed these brutal crimes, many of the dozen or so books which have appeared over the last twenty-seven years have attempted to piece together – with the help of interviews with friends and relatives – factors which may have contributed to the killings, searching through the remnants of the past for 'significant' moments when the dynamics of the couple's relationship may have shifted. In keeping with our culture's Freudian cast of mind which seeks to explain everything from sexual proclivities to serial murder in terms of childhood and family life, much of this is based on facile psychology, the search for a cause, an event in their respective childhoods when the path towards a 'heart of darkness' may have been set. As the books have proliferated, so has the conjecture. The facts, as they stand, are these.

Myra Hindley was born in Gorton, a working-class area of Manchester, on 23 July 1942. When her sister Maureen was born in 1946, she was sent to live with her grandmother a few streets away. A practising Catholic, she attended church regularly, hung out with her girlfriends, and was of above-average intelligence. When she left school at fourteen she took a number of office jobs, and at seventeen she was briefly engaged to a childhood friend. She broke off the engagement because, she said, the boy was 'too childish'. In January 1961, when she was just eighteen, she went to work as a shorthand typist at Millwards, a chemical factory. It was there that she met Ian Brady.

Brady's own background was very different. He was born in Glasgow on 2 January 1938; his unmarried mother handed him over to the care of foster parents who lived in a tenement building in the Gorbals slums. By the time he was thirteen Brady had appeared in court charged with housebreaking and theft, and was given two years' probation. A string of other convictions followed, until 1957, when a court ordered him to live with his mother and stepfather in Manchester. The following year, he was sent to borstal for two years. A few months after his release he joined Millwards as a stock clerk.

Hindley was immediately attracted to the enigmatic Ian Brady. A diary she kept during her first year at Millwards, written in breathless teenage prose, charts the progress of a classic romance: the girl wilting at his every glance, he older, mysterious, dominant:

Ian looked at me today . . . He smiled at me today . . . Not sure if he likes me . . . Gone off Ian a bit . . . Wonder what Misery will be like tomorrow? . . . I love Ian all over again. He has a cold and I would love to mother him . . . He hasn't spoken to me today . . . I hope he loves me and will marry me some day . . . Ian still ignores me. Fed up. I still love him.

Then, just before Christmas 1961: 'Eureka! Today we have our first date. We are going to the cinema.'

One apocryphal story – repeated in numerous books, from novelist Emlyn Williams's *Beyond Belief* (1967) to journalist Jean Ritchie's *Myra Hindley: Inside the Mind of* a *Murderess* (1988) – tells how on that first date, Brady took Hindley to see *Judgement at Nuremburg* at the local cinema. The pair shared a mutual interest in Germany, and Brady quickly initiated his girlfriend into his various obsessions – his personal library included *Mein Kampf*, *The Life and Ideas of the Marquis de Sade*, de Sade's *Justine*, *The Kiss of the Whip*, Dostoevsky's *Crime and Punishment*, *The Pleasures of the Torture Chamber* . . . The couple regularly visited Saddleworth moor in Yorkshire, camping out and drinking bottles of German wine. Brady nicknamed Hindley 'Hess' after the German pianist Myra Hess – a moniker which, given his fascination with fascist philosophy, must have seemed particularly apposite.

By 1963 Brady had moved into the house where Hindley lived with her grandmother, in Bannock Street, Gorton. The following year, as part of the postwar reconstruction taking place all over Britain, the old back-to-back slums of Gorton were cleared to make way for new estates of terraced houses and tower blocks linked by walkways. Hindley's grandmother was moved out of Bannock Street and into a spanking new house in an overspill estate in Hattersley, another part of Manchester. It was in that house, 16 Wardle Brook Avenue, that the body of Edward Evans was found in 1965.

The late 1940s and 1950s, when Myra Hindley was growing up, was a particularly oppressive period for women. In *Only Halfway to Paradise*[4] Elizabeth Wilson suggests that the atmosphere of democratic consensus which pervaded the period immediately following the war was in fact the 'achievement of a deceptive harmony . . . the orchestration was harmonious in covering up what was really a silence, what was not said'.[5] She goes on to argue that this process focused on women through ideologies of 'correct' or 'normal' sexuality and of the family as primary sites where the politics of 'social reconciliation' between classes, genders and generations were played out. The theory and practices of the new welfare state embodied conservative assumptions about the family and motherhood, seeing them as the central unit of a society which would focus on women's 'special qualities' – their roles as nurturers and arbiters of morality – as a stabilizing and civilizing influence. The concern with reinforcing and encouraging the institution of marriage as a 'vital occupation and career'[6] for women went hand in hand with official and unofficial disquiet about the future of the family.

In the 1950s, for the first time, marriage was viewed as an equal partnership between men and women. Sex manuals and pamphlets designed to help married couples recognized the importance of mutual sexual pleasure *within* the confines of monogamous marriage, while focusing on the husband as the active sexual partner – in bed, as in the workplace, women were consigned to a passive role.

The probable destiny of a working-class girl like Myra Hindley would have been marriage to the boy next door and life in a back-to-back slum, doing menial jobs and struggling to bring up her children. But it is clear from her own accounts of her fascination with Brady and her later attempts to educate herself in prison, passing German and English O levels and gaining an Open University degree, that her own ambitions were rather less conventional.

At the trial, her sister Maureen described how, since meeting Brady, her sister had changed: 'She stopped going to church. She said she didn't believe in it. She didn't believe in marriage. She said she hated babies and children and hated people. She began to keep things locked up.' The once-devout Hindley had become a confirmed atheist; when she took the witness stand at the trial, she refused to take the normal oath on the Bible, preferring instead, in keeping with the faithless monster image she later acquired, to affirm. Later, in prison, she returned to the Catholic faith, and in 1971 she broke off contact with Brady.

In 1979 Hindley wrote a 21,000-word statement for the Parole Board which was leaked to a newspaper. It is a curious document – full, we now know, of evasions about her actual involvement in the killings[7] – but what she wrote about her relationship with Ian Brady is oddly consistent with the sentiments expressed in the diary she kept in 1961 and – in the light of her 1986 confessions to the murders of Pauline Reade and Keith Bennett – with her later appraisal of the power of the romantic fantasy he seemed to embody. In it she wrote: 'Within months he had convinced me that there was no God at all (he could have told me that the earth was flat, that the moon was made of green cheese, that the sun rose in the west and I would have believed him). He became my god, my idol, my object of worship and I worshipped him blindly.'

In her 1986 confessions Hindley spoke of her fear of Brady, claiming that he had drugged her in order to take pornographic photographs and then blackmailed her with them. After that, she said, she gave a letter to a friend, telling her that if anything happened to her, she should give it to the police. In 1992 she was to say:

> When I met Ian I was eighteen and a half. He was
> cultured, he listened to classical music, he read classical
> literature. They were things that interested me too,
> but I had no one to share them with. And he was
> good-looking. I was very impressionable. I thought I
> loved him, but I realise now with 20 years' hindsight
> that I was infatuated, and that infatuation grew into an
> obsession. He was God. It was as if there was a part
> of me that didn't belong to me, that hadn't been there
> before and wasn't there afterwards. I'm not saying
> he took over my mind or anything, or that I wasn't
> responsible for what I did, but I just couldn't say 'no' to
> him. He decided everything; where we would go for our
> holidays, everything.

In her discussion of mass-market romance fiction for women, American academic Ann Snitow has remarked that the kinds of romantic fantasy described in these novels 'can deal women the winning hand they cannot hold in life'.[8]. In the context of the limited options available for most women in the 1950s and early 1960s for fulfilment through education or career, submission to a mysterious, unknowable Other, the embodiment of the power she, as a woman, is lacking, must have been particularly potent. For Myra Hindley, Ian Brady became the God that replaced her Catholicism. But why she was attracted to his 'theology' of fascism and nihilism, and why she became a participant in those brutal murders, are questions which have vexed her friends and commentators alike. It is around this absent centre, the point at which knowledge and understanding fail, that representations by and about Myra Hindley have proliferated, and the myth of a she-devil has found fertile ground.

Moors killer sensation

From the outset, the Moors Murders, and the contest over Hindley's status as a criminal and a woman, took place in a blaze of publicity. The committal proceedings were open to the public and journalists were permitted to report what went on (the law restricting press coverage of committals was not introduced until 1967). As the trial judge, Justice Fenton Atkinson, pointed out to the jury in his summing-up: 'The committal proceedings were reported very widely. I expect you had probably read all about one side of the case before you had any idea you might find yourself on the jury.' In other words, it was impossible that any of the twelve jurors would have been untouched by the publicity.

At the trial it emerged that David Smith – who had a number of convictions for violence and petty crime and had a close relationship with the couple, particularly Brady, in the months preceding the couple's arrest – had been promised £1,000 from the *News of the World* for his story, and that his hotel bills were being paid by the paper.

Since then, the case – and the figure of Myra Hindley in

particular – has taken its place in the front line of the increasingly virulent circulation wars between the tabloids. As Keith Soothill and Sylvia Walby point out in *Sex Crime in the News*: 'The Moors Murderers, despite the time since their convictions, figure in the media more than all the rest of the sex criminals in custody put together.'[9]

There are several logical reasons for this persistent interest. One is that the death penalty was abolished while Brady and Hindley were awaiting trial; it was the first mass-murder trial held since then, and as several contemporary commentators noted – echoing the feelings of the 42,000 signatories on a petition for restoration of the death penalty – there was a sense that aesthetic justice was lacking. As Pamela Hansford Johnson put it: 'When the Moors Trial ended, we did feel a lack of catharsis: something violent should have happened to put an end to violence. Throughout, we were missing the shadow of the rope.'[10] Had the couple been hanged, it is unlikely that they would have continued to haunt the public consciousness a quarter of a century later. As it is, they, and Hindley in particular, remain the subjects of constant surveillance, scrutinized for visible signs of badness or madness which might explain the inexplicable or match – aesthetically, at least – evidence of their inner disquiet to their moral outrages.

The location of the murders has a special resonance too. A few miles from the densely populated industrial cities of north-west England, the Yorkshire moors have – since Emily Brontë wrote *Wuthering Heights* – become a place of mystery in the national imagination, their wild beauty an invitation to fantasy. Now a popular holiday area for walkers, they have been reclaimed as a National Park, but the climate is volatile: they are green and rolling in summer, but in autumn and winter mists come down suddenly, and the world falls silent. You can lose your bearings completely, wander in circles for hours before finding a road to take you back home. Situated on a psychic boundary between civilization and wilderness, the moors, as the locus of murder, are themselves suggestive of the horror and the otherworldly metaphors which the case continues to invoke.

Another reason is the involvement of Lord Longford, a Catholic peer who befriended the couple soon after they went to prison. In the early 1970s Ian Brady went on hunger strike to protest the Home Office's refusal to allow him and Hindley to meet. His campaign was backed by Longford, who as early as 1973 further inflamed public opinion by writing to the *Guardian* claiming that 'The more one looks into the case, the more one comes to accept her [Hindley's] insistence that she was never directly involved in any act of murder. The tapes, horrible though they are, prove nothing in that respect.'[11]

Two years later, Longford, along with John Trevelyan, ex-chair of the British Board of Censors and the writer Robert Speaight, released letters they had received from Hindley to *The Sunday Times*, in support of their claim that she was a reformed character, remorseful and fully rehabilitated, and that the Home Office should begin to consider her eventual release on parole. The tabloids had a field day. Longford was branded a 'loony' and – their worst insult – a 'do-gooder'. Myra Hindley, they said, was 'evil' and should never be released.

But the tabloids, quite independently of Longford's misguided attempts to publicize the case, have continually goaded the public with mostly unfounded reports that Myra Hindley herself was 'campaigning' for parole, along with regular 'You the Jury' surveys, which canvassed readers' opinions on whether she should be released. In 1972, for example, reports that Dorothy Wing, the governor of Holloway prison, had taken Hindley for a ninety-minute walk in a north London park to prepare her for early release, were splashed all over the front pages. The Home Office was quick to react, denying that it was considering early parole[12] and publicly rebuking Mrs Wing for an 'error of judgement'. In her defence,

Wing responded that prisoners had been taken out for short trips from the prison for at least a decade, and had benefited considerably from the experience. While some of the broadsheet papers supported Mrs Wing, arguing that rehabilitation was an important part of the penal process and that 'Mrs Wing was appointed to exercise her judgment by a Home Office which obviously found her well qualified to do so',[13] public opinion was satisfied that Mrs Wing was firmly in the wrong.

The tide of rumour and speculation which surrounds the case of Myra Hindley has continued unabated for twenty-seven years, making it one of the longest-running stories in the history of British journalism. Both Hindley's family and friends and the families and friends of the victims continue to be hounded by the tabloid press; some have sold their stories, some have lucrative contracts with individual papers. Ex-prisoners have obligingly embellished tales of Hindley's sex life in prison and smuggled out photographs and letters. Even a police officer, Chief Superintendent Peter Topping, who heard Hindley's confessions to the murders of Pauline Reade and Keith Bennett in 1986, has profited from his involvement in the case, publishing tapes and notes made of the confessions in a book which was then serialized in the *Sun*, a right-wing tabloid.[14] Hindley's attempt to have the book withdrawn on the grounds that it breached confidentiality was dropped due to lack of funds, but Manchester police issued its own writ against him in 1989. The case is still pending.

At regular intervals, 'psychologists' are wheeled out to beef up thin stories with 'expert' analysis of Hindley's handwriting, which invariably concludes that despite the fact that numerous psychiatrists have failed to find anything wrong with her, Hindley is dangerous. Tales abound of her 'cushy', '5-star' hotel life at Cookham Wood Prison, where she was moved in 1983, detailing what kind of make-up she wears, the size of her cell, how much money she earns, the way she dresses . . . This fascination has spilled from the pages of the press into all areas of popular culture. In 1991 the infamous photograph of Hindley appeared on the cover of Gordon Burn's novel *Alma Cogan* – a cynical marketing ploy, given the spurious narrative connection between the 1950s singer and the murderess. Several plays have also been written about the case, most of which Ann West, mother of Lesley Ann Downey and a vociferous media campaigner, particularly against Hindley, has succeeded in stopping. She also tried to ban the 1984 single about the murders, 'Suffer the Children', by the pop group The Smiths, which appeared with a photograph of an uncanny Hindley lookalike on its sleeve.

In their clamour for new angles to satisfy a perceived need for public vengeance, the tabloids, assisted by the 'true crime' pundits, have, like a latter-day Frankenstein, created a monster and labelled it Myra Hindley. In the process, Hindley has become a scapegoat for some of society's greatest anxieties: through her, moral panics – about the relationship between 'obscene' literature and crimes of violence, natural and 'deviant' sexuality, class, and the role of the penal system – have found a flickering register.

Moral panics

Throughout the late 1960s, national press coverage of the Moors Murders was fairly sober by today's standards, although it was then – as it is still – given dramatic treatment in the regional papers in Manchester and Yorkshire, where the relatives of the victims continue to live. At this time, the tabloid press, with its gung-ho formula of mindless patriotism, tits and TV gossip, was in its infancy (the *Sun* was not relaunched as a tabloid until 1969; the *Daily Mail* in 1971, followed by the *Express* in 1977 and the *Star*, which went national in 1981 and the broadsheets largely restricted themselves to straight reportage of evidence given at the trial and to commentaries debating the ethics of publishing some of its more sensational details, such as the transcript of the tape on which Lesley Ann Downey pleaded to be let free.[15] It was in the five books published in the two years following the trial that the seeds which have made Myra Hindley the most notorious female criminal in modern British memory were sown.

In 1960, the Director of Public Prosecutions brought a case against D.H. Lawrence's novel *Lady Chatterley's Lover*, which Penguin books planned to publish in its first unexpurgated version in English. As much a test case for the recently passed Obscene Publications Act (1959) as a reflection of contemporary attitudes towards sexuality, the trial resulted in an acquittal. Commentators have since pointed out that since the book showed a woman as agent of her own desire who had a sexual relationship with a servant, 'it was not Lawrence's book, so much as the woman, Lady Chatterley, who was on trial'.[16] Such was the impact of the debates around natural and unnatural sexuality that raged throughout the Chatterley saga that they found echoes six years later in a very different trial at Chester Assizes.

Novelist Pamela Hansford Johnson covered the Moors Murders trial for the *Daily Telegraph*. Her book *On Iniquity*, published the following year, focused on the fifty books on sadism, torture and Nazi philosophy found in the house in Wardle Brook Avenue which Hindley had shared with Brady. Cited by the prosecution as evidence of the couple's 'moral corruption', passages from de Sade's *Justine* were read out in court. Taking this argument further, Hansford Johnson saw in the crimes of Brady and Hindley a symptom of an 'affectless society' where 'a swelling violence is in the air' and vandalism, mugging and promiscuity were rife. In a strenuous attack on the new 'realist' theatre of Harold Pinter and Edward Bond, she argued that the role of the artist is to impose some kind of moral discrimination on the ignorant masses. Echoing the words of Mr Griffith Jones, counsel for the prosecution at the Chatterley trial

– 'is this a book you would even wish your wife or your servants to read?' – Hansford Johnson explicitly linked the perverse sexuality of Brady, in his sexual assaults on children, and of Hindley, in the photographs of her naked that were recovered by police, with the couple's working-class origins. 'Depraved material' like that of de Sade, she argued, should not be available 'to minds educationally and emotionally unprepared'.[17] Noting that Brady and Hindley had acquired all the symbols of the 'affluent, affectless society' – a car, transistor radio, a tape-recorder, German wine, cameras, 'pornography' – she concluded that it is only in a climate where the educated, bourgeois elite have relinquished their responsibilities that crimes like these can flourish: 'It is to me, the purest self-deception to pretend that our Ugly Society played no part in what happened on the estate at Hattersley, Cheshire.'[18]

Today this view – which was shared, at least in part, by other contemporary writers [19] – seems antiquated, symptomatic of a society in crisis, where old bourgeois and moral values were threatened by the onward march of stiletto and brothel-creeper. A sexually active, newly affluent, working-class youth had already begun to invade the territory of the educated middle classes, taking its place in their universities, in their offices and on their stages. None the less, arguments like these are indicative of how the search for a cause – why did they do it? – centred on a presumed correlation between 'deviant' sexuality, criminality and class.

Some of these early accounts, unable to conceive that a woman might be capable of such heinous crimes, argued that the relationship between the couple must have been a *folie à deux*, by which one partner becomes 'infected' with the unhealthy obsessions of the other. According to this theory, Myra Hindley became a kind of tragic anti-heroine: the victim of a sick, clever male mind. As long as Hindley could not be seen to think for herself, her acts could be made comprehensible. But in recent years, in tandem with the growth of second-wave feminism and its principles of self-determination for women, that argument has all but died. While Brady has faded from view, largely because psychiatrists have labelled him insane (to name the disease is a substitute for having to know it or to understand what he did and why), and because he has said he never wants to be released, Hindley has become the arch-villain, her active desire to gain eventual freedom cited as evidence of her lack of genuine remorse and of her 'evil' nature – evil as it pertains to femininity, implying deviousness, manipulation, duplicity. Yet the source of this 'evil' has never been defined. Is it natural, a creeping cancer which grows invisibly behind a faultless façade? If so, Myra Hindley can hardly be held responsible for her crimes. Is it acquired? And if so, from where or from whom? Not, we cannot think, from a social order which works so hard to invest its female subjects with goodness and moral responsibility. Or is it imposed, as Christian thinking would have it, from elsewhere, by which interpretation Myra Hindley ceases to be human, much less *a woman*, at all?

The idea of a correspondence between sexuality and criminality was strengthened when, in 1974, Myra Hindley went on trial charged with her lover, prison officer Pat Cairns, a former Carmelite nun, and a fellow inmate, Maxine Croft, of conspiracy to escape from prison, and again made the front pages. Nicolson Freeman, counsel for Croft, painted a picture of a weak, frightened woman who had fallen under the influence of a calculating, Mephistophelean murderess: 'She has persuaded some of the highest in the land that she is a reformed character who merits special consideration. Such is the woman who brought Croft into her thrall.'[20] Cairns, for her part, was labelled a 'very wicked woman' by the judge.

In her 'biography' of Hindley, *Inside the Mind of a Murderess*,[21] written without the co-operation of the vast majority of Hindley's friends and supporters and published in 1988, ex-*Sun* journalist Jean Ritchie (who also ghost-wrote Chief Superintendent Peter Topping's book) takes the argument further. She cites the 'jailbreak plot' as evidence of Hindley's unsavoury promiscuity, her power to manipulate others and use them to protect her from less sympathetic prisoners. Questioning her status as a 'real' lesbian, Ritchie joined numerous other journalists[22] in presenting Hindley as a she-devil, who has duped all those who feel that her remorse is genuine and 'believed her own lies'. While admitting that many women prisoners engage in sexual relationships with other prisoners, she insists that Hindley's own were perverse, tainted, and implicitly links her 'unstable' sexuality with the deviance that led her to murder.

Inside the Mind of a Murderess was serialized in the *Sun* in February 1988. The notorious photograph was cropped to show just the eyes, dark and ominous above the headline 'Sex Romps with an Ex Nun on E Wing'. The parts of the book chosen for extract focused on the affairs in prison, the 'jailbreak plot' – and were heavily edited to retain only the most salacious details. One piece, headlined 'Mad or Bad', accuses Hindley of 'moral corruption'; another went on to define just what that means for women: the news that Hindley posed for 'pornographic photographs' is immediately followed by her sister Maureen's statement in court that 'she hated babies and did not believe in marriage'. Sexual 'deviancy' again aligned with depravity; female sexual desire with violent transgression.

Remorseless blondes

In her autobiographical book about Nazi atrocities at Belsen, Olga Lengyel describes Irma Grese, the notorious camp guard, who was hanged in 1945:

> She was of medium height, elegantly attired, with her hair faultlessly dressed. The mortal terror which her mere presence inspired visibly pleased her. For this 22-year-old girl was completely without pity . . . during

the 'selections', the 'blonde Angel of Belsen' as she was later to be called by the press, made liberal use of the whip . . . Our shrieks of pain and our spurts of blood made her smile. What faultless, pearly teeth she had.[23]

Apparently, Myra Hindley carried a photograph of Grese in her purse.

A little over a decade later, Ruth Ellis, a working-class woman who worked as a hostess in a Soho club in London, was hanged for the murder of her upper-class playboy lover, David Blakely. The public was shocked when she appeared on the witness stand in a fur coat and with bleached hair and stated coolly: 'It was obvious when I shot him that I intended to kill him'. Feminists have since argued that one of the reasons Ellis was sent to the gallows was that in the eyes of the all-male jury, her appearance did not match the line of her defence.[24]

During her own trial, Hindley sat impassive, in smart clothes, full make-up and with newly peroxided hair, and took copious notes of the proceedings. Remorseless, unrepentant, and certainly not a victim. In *On Iniquity*, Pamela Hansford Johnson wrote of Ian Brady:

> on the whole he looks ordinary . . . Myra Hindley does not
> . . . she could have served a nineteenth century painter as
> a model for Clytemnestra, but sometimes she looks more
> terrible, like one of Fuseli's nightmare women drawn
> giant-size, elaborately coiffed, with curled and plaited
> maidservants reaching no higher than her knee . . . Her
> hair is styled into a huge puff-ball, with a fringe across her
> brows . . . Now in the dock, she has a great strangeness,
> and the kind of authority one might expect to find in a
> woman guard of a concentration camp.[25]

This invocation of excess – mythic, unconscious, Nazi – is symptomatic of how the attempt to represent the woman who killed children circulates around a linguistic vanishing point – here, evidently, is femininity as masquerade (there is nothing natural, 'ordinary', about her appearance), yet the words, the hyperbolic metaphors deployed to penetrate the mask and make it yield the truth, only enhance the enigma.

The spectacle of the treacherous, sexually active blonde has become a popular cliché since the Second World War. The sirens of *film noir* – Barbara Stanwyck in *Double Indemnity*, Rita Hayworth in *Gilda* – set the tone for a period in which the most potent cinematic representations of women linked the blonde with perverse sexuality and social aberration. And from there, these films implied, it was just one more metaphoric step to murder. Above all, though, as cultural critic Richard Dyer has pointed out, it was through the (usually blonde) *femme fatale* that the world of *film noir*, mimicking that of a culture defined by men, was divided into the unknowable (female) and the knowable (male). It is, he says, 'not so much their evil as their unknowability (and attractiveness) that makes them fatal for the hero'.[26]

So powerful is this fantasy that it has become – with minor nods towards social changes – a staple of Hollywood cinema since the 1940s. In 1986's *Black Widow* (which Christine Holmlund discusses in 'A decade of deadly dolls') Catherine, played by Theresa Russell, poisons a succession of rich husbands in order to inherit their money. Her success at this is thwarted only by the intervention of another woman – the implication being that it takes one to know one. And in the 1992 film *Basic Instinct*, the blonde, ice-pick-wielding murderess played by Sharon Stone is both bisexual ('deviant') and possessed of formidable powers of psychological manipulation. The image also has echoes in the popular perception of Margaret Thatcher who, despite the best efforts of the spin-doctors, failed to match her softer, ash-blonde persona to her style of government – ruling her party, we are asked to believe, like her country, with a rod of iron and symbolically castrating her all-male Cabinet.

It is into this tradition of the unknowable blonde with a heart of steel that the image of Myra Hindley has been co-opted, and from which it has acquired some of its force. But her own account of how the notorious photograph was taken is instructive. After four sleepless nights, she says, she went to the police station and was ushered into a bare room with a single chair in the middle. Images flashed through her mind of the interrogation scenes from films, and she was terrified. To hide her fear, she glared at the policeman; then a flash gun went off, and the image of the 'most evil woman in Britain', as the *Sun* has dubbed her, was made.

A chilling reminder of the gap between what we see and what we know, that photograph, counterpointed by articles which often unwittingly interrogate its meaning – mad or bad? devil or dupe? – opens up a chasm between the idea of femininity as guarantor of idealism, nurturance and nature and its opposite: violence, depravity and nihilism. It serves to distance us from the 'monster' it depicts, while reminding us of our own potential for 'evil'. This is perhaps one reason why we find the gaze of a sexually active, childless woman who killed children so profoundly disturbing. It is the ultimate outrage against (and rejection of?) the much-vaunted maternal instinct; as such, it tears across the boundary of sexual difference.

French psychoanalyst Julia Kristeva explains this kind of disturbance in terms of her concept of the abject. She argues that to attain a stable position in the social order – the world she calls the symbolic – the human subject must disavow improper, unclean or taboo elements such as incestuous desire, blood and the violence of our birth, which belong properly to the pre-Oedipal or semiotic universe. But we can never fully expel these things, and for that reason any identity we assume is provisional; it is always threatened with disruption. The subject's recognition of the impossibility of a coherent, stable identity through which all these elements are completely banished is the attitude that she calls abjection. It may recur in a kind of 'return of the repressed', and crucially it is intrinsic to linguistic and visual representation – to the production of art, literature and philosophy. It is a boundary, an abyss which both attracts and repels us.[27] It may be our recognition of the abject in that photograph, the threat it invokes of all boundaries destroyed, the collapse of rationality, the triumph of moral anarchy, that reminds us of our own precarious position in the social order.

'The decency to go mad'

The public duel between Myra Hindley and Ann West, mother of Lesley Ann Downey, that has raged in the tabloid press has become a kind of modern morality play, starring the 'bad' mother (I am, of course, using the term metaphorically) who killed children, and the 'good' mother, whose 'innocent' fantasy of cosy family life has been destroyed by the brutal murder of her daughter. Horribly exploitative as these excavations into Mrs West's personal tragedy are, none the less, each time the press seizes on a new Hindley story – particularly if it pertains to the possibility of her eventual release – Ann West is drafted in on the flimsiest of pretexts, to give the public the condemnation it wants. And while this has done nothing to heal the wounds for the relatives of the victims, the spectacle of the grieving mother pitted against the 'devil's daughter', as West has called Hindley, serves the purpose of reminding us of what 'natural' femininity is – and, significantly, is not. In this black-and-white drama there is no space for a third term; as woman terrorizes woman, the man is written out.

Since the trial, Mrs West has campaigned hard to keep Myra Hindley in prison, believing, along with a substantial sector of the public, that she is the more 'evil' of the two. When, in 1989, Peter Timms and David Astor, regular visitors to Myra Hindley, decided to try to break the spell woven by that 1965 photograph by releasing pictures of her at her degree ceremony, West's response was swift. The black gown Hindley wore was, she said, 'The Cloak of Satan', echoing the words of Paul Reade, Pauline's brother, that 'Satan in satin is still Satan'.

In 1985, after a long period of illness, Ian Brady was transferred from Gartree prison to Park Lane psychiatric hospital, diagnosed as suffering from paranoid schizophrenia. He had, remarked West, 'at least had the decency to go mad'. Hindley, on the other hand, is viewed as sane, a 'tough nut' who for twenty-one years stuck to her line that she was less involved in the killings than she subsequently admitted. And as sketches of a thin, ravaged Brady, his body apparently displaying the signs of inner torment, began to appear in the press, those of Hindley showed a softer, prettier, *happier* image.

The logic goes that if Hindley was, as she insists, a naive and infatuated young woman who acted as Brady's lieutenant and not in any way as the architect of the crimes, how has she survived in prison, how has she not gone mad? And if Hindley is not mad, clinically *insane*, how can we know that she now is genuinely reformed and rehabilitated, clinically *sane*, as her supporters claim? Ironically, if Myra Hindley had been sent to psychiatric hospital, it is possible that she would have been released by now. Instead, the popular assumption remains that by virtue of her sanity, Hindley has not changed one iota in twenty-seven years.

But madness also implies lack of responsibility, dispossession of the self. Faced with terrible crimes like these, and without a language to explain them, to label their perpetrator 'mad' allows us to push the horrors, our fear of the abject, away, settling the questions which – as the disappearance of Ian Brady from the headlines and the contingent vilification of Myra Hindley show – otherwise continue to nag at the public consciousness. In this context, the virulent loathing that Ann West still holds for Myra Hindley is understandable, but there can be little doubt that it has also been fostered by the press and, possibly, by West herself.

In 1989, Ann West wrote a book, *For the Love of Lesley*. It is a confused account, both a tirade against Hindley and the tragic story of her grief. When Lesley was killed, there were no victim support schemes to help relatives come to terms with the death of a loved one. Instead, West was prescribed tranquillizers and has, by her own admission, developed a chemical dependency. Her hatred of Hindley has become her *raison d'être* – 'my struggle to keep Hindley behind bars gave me a will to live and a sense of purpose'[28] – and she reiterates her threat, repeated many times in the press, that if Hindley is ever released, she will kill her. This may be one reason why Myra Hindley is still in prison.

Confession

Another portrait of Myra Hindley emerges from the accounts of her friends and supporters, and from the 1987 confessions she made to her involvement in the murders of Pauline Reade and Keith Bennett.

In 1984 (he is unsure of the exact date), Peter Timms, a Methodist minister, an experienced counsellor and an ex-prison governor, was approached by Hindley with a request for counselling. With permission from her Catholic priest and her governor, he began seeing her once a week. 'My impression was that she was a normal working-class girl, bright, articulate, intelligent, underachieved, who got involved, felt flattered by this man who was very clever,' he said. 'I felt that she had the enormity of the problem locked up inside her, and as she began to trust me, she began, very, very slowly, to unlock bits of her life.' Then as suddenly as they had started, the counselling sessions were stopped. Timms wrote to the Home Office to find out why, but was given no satisfactory answer. He is convinced that the reasons were political: 'They were afraid of the press, they weren't going to take risks with giving her privilege of any kind – even though there are people like me up and down the country giving counselling to prisoners. It's absurd to think that helping somebody come to terms with their offence and imprisonment is a privilege.'[29]

Then, in 1986, spurred by a book written by journalist Fred Harrison which claimed that Brady had begun talking about two more murders,[30] Manchester police began to show an interest in reopening the case. Timms received a phone call from Chief Superintendent Peter Topping, asking him if he would intervene with Myra Hindley to help police with their investigation. Timms agreed to discuss it with Hindley: 'I saw her for one visit and told her that my only interest was to help her resolve her conflict. I warned her that the authorities might try to pull the carpet from underneath her. We might start working again and get into something significant and then the counselling would be stopped. She said that the governor had agreed that the sessions would be open-ended and that Topping had promised the same.'[31]

During those sessions, Hindley spoke of her involvement in the killings of Reade and Kilbride, and of her obsession with – and fear of – Brady. She also said that she had been given legal advice not to co-operate with the police before she was arrested and when she was on remand. During the committal and trial she described how she felt she was the subject of intense scrutiny and so cultivated an expressionless face, since interpreted as evidence of her callousness. In the early 1970s, she said, she had requested permission to write to Ann West to allay her worst fears; that the infamous tape-recording was made not while her daughter was being physically tortured, but while she was being photographed. The Home Office refused to allow it.[32] (Hindley did write to Ann West in 1986, and the letter was released to the *Daily Mirror*, which printed extracts, along with a picture of a tearstained Mrs West. Angry at this splitting of hairs on the subject of torture, West claimed that Hindley's expression of remorse was fake.)

After speaking to Timms, Hindley wanted to talk to Peter Topping, but said she felt she couldn't go through the process of confession again without Timms being present. For two days she repeated what she had told Timms, and then said that she wanted to go on the record. 'She felt', said Timms, 'that she'd held on to all this for twenty years and wanted to get it over with. She also knew that she might face another trial.' She examined photographs taken by Brady back in the 1960s and tried to pinpoint locations where the bodies might be buried. Following her leads, police began to search the moors. The setting for this new episode in the drama was suitably macabre. The search, which had begun in November 1986, was hindered by mist, rain and frozen ground – as if the land itself was reluctant to yield its secrets. Then, in March 1987, amid a blaze of international publicity – some of which alleged, falsely, that she had been granted immunity in return for her confessions, and that they were just another ruse to gain public sympathy – Hindley was taken back to the moors to help identify the graves. As a direct result, the body of Pauline Reade was finally laid to rest. The body of Keith Bennett has still not been found.

The Director of Public Prosecutions decided not to prosecute Brady or Hindley for these two murders, on the grounds that to do so would be unnecessarily painful for the relatives. Immediately after securing the confessions, the Home Office, contravening its agreement with Hindley and Timms, stopped the counselling. Meanwhile, Hindley wrote to the Parole Board requesting that she not be considered for parole when her next review became due in 1990.

It must have taken courage for Myra Hindley to make those confessions twenty-one years after the event. Timms believes that she found them intensely traumatic, and that the attitude of the Home Office was callous in the extreme. He is also convinced that what she told him was the truth. Public opinion, to the extent that it is shaped and can be measured by the tabloids, still does not. In

1989, shortly after the release of the degree photographs, a *Sun* 'You the Jury' poll found that '42,000 Say Let Her Rot' (in jail).[33] It seems that Myra Hindley is damned if she speaks, and damned if she does not. Her attempts to represent *herself*, to locate an explanation for her actions somewhere between the polarities of victimization and evil, are doomed to failure; at once too subtle (I was obsessed, but I was still a separate person) and too contradictory (I knew what I was doing, but there was a part of me that didn't belong to me) – possibly even too *human*: they do not tally with the need to distance ourselves. This is not me; this has nothing to do with me. I will not countenance her.

Timms explains the reason for Hindley's twenty-one-year silence thus: 'The tragedy of all this is that she wasn't given help at the time of the trial; instead the focus was simply on whether she was guilty or not. Had she had help, perhaps all this would have come out then. Instead she gave a defensive face. That's what people saw, a hard person. But it's not unusual for lifers to refuse to acknowledge what they have done. I think in her case it was the least painful thing to do and that there was no one she felt comfortable enough with to trust with that terrible information. She knew that I knew how prisons operate, and the grapevine said that I was someone who could be trusted and that counselling prisoners was a job I was good at.'

Hindley herself has this to say: 'I knew what we were doing was wrong. But I can't explain it. When we were arrested, it was a relief, although I couldn't admit it to myself at the time. I was so terrified, and what we'd done was so terrible. For years I just blocked it; I couldn't talk about it or even admit it to myself. When I made the confession it was as if a weight had been lifted. I just wish I could have done it twenty years before. The wounds began to heal, then my counselling was cut off, and I was left with the enormity of what I'd done, but I couldn't go any further. I tried writing it all down, but apart from the fact that I could only write in privacy at night when we were locked up and I had terrible nightmares, I didn't understand it myself. I feel a terrible guilt. It's as if the wound opened up and then scarred over but the pain was still there. There's still a blockage. I just wish I could explain it somehow.'

It is tempting to believe, as do Timms and Hindley, that were she able to explain why, after the first murder, she didn't go to the police, public opprobrium might be stilled. While there is little doubt that for Myra Hindley to have continued access to therapy would have been of considerable benefit both to her and to our understanding of why people commit crimes like these, public feeling, exacerbated by the tabloids, runs much deeper than logic or reason will allow. It is the recognition of this which perhaps lies behind the Home Office's belligerence.

Loose ends

The British penal system is based on three tenets. The first is rehabilitation. Hindley's friends and supporters cite her degree as evidence that she has benefited from her time in prison, along with the fact that since the escape attempt in 1973, she has been a model prisoner. Another is whether a prisoner would be a danger to the public if he or she were released. There appears to be no evidence, psychiatric or otherwise, to suggest that this is true of Hindley. The third – and this is the major issue – is punishment. How long is long enough?

Myra Hindley has been in prison for close to twenty-seven years. Most lifers serve between ten and eleven years. Unless there is a psychiatric reason for keeping a person incarcerated, it is unusual for prisoners to serve more than twenty-five years.[34] For the victims' relatives – especially the family of Keith Bennett, whose body still lies somewhere on the moors – life should indeed mean life. But Hindley's supporters argue that the decision not to release her is a political one, based entirely on the necessity for the Parole Board to take public opinion into account, and one for which no Home Secretary would want to take responsibility. She should, they say, be treated like any other life prisoner. As David Astor, ex-proprietor of the *Observer*, put it:

> If Whitehall suggested that it was not that they feared the press, but that they cared about the feelings of the victims, why has that sensitivity not been shown in other cases? Presumably because if all relatives of all victims had a right of veto over the release of their particular criminal, few releases would ever be made.[35]

Although there is a long history of certain prisoners being held as scapegoats, the case of Myra Hindley and its attendant publicity presents a problem for a criminal justice system which must be answerable to rational principles and which prides itself on its basis in empirical judgement rather than speculative assessment. But beyond this lie other, deeper questions: about the standards by which femininity is judged and the ways in which the reality of a female serial killer unhinges our assumptions about women. Perhaps we will never know the extent of Hindley's involvement in the killings – although the available evidence suggests that she may be speaking the truth, as far as it is possible to do so – but we can see how the logic of opposite extremes and ideological norms of female behaviour combine either to deny her any agency, to make her the 'innocent victim' of a psychopathic megalomaniac, or to cast her as essentially wicked. The mythology of Myra Hindley reveals, above all, that we do not have a language to represent female killing, and that a case like this disrupts the very terms which hold gender in place.

The trials of motherhood

*The case of Azaria and
Lindy Chamberlain*

Briar Wood

Around 8 p.m. on the evening of 17 August 1980, at a
camping ground near Uluru, also known as Ayers Rock,
Azaria Chamberlain, the daughter of Lindy and Michael
Chamberlain, disappeared from the tent where her mother
had put her to bed only a few minutes before. There
was blood on the bedclothes as well as on the tent,
and Lindy Chamberlain saw a dingo emerging from the
tent shaking its head seconds before discovering her
daughter's absence. Reports of dingoes attacking people
the day before were circulating, and July and August had
seen many such reports.

A dingo, for anyone who doesn't know, has been defined
as:

1. the Australian wild dog, *Canis familiaris dingo*,
introduced by the Aborigines, often tawny-yellow in
colour, with erect ears, a bushy tail and distinctive gait,
and with a call resembling a howl or yelp rather than
a bark. 2.a. a contemptible person; coward. b. one who
shirks responsibility or evades difficult situations. – *v.i.3.*
to act in a cowardly manner.[1]

Skilled Aboriginal trackers testified that there were dingo
tracks leading into and out of the tent, and imprint marks
in the sand consistent with the baby's clothing where the
dingo could have put the child down.

The Chamberlains spoke openly to journalists and did television interviews, hoping to warn other parents of the dangers of dingoes and to speak about the strength in adversity they believed their religious faith had given them. I don't remember exactly when the Azaria Chamberlain case surfaced in my personal consciousness, but I do remember following it daily, with a feeling of deep unease, in the newspapers at the time of the second inquest. I recall being aware – as were a great many people living in Australia and New Zealand, and possibly further afield – that something very peculiar was going on, and that there was a lot at stake. The fact that only last year Lindy Chamberlain was awarded the equivalent of £380,000 and Michael Chamberlain £170,000 compensation (they had claimed £2.2 million) by the Northern Territory government means that the case dragged on for over ten years, and the Chamberlains will always be a focus of media attention.

My reasons for wanting to return to it yet again are that despite the fact that I have read a lot of material, there are still nagging questions. Those questions, already raised many times, are explored from a different perspective in this chapter: Why was there a second inquest, quashing the findings of the first, followed by a trial, and how did Lindy Chamberlain come to be imprisoned for the murder of her child? Why was it that despite such strong evidence to the contrary, Lindy Chamberlain was accused of murdering her daughter? And finally, how is it that the case has produced so much discussion and visual or written material?

Various explanations, emphasizing the part played by factors such as the attitudes of the press, ideological stereotypes of women, clashes between federal, national and international systems, city/country hostility and uneasiness about religious beliefs in Australia, have already been offered. I will draw and expand on several of these explanations. In particular, I will return to the question of Lindy Chamberlain's role as woman and, especially, mother, and her position in terms of Australian discourses about Australian nationality. Some of these issues will be linked to a discussion of the mechanism of scapegoating. I have focused on a number of texts that attempt to deal with and interpret the facts of the case: John Bryson's book *Evil Angels* (1985), Ken Crispin's *The Crown Versus Chamberlain 1980–1987* (1987), Dianne Johnson's 'From Fairy To Witch: Imagery and Myth in the Azaria Case' (1984), Jennifer Craik's 'The Azaria Chamberlain Case and Questions of Infanticide' (1987) and Lindy Chamberlain's autobiography, *Through My Eyes* (1990).

Motherhood on trial

On 24 August 1980, Azaria's clothing (except a jacket) was found by a tourist, Wally Goodwin. Constable Morris, who visited the scene, picked up the jumpsuit when he got there, so that later photographs of it did not, according to Goodwin, accurately represent its position when he had first seen it. Paw prints found on a blanket that had been in the tent on the night of Azaria's disappearance, seen by several members of the Chamberlain family, disappeared in police hands. Lindy Chamberlain was to claim that the policeman who testified at the trial to having picked up the blanket was not the one who did so. These are just a few of the tales of police mismanagement in what was already emerging as a controversial case.

There were suspicions amongst police and journalists about the Chamberlains' version of events. At the same time, rumours were spreading that Lindy Chamberlain had been a careless mother, that she had dressed the baby in black, that Azaria meant 'sacrifice in the wilderness', and many more. The Chamberlains were openly abused and received mail and calls from members of the public who believed they had killed Azaria. A task force headed by Detective Sergeant Graeme Charlwood took over the investigation of the case in September 1980. He conducted a secretive operation, taping the Chamberlains without their permission and inquiring into many areas in their lives in the town of Mount Isa, where Michael was a Pastor in the Seventh-Day Adventist Church. Evidence was given by a forensic dentist, Kenneth Brown, of tests done with dingoes in Adelaide Zoo. According to him, the damage to fabrics by the dingoes' teeth did not tally with the marks on Azaria's clothing and bedding. Scientific tests were done on clothing, saliva and bloodstains.

An inquest opened in Alice Springs on 16 December 1980. Amid threats to the Chamberlains' lives, eyewitnesses, trackers and a number of scientists were called on to give evidence. Coroner Barritt took the unusual step of permitting the concluding statement on 20 February 1981 to be televised in order to quell rumours spreading across the country, the most persistent of which was that the Chamberlains themselves had killed the baby. It was the first time such a decision had ever been made in the Northern Territory. The conclusion reached in the inquest was that a dingo had taken Azaria and that her body had been 'taken from the dingo and disposed of by a person or persons unknown'. The Coroner publicly rebuked both the conservation authorities at Uluru for failing to take sufficient precautions to protect the public against the increasing presence of dingoes at the camp site, and criticized the Northern Territory Police Force Forensic Science Section for less than stringent standards in their testing procedures, and for their lack of objectivity.

Many of those whom these criticisms touched did not take them well. Kenneth Brown was one. He got permission to have the jumpsuit Azaria had been wearing at the time of her death examined by Professor James Cameron, a forensic pathologist in London. Cameron concluded that Azaria's neck had been cut with a sharp instrument, that there were prints from an adult female hand on the back of the jumpsuit, and that she had been buried in the jumpsuit. After receiving this report, the Northern Territory Police called a high-level conference at which they planned to resume investigation of the case, reinterview all the witnesses and tape every interview, including conversations between policemen. The Chamberlains' home, car and private property were examined, as well as many medical and personal records. The police leaked limited information to the press, but refused the Chamberlains' counsel access to any information about the reasons for the renewed investigation. Police also conducted an exhaustive search of the camping ground at Ayers Rock. An application to the Supreme Court of the Northern Territory for the suppression of the findings of the first inquest was made on 20 November 1981 and a second inquest opened on 14 December 1981.

The inquest was organized in preference to the arrest and charging of Lindy Chamberlain because the police, having gathered a large amount of 'scientific' evidence against her, wanted to question her without having to make a case openly. They hoped that during the intense questioning that would take place before they tendered their evidence, she and other witnesses would make statements corroborating their evidence. Towards the conclusion of the inquest, it became obvious that the Crown's material was leading to the construction of a sequence of events quite different to the conclusion of the first inquest. According to the Crown, Lindy Chamberlain had cut Azaria's throat in the front seat of the car, hidden the body in the car, buried it, dug it up later, taken the clothing off, reburied the body and planted the jumpsuit at some time, with her husband's assistance. Meanwhile, in the country at large, rumours were increasing, with new stories appearing – some of them circulating via police and press, others springing up from alternative sources. At the conclusion of the inquest, Lindy Chamberlain was charged with Azaria's murder and Michael with being an accessory.

By the time the trial opened in Darwin on 13 September amid intense public hostility against her, Lindy
Chamberlain was six months pregnant. The jury consisted
of three women and nine men. In preparing for the
defence, Stuart Tipple, the Chamberlains' solicitor, consulted Professor Barry Boettcher, head of the Department
of Biological Services at the University of Newcastle, who
had examined and contested the findings of tests done
by a forensic scientist working for the New South Wales
Health Commission, Joy Kuhl. The original plates used
by Kuhl had been destroyed and had not been photographed. Consequently, they could not be re-examined.
Unlike Lindy Chamberlain's counsel, the Crown made
little attempt to address the case in terms of the statements
by witnesses. Instead, it concentrated on attempting to
provide overwhelming scientific evidence of the couple's
guilt, in which Kuhl's tests played an important part. Other
factors also worked against the Chamberlains, such as the
strong feeling running against them – as outsiders and as
outspoken Christians – in the city of Darwin, from which
the jury was drawn. On 28 October 1982, the jury passed a
verdict of guilty and Lindy Chamberlain was sentenced to
life imprisonment with hard labour. Michael Chamberlain
was sentenced to eighteen months.

Lindy Chamberlain was taken to Darwin Penitentiary,
at Berrimah, where she gave birth to Kahlia on 17 November 1982. Groups had been formed to petition for her
release, and an appeal was lodged. She went, on strict
bail conditions, to Avondale College at Cooranbong on
21 November 1982, but on 30 April 1983, the appeal
was dismissed. Lindy Chamberlain returned to Berrimah,
where she remained for three years, after a final High
Court appeal was turned down. Outspoken public support
for the Chamberlains continued to mount, including that
of other scientists prepared to challenge the Crown's
evidence. The Martin Report, a document containing new
evidence against the Crown's case, was dismissed, and

not until Azaria's missing matinée jacket was found in February 1986 was the need for a judicial inquiry established. The decision was also taken – suddenly – by the Executive Council of the Northern Territory Government to release Lindy Chamberlain from prison, amid widespread criticism of the conduct of government officials involved with the case.

The Northern Territory Parliament had to pass a bill to enable the selection of a judge from the Federal Court of Australia to review the Chamberlain case. Mr Justice Morling opened a Commission of Inquiry in May 1986. The matinée jacket was examined by the Victorian Forensic Science Laboratory, which had not previously been involved in the case, and both the Crown and the Chamberlains' representatives gave evidence. Aboriginal trackers had their own legal representative and gave careful evidence with the help of interpreters. The Crown's scientific evidence, intended to establish that Azaria had been killed in the car, was questioned, while the evidence of a dingo attack was given far greater validity. The Morling Report concluded that had the jury been given the evidence assembled before the commission, the couple had to have been acquitted.

Signifying motherhood

In his summing-up at the trial in Darwin, John Phillips, the Chamberlains' defence attorney, said:

> Ladies and Gentlemen, women do not usually murder
> their babies, because to do so would be contrary to
> nature. One of the most fundamental facts in nature
> is the love of a mother for her child. The love of a
> mother for her baby. A mother will make all manner of
> sacrifices for her baby. A mother will die for her baby.
> We all know that. It happens again and again. But we
> know too, from the evidence in this trial, that sometimes

mothers may harm or even kill their babies. But we know too, from the evidence in this trial, that that's not really contrary to nature when it happens, because we know that natural love of those mothers for their babies has been distorted and warped and removed by the effect of severe depressive illness. So that the killings can be said to be motiveless killings: killings without reason.[2]

Phillips's reasoning on the subject of motherhood and murder goes something like this: mother-love, up to and including the point of (self-) sacrifice, is the most natural thing in the world. Here, the category natural stands in for fixed or immutable. A woman who doesn't love her child to this point can't be called a proper mother; she must be mad and/or sick; she must be suffering from postnatal depression, and if she then kills her baby she can't have any reason for doing it except madness. Madness is illness, lack of reason, the failure of expressivity; and madness is motivelessness.

However narrow Phillips's reasoning, it must have met wide acceptance, since it was to these unspeakable categories – that of the mad and/or motiveless infanticide – that Lindy Chamberlain was publicly assigned after her conviction for Azaria's murder. Many continued to believe in her innocence, but the question remains open as to whether the case finally succeeded in widening the terms about the debate, or whether Lindy Chamberlain's innocence has closed it off again, returning her to the category of self-sacrificing (instead of child-sacrificing) and 'good' rather than 'bad' and selfish mother. Continuing his summary, Phillips reminded the jury of the fact that medical staff had not noticed any symptoms of postnatal depression in Lindy Chamberlain, and that the Crown prosecution had not managed to suggest any possible motive for her to kill her child. In terms of Phillips's argument, babies can't possibly be the cause of a mother's illness or distress; babies are innocent, and it is the mother who must still bear the burden of whatever responsibility she carries beyond the terms of her own ability to endure. If the mother isn't willing to die for her child, she's inhuman and unnatural, and if she does sacrifice herself she's annihilated herself; either way, she's as good as dead.

The Crown made little attempt to address the case in humanitarian terms. It did not even attempt to suggest a motive. Instead, it concentrated on attempting to provide overwhelming scientific evidence of Lindy Chamberlain's guilt. The evidence consisted of a barrage of 'facts' such as the claim that bloodstains found in the car and on Michael's camera bag were foetal blood, consistent with that of a child Azaria's age. The fact that some of this evidence was given by a woman, Mrs Joy Kuhl, who was quoted in *Evil Angels* as saying of Lindy Chamberlain: 'And all the time she was there behind me, staring. She just stares. She is, you know, a witch. I could feel her eyes burning holes through my back' [3] illustrates the degree to which a large section of public feeling was hostile to Lindy Chamberlain and the fact that women, too, participated in her vilification.

Although there were women writing in defence of Lindy Chamberlain, her position did not, perhaps, arouse the sympathy and admiration of women with more secular attitudes to life. Lindy Chamberlain appeared as a regressive figure rather than an obvious heroine of our times. None the less, her apparent acceptance of gender-role divisions was made problematic by events surrounding the trial. Her decision to be interviewed on television after the death of her child led, ironically, to accusations of heartlessness, self-aggrandizement and cynicism. In stepping outside the private role of housewife to become a public figure, Lindy Chamberlain's eagerness to speak to the media raised questions about what constitutes appropriate forms of mourning in a secular society.[4] It also earned her the hostility of many Northern Territory officials, police and members of the public whose territorial loyalties were aroused. Criticism of local authorities and rangers from visitors and tourists like the Chamberlains, who were ambivalently viewed as both unwelcome invaders and a necessary source of income, was regarded as an unwelcome intrusion into an area of federal jurisdiction.

A number of articles appeared by women exploring the intricacies of the case in terms of how it highlighted ideological constructions of femininity. Jennifer Craik's paper 'The Azaria Chamberlain Case and Questions of Infanticide' drew on previous texts such as Dianne Johnson's 'From Fairy to Witch: Imagery and Myth in the Azaria Chamberlain Case', which discussed the demonization of Lindy Chamberlain and her stereotyping as a witch. Craik suggested that Azaria's disappearance contextualized the 'implicit problematicity of the category "mother",'[5] and caused a re-evaluation of the status of maternity in its relation to the law. The Northern Territory, as a frontier society, did not have sufficiently sophisticated or subtle legislation to deal with a case of this kind, she wrote. All convictions of murder carried a mandatory sentence of life imprisonment, and this left no legal space for discussion of such mitigating circumstances as postpartum psychosis or the social welfare concerns which usually surround the death or disappearance of a child.

Craik's description of the case as one which raises prosaic issues about the law is, I think, a valid one. On the other hand, her discussion of the way events rapidly became mythologized is focused on restoring the importance of facts rather than investigating the power of fantasy to influence real events. One of the purposes of this essay is to expand on Craik's observations by picking up issues related primarily to what might be called a feminist interest in whether structural generalizations about the position of women – in particular, women as mothers – could be adduced from the fate of Lindy Chamberlain. The

Chamberlain trial was both quintessentially Australian (it couldn't have happened anywhere else) and transcultural in the way it produced a dilemma over the representation of women in and by the law. If only for the way in which it dramatized the local, national and international structures that circumscribe the lives of so many women in the past, present and possibly future, the Chamberlain trial has a crucial resonance. Why did the heaviest burden of responsibility fall on Lindy Chamberlain rather than her husband Michael? The most obvious feminist answer – that it is the mother who is ultimately held responsible for a child's safety – has, in this case, complex and multiple ramifications.

Related to this is the recurrent question of how the case reveals the way discourses – of the law, journalism, religion, nationalism – position and construct ideas about femininity and motherhood. The Chamberlain case, with its plethora of evidence – written, celluloid and spoken – testified to both the mobility *and* the fixity of the structures within which the lives of contemporary women are gendered. In opening up the lives of this God-fearing family, and in Lindy Chamberlain's subsequent and quite candid autobiography, the case raised questions about intra- and inter-gender relationships – between Michael and Lindy, Lindy and Azaria, Lindy and her sons, Reagan and Aidan. In both the way Lindy Chamberlain was represented and the way she represented herself, the case highlights the ideological contradictions between various constructions of female identity – housewife, mother, daughter, and professional woman. The death of Azaria Chamberlain caused a wide variety of attitudes towards maternity, the figure of the mother, parenting and the role of the state in the parent–child relationship, to be publicly aired.

The unprecedented degree of publicity surrounding the case can be read as an effect of the foregrounding of discourses about the maternal, in which the maternal stands as a signifier for both origin and end of the linguistic drive to generate meaning. Critic and psychoanalyst Julia Kristeva describes the maternal as a site of rapid and radical alteration both in the body and at the level of representation:

> Cells fuse, split and proliferate; volumes grow, tissues
> stretch, and body fluids change rhythm, speeding up
> or slowing down. Within the body, growing as a graft,
> indomitable, there is an other. And no one is present,
> within that simultaneously dual and alien space,
> to signify what is going on. It happens, but I'm not
> there. 'I cannot realize it but it goes on.' Motherhood's
> impossible syllogism.[6]

American academic Mary Jacobus argues that for Kristeva, as for the discourses of Christianity, 'the maternal body is the place of splitting', and that 'the discourse of maternity is another name for the movement of parturition which (re)produces the subject in, and of, representation'.[7] The representation of the mother is the point where the distinction between the real and representation is often lost.

Theoretician and critic Jacqueline Rose has argued that in terms of Lacan's text 'God and the *Jouissance* of The Woman', the signification of woman and God as Other[8] is exposed for the way it has underpinned and fixed the signifier of 'man'. The God-term, with its fantasy of an omniscient and omnipotent being (often gendered as 'He'), secures an illusory coherence of the sign. It is with reference to 'God' as the source and final reference point of interpretation that man's 'place' in the world has been designated:

> As negative to the man, woman becomes a total object
> of fantasy (or an object of total fantasy), elevated into the
> place of the Other and made to stand for the truth. Since

the place of the Other is also the place of God, this is the
ultimate form of mystification . . . In so far as God 'has
not made his exit', so the woman becomes the support
of his symbolic place.[9]

As the good mother and God-fearing wife, Lindy Chamberlain did her very best to fit this description of the
fantasy woman whose support of the male-led institutions
of Church and home guarantees their continuity. But in
the sense that this identity *is* a fantasy, no real woman
can fulfil it. In so far as – in a system where logic is
based on the contrast between extreme oppositions –
God represents all that is right and good, woman, as
not-God and as a diametrical opposite of the God term,
can stand in as a representation of evil. The extremes of
representation manifest in public and official attitudes to
Lindy Chamberlain indicate the operation of such a split –
'witch or fairy', good mother or infanticide – these were the
poles around which the discourses sometimes circulated.

John Bryson's *Evil Angels*, the first major study of the
case, begins with a history of the Seventh-Day Adventist
Church and a description of a night in 1844 when several families in Pennsylvania unsuccessfully awaited the
Second Coming of Christ. In spite of the Great Disappointment – as it came to be known – the Church survived, and
it was this group to which Michael and Lindy Chamberlain
belonged. By juxtaposing this story of the failure of revelation beside that of the Chamberlains', and in laying it out
as a narrative about the origins and limits of the Church,
Bryson attempts to explain the Chamberlains' behaviour.
What is particularly noticeable about Bryson's book is
that it avoids sceptical or ironic commentary – about
the police, the judiciary, or the Chamberlains. Despite
his avowed intention that his book was to contribute
to the clearing of Lindy Chamberlain's name, Bryson's
approach could be interpreted as having simultaneously
fuelled the discussion about mysticism that made the

case a locus of heated public opinion. Its circumlocutory narrative approach cast the case in terms of a grand debate about the meaning of life, death and spirituality. The title, for example – 'evil angels', with its hint of black magic – might have been chosen with an eye as much to publicity as to dispelling public fantasies. The title might, in fact, have contributed to keeping such ideas as the rumour that Azaria's name was said to have meant 'sacrifice in the wilderness' in circulation rather than halting them.

The term 'evil angels' was used by Ellen White, prophet and founder of the Seventh-Day Adventist movement in Australia, to describe secular opponents, but this reference would be known only to someone who had read the book (which is 550 pages long) very carefully. The publicity brochure released by Cannon Entertainment Inc. – distributors of the film *A Cry in the Dark*, which was based on Bryson's book – quotes him as saying: 'I knew two books would have impact: the first and the best. And I was going to write the best.' But despite this unseemly hurry to produce an outstanding first account of the case, the reader was assured that Bryson wanted the film to 'be good, in a writing sense'. The extent to which a good scoop, a good story and a literary work are compatible was at stake, and the question must be asked as to whether Bryson's metaphorical method, his very literariness, was, in fact, the most effective way of securing Lindy Chamberlain's release. On the contrary, it may have been that the attempts to universalize the case through apocalyptic rhetoric and grand thematic trajectories resulted in a vagueness that confused rather than clarified the issues.

The film title was originally *Evil Angels*, but it had to be altered for its US release because it was thought that the public would link it to the Hell's Angels gang – that they would, in other words, give it too literal a reading. Bryson, a lawyer and writer, emphasizes the power of the media, suggesting that the press was responsible for ensuring Lindy Chamberlain's conviction and later, when better advised, securing her release. The film publicity praises Bryson for modestly 'downplaying the issue of how much influence his chronicle had in accelerating Lindy Chamberlain's release, but there can be no doubt that the book's publication in 1985 had an enormous impact'.

Bryson's concern with the impact of media politics on the criminal justice system emerges as a major theme in the film. He strongly criticizes the public-relations exercises carried out by investigative teams, with apparently little awareness that the circulation of his own writing is caught up in similar (PR) mechanisms. Police, lawyers and scientists do emerge as culpable in Bryson's summary, yet the push to make the general public more aware of its own manipulation through the media leaves out the question of where the PR stops. The Chamberlain trial was a spectacular illustration of the power of press and media:

It's something that has already happened in the United States, where the hearts and minds of a jury are being fought for from the moment that news of a crime hits the television screen. The police, the personable lawyer, the district attorney . . . all of them are using public relations methodologies.[10]

This reference to the USA as exemplary media-dominated society is an important factor in considering how the film *A Cry in the Dark* represented the case. The American actress Meryl Streep, who specializes in playing the eternal feminine, was chosen for the role of Lindy Chamberlain. Many of the specific references to Australian culture were diffused and signified only on a visual level. Lindy Chamberlain was represented as any and every outspoken woman. But the overt attempt to present her as 'ordinary' was undermined by the fact that the role was played by Streep made up to look suitably Australian-housewifey – i.e. 'homely' on the outside but extraordinarily capable underneath. In terms of the PR, Streep's decision to take the role increased media speculation about the contrast between the two, rather than setting out to explain the facts of the Chamberlain case to an international audience. Streep was reported in the British tabloid *Daily Mail*, for example, as saying of Chamberlain: 'I've met tough guys but she is formidable. I had a lot of fears about meeting her. I think she thought I was too tall, too blonde, my nose was too long and, of course, I'm American.' The failure to situate Lindy Chamberlain in terms of a personal, familial or social past meant that she was once again made mysterious and enigmatic. The black wig worn by Meryl Streep in the film which caused so much mirth among reviewers replaced Lindy Chamberlain's brown hair and mobilized the witch-hunt motif through the reproduction of a visual stereotype.

Multiple myths of origin: maternity and nationality

The signifier/signified 'Lindy Chamberlain' has come to stand in popular consciousness for a cluster of fantasy and linguistic relations. In a number of collective imaginations and a variety of moments she has represented the phallic mother, the unnatural mother, a 'good-enough' mother, a Christian mother and the mother who 'eats', or consumes, her own babies. In the collapse of sign systems that occurs on the borders of representation – and I'm thinking here of Julia Kristeva's notion of the abjected mother[11] – the boundaries between nature and culture, the human and the animal, dissolve.

In traditionally male-dominated Western signifying systems such as Romantic writing, for example, women often represented a transitional or intermediary category between nature and culture. The T-shirts depicting a dingo with Lindy Chamberlain-style hairdo and dark glasses with the caption 'The Dingo is Innocent' that appeared at the time of the trial represent a moment when categories of meaning collapse. They make a joke of the emergence into public discourse of a terrifying fantasy about consumption and being consumed by the mother/nation. Ian Barker, senior prosecuting counsel, discredited the idea that a dingo had taken Azaria and implicated her houseproud mother by commenting: 'it was not only a dexterous dingo, it was a very tidy dingo . . . It managed to cut the collar and the sleeve with a pair of scissors.'[12]

The dingo as totem came, in various ways, to represent Australia, and the argument about its innocence poses the question of how responsibility for the maintenance of law, order and modernity is to be maintained in Australia – and at what price. Some of the jokes that emerged at the time – and I intend to represent only one of many here – signal a mixture of anxiety and confidence about the signification of a subjectivity that could be called distinctively Australian. Q: What would have changed the course of history? A: A dingo at Bethlehem. To point out how the word dingo stood in for a spurious Australian identity within an international framework, I need only remind readers of an advertisement for low-alcohol lager that was trundled about on London's double-decker buses a couple of years ago. 'Swan', read the sign. 'It won't make your dingo limp.'[13]

Aidan Chamberlain's poignant response to the loss of his sister, 'the dingo's got my bubby in its tummy', articulated what became a national obsession. As wild dogs, dingoes occupy an ambivalent space between nature and culture – they exist on the threshold of and in constant contact with human habitation, but have not been entirely domesticated by it. The domestic guard dog such as the the Rottweiler or pit bull terrier might be said to occupy a comparable, but significantly different, position in contemporary British society. The opposite of the nurturing mother who carries the child in her belly is the savage dingo – though dingoes, too, can be 'mothers'.

Positioned in the centre of Australia where Azaria disappeared, Uluru became the belly or omphalos of the nation, and at this ambivalent (a place of both birth and death) centre, the figure of Lindy Chamberlain was transposed on to the figure of the dingo – and vice versa. This transposition occurred most frequently and readily in the minds of those who knew little of outback lore/law. Professors in London, journalists inhabiting a Sydney high-rise, policemen for whom detective work is primarily an urban activity – such people were unable to accept the dingo explanation. On the other hand, rangers and locals, including Aboriginal people, had no doubt that a dingo could, would and did take and eat the baby.

Writing on 'Nostalgia in Australian (Migrant) Writing', Sneja Gunew states that for white Australians:

> Life . . . exists in cities, on the edge where the land is covered over, pressed under, and where the subject is lost in the automatic, automaniac maze: life-in-death and death-in-life. The real mother is always elsewhere, though repressed, in other cultures, though disavowed.[14]

It was within this context of urbanization that the Chamberlain case surfaced and assumed the dimensions it did, at a time when, for a majority of white Australians, the representation of the outback was once again a contentious issue. As Australia became increasingly a nation of city-dwellers, the old myths about the outback needed to be reworked; the international success of *Crocodile Dundee* was one strikingly obvious example. *Evil Angels* also staged various aspects of this urban/rural divide. While the film drew on the popular formula of the courtroom drama, it also had successful mainstream precedents like *The Last Wave*, *Picnic at Hanging Rock* and *Walkabout*, which represented the intersection of white Australian culture with Aboriginal cultural elements. *A Cry in the Dark* locks into narratives like these, where Australia becomes synonymous with the outback and the threat of losing the standards and norms of modern American/European life.

Australia Live, a bicentennial production that televised a day in the life of Australia, has been described by cultural critic Meaghan Morris in '*Australia Live*: Celebration of a Nation' as an attempt to reshape an Australian image as object for consumption in which 'a surveillance space where nothing secret, mysterious, troubling or malcontent could find a place to walk or hide'. It 'celebrated Australia as a vast reservoir of exotic yet familiar (cross culturally accessible) resorts and photographic locations . . . It produced Australia as a space for visiting, investing . . .'[15] Morris points out, however, that the reordering of history is not equivalent to the abolition of history. The recording and interpretation of the Chamberlain case, as historical event, has been up for grabs and to some extent still is. Sneja Gunew suggests that for immigrants who acknowledge the importance – even the primacy – of other countries of origin, other languages, 'Australia is the mother who is not mother, the uncanny place that will never give birth: the still-born. For white Australians, the country is the dead centre, the mother who ingests life.'[16] A footnote adds the suggestive remark: 'This resonates with new mythic significance as a result of the Azaria Chamberlain case.'[17]

Sneja Gunew explores the relationship between psychoanalytic theories of the subject and fantasized representations of parents, parent culture and language. Using the terms of the psychoanalyst Jacques Lacan, she proposes that the entry into language is synonymous with the Symbolic Order, which is the domain of the father. The mother is linked to the field of the Imaginary, in which the child attempts to fantasize an integrated identity. The Symbolic Order is modelled on the language system, and access to this system is gained by passing through the Oedipal crisis. If the entry into language is superseded by a move to another country, the country of origin (since its signifying systems have to be repressed to make way for those of an alternative community) might then be signified in migrant consciousness in maternal terms. The resurfacing of the fantasy of the maternal/(m)other country into national discourses brings with it disturbing elements.[18] Lindy Chamberlain was born outside the geographical borders of Australia – in New Zealand. Paradoxically, it is the proximity of her origins and the ambivalence of her 'Australianness', since she was brought up in Australia from the age of twenty months, that made her both typical and an outsider by birth, and only by birth. Lindy Chamberlain's autobiography can then be read as a bid to enter the Symbolic constructions of Australian identity. She did this at the price (through no fault of her own) of losing her baby daughter, who then came to signify a lost and silenced femininity.

Gunew is primarily concerned with what writers reveal about the psychic process of moving from one country to another, one language to another. In her terms the Chamberlains had not moved from one language to another but as migrant New Zealanders they had constantly to negotiate their own displacement in the shifting terms that construct cultural and national identities. They too were migrants in what she describes as a migrant society. And typically, at the time of Azaria's disappearance, they were, by travelling as tourists and holidaymakers, engaged in the act of (nationally) contemplating the country's navel. In her autobiography, in the chapter that leads up to the moment when the baby was taken, Lindy Chamberlain ironically refers to the trip as 'The Holiday of a Lifetime'. This self-conscious and avid interest in exploring and discovering their 'own' country on holiday/holy days exemplifies the way in which ideologies may focus on the need to keep currency circulating within the boundaries of the national culture in order constantly to reinforce the idea of nationhood. Being a tourist in your own country becomes an act of national loyalty and commitment.

Parents take their children to view sights, landmarks and buildings to establish, both in their own minds and those of their offspring, the enduring importance of nationally significant structures and sites. In the case of the Chamberlains they were distanced from this process while participating in it – their status as tourists was emphasized by their New Zealand origins.

Writing for her life

Michael Chamberlain's interest in photography and Lindy's buying of souvenirs of Ayers Rock for her sons even after the death of her daughter there reveal them as participants in the continuous process by which individual subjectivities attempt to align themselves with national ones. The national subject must be represented through images, symbols or words. However, because these processes of representation involve different signifying systems, governed by differing codes and relations, national and individual discourses often cannot be exactly mapped on to each other. The Chamberlains' position as both insiders and outsiders – and, above all, Lindy Chamberlain's status as a mother whose 'origins' and whose husband's 'origins' were elsewhere – rendered the couple ambivalent as loyal subjects to the constructions of Australian law, and beyond that, the law of a(n) (m)other country, Great Britain. Even the religion they followed was a marginal one in terms of national and international institutions.

Ken Crispin has described a degree of 'paranoia' in the police handling of the case, and police reactions were matched by rising public controversy over it. Not only did the Chamberlains experience the full glare of public gaze on many aspects of their private lives, but they were inspected, analysed and studied by the police to a remarkable degree. Plans made to reinterview all witnesses and to tape-record all conversations about the case, even those between police officers themselves, can be understood as a desire for the law to be able to achieve total surveillance of its subjects. This desire is also reflected in the enormous variety of technological machinery wheeled out to record the case: recording tapes, videotapes, books, letters, legal papers, newspaper and magazine articles, television and, of course, the movie, with its attendant posters, postcards and stills. Ken Crispin, whose book was published in 1987, noted: 'As the Attorney General told the Northern Territory parliament, "the amount of evidence, exhibits, transcript and other items which were freighted from Darwin to Sydney, and back again, weighed an estimated five tonnes."'[19]

When, at the the first inquest, Coroner Barritt took the step of permitting the concluding statement to be televised, it was with the specific intention of quelling rumours. The conclusion that the dingo had 'appropriated the baby into the unknown', as Craik points out,[20] allowed for the possibility that there was 'human intervention in the burial of the body', but also works to reincorporate this horror back into the known. By such a strategy, 'the fear and threat of the unknown could be "tidied up" in an account which incorporated the events back into the social'. It also meant that the threat of the abject corpse of the child – the absent body – could, at a fantasy level, have been 'buried' with due ceremony. This was confirmed by the fact that the subsequent reappearance of the matinée jacket was the cause of the resurgence of massive public, legal and police concern over the events which preceded it.

Coroner Barritt's study of a transcript in which Sergeant Saundry from the Northern Territory police questioned Dr Corbett, a dingo expert, caused him to remark that 'when Dr Corbett made a statement in any way supporting the Chamberlains' account of this tragedy, the topic was immediately changed, obviously to avoid any further evidence that might support the Dingo Theory'.[21] The fact that

Professor James Cameron's conclusion that there was the print of an adult female hand on the back and shoulder of the jumpsuit was ever taken seriously (how can the gender of a hand be determined from a smeared print?) reveals the blatant degree to which sexist judgements were operating. Crispin describes the alacrity of the police response to this report as extraordinary, but given the predominantly male composition of the police force, the Chamberlain case is one more among many in which male fantasies are so overdetermined as to become publicly revealed as fantasy. Another parallel can be drawn between police surveillance and psychoanalysis in the sense that psychoanalysis, as a practice, had its beginnings in a situation where the observation of women was presided over by male authorities. Detective Sergeant Charlwood, for example, suggested to Lindy Chamberlain that she submit to hypnosis. She refused on 'religious grounds' – and it is around the delineation of what constitutes the religious and the sacred that so many of the rumours about the case turned.

The televising of the inquest decision disseminated rather than put an end to discussion. Meaghan Morris argued in *'Australia Live'* that 'Thanks to satellites, aeroplanes and computers (three enabling conditions of the show), one version of history, at least, was repeatedly declared dead: Australia as a space of isolation, slow development, and eccentricity.'[22] Although this idea seems applicable to the Chamberlain case, it could equally be argued that the events surrounding it have in many ways fixed Australia again in an international imagination as a place where strange and inexplicable events occur; a lawless frontier inhabited by weirdos, cranks, Aboriginals, and wild animals. Morris quotes feminist academic Alice Jardine's description of paranoia as involving both a 'fear of the loss of borders' and an experience of such a loss, and suggests that the work of postmodernist theoreticians like Fredric Jameson points to the way in which, in media-dominated space, the 'practice of discrimination seems to have become more difficult'.[23] In terms of national identity, the question of who or what was defined as Australian resurfaced in the case of Lindy and Azaria Chamberlain.

Even after the Morling Commission had systematically deconstructed the Crown's case, Barker, the senior prosecuting counsel for the Crown, persisted in locating responsibility for events with Lindy Chamberlain:

> The Crown's position is that all the facts are not known
> and never will be known because the sole repository
> of all facts is Mrs Chamberlain and she will not
> disclose what happened . . . In suggesting possible
> murder scenarios, we are not inventing hypotheses.
> If there is or are a possible scenario or scenarios, it
> follows that murder, if otherwise proved, is not to
> be disproved on the basis that there was no place or
> means or opportunity for it to have happened. The
> Crown says it did happen because that is the only
> rational conclusion capable of accounting for the
> demonstrated facts.[24]

This statement is tantamount to a denial that the discourses of the law can have an unconscious or hidden agenda. The narratives the Crown constructs to prove Mrs Chamberlain a murderess must be logical because the Crown has proposed them. They cannot be scenarios because that term introduces the possibility of a fantasy life and its intrusion into the administration of justice. But the repeated negatives and tortuous grammar are an indication that something else is going on. In fact, collective versions of fantasy life *did* break through in this case, and affected events in and around the trial. The refusal to abandon the interrogation of Lindy Chamberlain stemmed from the prosecution's *idée fixe* that as mother she *must* know and *must* be made to speak the truth. And Lindy Chamberlain both fulfilled this function and could not. As exemplary Christian, she had to speak the truth, the whole truth and nothing but the truth; yet her discourse produced silences, inarticulacies, denials, contradictions, lapses in memory. Her pronouncements both inspired and frustrated the police, media and curious public. As mother, she was held ultimately responsible on a personal (though often unstated) level, by male individuals in the police force (some of whom she points the finger at by naming in the autobiography), for her child's welfare. Her failure to protect Azaria from death stamped her as guilty – at least of negligence, at worst of murder; and in terms of the male-dominated structures of the law, she had to be made to pay.

The closeness between Lindy Chamberlain and her first daughter Azaria, as well as her second daughter Kahlia, was spliced by the intervention of patriarchal law: a law which denies to the mother total control over the child and denies to both of them the fluid exchange of identities operating in the pre-Oedipal. In the Crown's accusation that Lindy Chamberlain had cut her child's throat, a fantasy of the female as castrator and the feminine (daughter) as castrated came into play. This moment of division, or separation, is one in which double images of the mother of oppositional patriarchal logic came into operation – the mother's femininity was regarded as both/either harmless and/or innocent, like that of her baby daughter, and different – that is, omnipotent and sexualized (in relation to the baby).

Lindy Chamberlain fought and contested this intervention in a variety of ways, particularly where it seemed especially harsh, unreasonable or unjust regarding women. She argued on a personal level with police, legal representatives, members of the Church hierarchy, her own counsel, press representatives and her own husband. There are many examples of her resilience. There was, for example, her retort to the Sergeant Charlwood when he hinted at Dr Cameron's 'findings': 'I didn't know there were dingo experts in London.'[25] She may have lost many times on the way, but arguably, with the granting of financial compensation, she did finally, and with considerable reinforcement from sympathetic pressure groups, win some of the battles.[26]

Part of Lindy Chamberlain's struggle to retain some power to represent herself was her decision to write her own story. The book title sets out to subvert the accusations of evil by inviting the reader to see events through her eyes. This move can be read as one in which Lindy Chamberlain, for so long an actor in a drama written for and around her, got to tell her side of the story. Yet it is only through the brutality of the system, its visibly pushing her to the limits of a meaningful identity, that what she had to say became meaningful to others. Paradoxically, then, it was by taking up a position as the silenced and wronged (and on the wrong side of the law) but now articulate and competent – by her entry into the Symbolic world of *written* public discourse – that her own version of events became widely relevant. And the question of what category her autobiography, her testament, her writing, can be regarded as belonging to again constitutes a troubling of boundaries – this time of the boundaries of institutionalized discourses through which national and literary identities assert (in retrospect) a spurious validity.

To what categories of writing does the text that Lindy Chamberlain has authored belong? Discussing the difficulty of categorizing the work of a popular Australian woman writer of the 1930s, Ernestine Hill (is it travel writing, romance, history?), Meagan Morris describes its inclusion in the term 'Australiana', which can include 'anything from undisputed literary classics to coffee table books to wildlife magazines and politicians' memoirs' – and, I would add, postcards, stuffed koala bears, T-shirts and perhaps Lindy Chamberlain's autobiography.

The term Australiana, Morris posits: 'openly allows for a *promotional* concept of reified Australian identities: it admits that producing images of Australianness is a commercial activity, a mode of entertainment and a genre of cultural practice.'[27] As a subject with a foot in more than one camp, the migrant becomes at once object, medium and subject of exchange.

Migrant writing, because it examines a relation in which the representation of home has been severed from a relation to the land, releases the uncanny. In Freudian terms, as Gunew explains, *heimweh*, like nostalgia, is a 'pregnant term, containing the home, the mother, sickness for but also of the home ... '[28], and it refers to the *unheimlich* or uncanny, where what has been repressed surfaces. The uncanny is the site of doubling, and the double is both 'insurance against, but also a harbinger of, death'.[29] The mother – who represents the home, and with it all that is familiar and reassuring – who becomes estranged or unfamiliar is then, in fantasy structures, an indissolubly duplicitous figure. The radical split in subjectivity represented by this set of associations can be located in a statement like that of Chester Porter, senior counsel assisting at the Morling inquiry, who described two extreme positions which permitted no intermediate ground: 'Either this lady when she gave all these statements was a murderess, or she was a mother who had suffered frightfully and was being accused of murder.'[30]

Sacrificing the scapegoat

To turn, now, to Girard's *Violence and the Sacred*, the application of which, in the case of Lindy Chamberlain, is not especially satisfying or appropriate from a feminist point of view; but it contains a number of theories that have some relevance to a discussion of the trial. Central to Girard's discussion of the relationship between acts of violence in what he labels 'primitive' societies and their social ordering are the notions of the scapegoat and the sacrificial crisis. To say that Lindy Chamberlain was a scapegoat may seem like stating the obvious, but an examination of the way Girard describes the mechanisms of scapegoating has particular relevance in the Chamberlain case. Where did the notion come from that Azaria had been sacrificed? Why did the rumour that Azaria meant 'sacrifice in the wilderness' prove so acceptable to members of the general public?

Scapegoats, according to Girard, are surrogate victims – animal or human – on whom a society vents its communal frustrations in order to 'quell violence' and 'prevent conflicts from erupting'.[31] If they are animals, they are often those animals closest to human beings; if they are human, the victim might be any member of a group. In many cases, human and animal sacrifices are interchangeable. 'The relationship between the potential victim and the actual victim cannot be defined in terms of innocence or guilt,' writes Girard, because the victim is a substitute for the collective, and it is therefore irrelevant what he or she has done. The actual event remains mysterious: 'celebrants do not and must not comprehend the true role of the sacrificial act', Girard insists. The frequency of infanticide as sacrifice is, he argues, well documented: 'In many primitive societies children who have not yet undergone the rites of initiation have no proper place in the community; their rights and duties are almost non-existent.' The backlash against Lindy Chamberlain after the death of Azaria might therefore be read as a response to the fact that a human child might be killed or eaten, like any other victim, by a wild animal.

Powerful members of the community such as kings might be sacrificed; on the other hand, 'exterior or marginal individuals capable of establishing or sharing the social bonds that link the rest of the inhabitants might be selected'. In Australia, Lindy Chamberlain was just such a person. There are problems with Girard's model, since he maintained that women are not usually chosen as sacrificial victims.[32] On the other hand, Girard's work has been criticized for its male-centred focus.[33] The 'sacrifice' of Lindy Chamberlain (fortunately) was never achieved in any final way, since she was released from prison and financially compensated. There were protests in New Zealand, where her own family proclaimed her innocence, while the Church to which she belonged also formed a community which resisted and challenged the charges laid against her.

Lindy Chamberlain's religious community and many of her family ties could, therefore, be described as marginal. Arguably, she was rejected by a powerful section of the community only to be reabsorbed by it as a prisoner. Sneja Gunew describes national identity as a pastiche of personal and public memories, using the metaphor of a scrapbook to describe the sometimes coincidental associations made by bringing together the public and the private. She asks who or what gets left out in dominant versions of national identity:

> In some versions of this scrapbook, our mental
> landscapes, our oneiric projections, are piously left to
> the Aborigines, to their dreaming, suitably and invisibly
> mediated from within the confines of expensive
> galleries, anthropological studies etc. Presumably,
> we hope that they may redream us after the event –
> purified, absolved.[34]

'Uluru' or Ayers Rock has been described by the writer Robin Davidson as 'the most symbolically charged object in the country'.[35] Despite the depredations of tourists, it is, she claims, 'too ancient to be corruptible'. (As Azaria was too young?) Jennifer Craik discusses 'a tension between tourism and conservation' relevant to the issues raised by the Chamberlain case; this straining between the desire to preserve and the desire to exploit (e.g. natural resources) is particularly marked in 'new' settler societies like Australia, Canada and New Zealand.

The Azaria Chamberlain case revealed a society in the process of re-negotiating the social and legal status of its citizens. The way the jury was bombarded with forensic evidence by the Crown during Lindy Chamberlain's trial can also be read as evidence of the postmodern condition in which societies articulate an 'incredulity toward metanarratives'[36] and undergo a crisis of legitimation. In Australia, Aboriginal, Christian and many more religious beliefs circulate – if not on an equivalent footing, then at least in an environment where faith is nominally optional rather than enforced.

For the Pitjanjantara people, Uluru is sacred and religious ground; caves on the rock are of central importance in fertility rites. It is also, Davidson has written, 'particularly rich in Dreaming stories, being an intersection of many different odysseys. Wallaby people, spirit dingo and willy-wagtail woman all contributed to its topography.'[37] In a society where modernity exists side by side with tribal beliefs, the incompatibility of belief systems constitutes dilemmas in everyday life. Scientific narratives were not able to produce a truth about what happened to Azaria any more than Aboriginal beliefs, despite the lengths to which the police and government officials were prepared to go.

In the period in which the trial of Lindy Chamberlain was taking place, Uluru was ceremonially returned to Aboriginal groups. This was a gesture of recognition that there is a need for adjustment in the relationship between Aboriginal groups, government bodies and a non-Aboriginal public. It might also be regarded as an example of the tendency to relegate the realm of the mysterious and the spiritual to Aboriginal groups. The fact that there has never been a clear statement of what happened at Uluru means that the secret of what happened to Azaria is cordoned off and can be regarded as beyond the bounds of a non-Aboriginal public's comprehension. Sacrifice, then, in a non-Aboriginal imagination, can be regarded as an Aboriginal concern.

At the time of the inquest in Alice Springs, there was a rumour that a Kadaitcha man had taken Azaria. 'Such legendary Aboriginal executioners are said to strike suddenly and then vanish, sometimes leaving the tracks of a wild animal behind in an attempt to deceive the relatives of the victim.'[38] However, as Ken Crispin suggests: 'There was, of course, no evidence to support such rumours and Stuart regarded them as far-fetched.' Far-fetched was a term used by Barker at one point in the Darwin trial to describe the dingo theory. Crispin opens his study of *The Crown Versus Chamberlain* with a description of the mythological significance of Uluru, including the legend of Kurrpanngu, a devil dingo which occasionally 'inhabits the body of a living dingo, causing it to act with uncharacteristic malevolence and ferocity'.[39] His text reproduces the double bind of liberal non-Aboriginals who on the one hand attempt to respect and accept the credibility of Aboriginal beliefs, and on the other stand as outsiders in relation to Aboriginal culture.

As Girard writes: 'Because the very concept of a deity, much less a deity who receives blood sacrifices, has little reality in this day and age, the entire institution of sacrifice is relegated by most modern theorists to the realm of the imagination.'[40] It was the mechanisms of psychic repression governing non-Aboriginal Australian culture that kept breaking down in the case of Azaria Chamberlain, with the result that suppressed fantasies about child murder as sacrifice resurfaced in order to be dispelled.

The sacrificial crisis, according to Girard, occurs when there is an alteration in 'the hierarchical classification of living creatures', which undermines the social. Dingoes that behave like domestic dogs might constitute such a change – as might women who demand the same rights as men. Defined as 'a crisis of distinctions – that is, a crisis affecting the cultural order', the sacrificial crisis reveals the cultural order as 'nothing more than a regulated system of distinctions in which the differences among individuals are used to establish their "identity" and their mutual relationships . . .'[41] The existence of the dingoes as a symbol of savagery and wildness has been threatened by the encroachment of modern technology and structures (camping grounds, motels and hotels) on to a space designated as the outback. In the case of Azaria Chamberlain, the animal world, in an arbitrary and irrational event, engulfed the human, causing a crisis in the way society envisaged itself. And for Lindy Chamberlain, the judicial system has been seen, publicly, to fail. Ian Tuxworth, Chief Minister in the Northern Territory Parliament, said of the campaign for the release of Lindy Chamberlain in November 1985: 'At stake is law and order and faith in the due processes of a legal system recognised as the fairest in the world.'[42] 'Fair' or otherwise, the case certainly drew attention to the need for legal reforms.

Writing of the links between sexuality and violence, Girard argued:

> The problem at hand is not the arrogance of Western science nor its blatant 'imperialism', but rather its sheer inadequacy. It is precisely when the need to understand becomes most urgent that the explanations proposed in the domain of religion become most unsatisfactory. Sexuality . . . is a permanent source of disorder even within the most harmonious of communities.[43]

Many factors combined to make the disappearance of Azaria Chamberlain and the trial of Lindy Chamberlain of central importance to Australian public life. As a media event, it staged a confrontation between differing versions of Australia. Lindy Chamberlain's imprisonment and giving birth in Darwin Penitentiary parallels the birth of the nation as a predominantly European concept and as a prison colony. The film made this point in the first prison shot, which focused on the faces of Aboriginal women and then moved to Streep/Lindy Chamberlain. It makes the task of continuing to establish different and less restricted versions of what it means to be Aboriginal, a mother and a woman in both an Australian and an international context seem all the more urgent.

Acknowledgements

Thanks to Sophie Tomlinson, Peter Barry, Ingrid Page, Helen Birch, Sue Joseph and Quentin McDermott.

Biting the hand that breeds

The trials of
Tracey Wigginton

Deb Verhoeven

> Perhaps blood will have the freedom of the city
> and the right to circulate, only if it takes the form of
> ink.
>
> (Luce Irigaray[1])

For the Australian public the story began inauspiciously
enough one Tuesday in late January 1991. A small, undis-
tinguished news report buried amongst the pages of the
Brisbane *Courier Mail* rewarded only the most persistent of readers with its solemn account of Tracey Avril
Wigginton's sentencing at the Queensland Supreme Court.
Tracey ('25, unemployed') had pleaded guilty to the murder
of Edward Clyde Baldock ('a council worker . . . a father of
five and a grandfather').[2] It all seemed perfectly straightforward – an open-and-shut case literally en-Gulfed by the
uncertain turmoil of international news.

This impassive newspaper item, however, did not even
hint at the intense media speculation that was soon
to follow. By the end of the week, Tracey Wigginton's
nine-minute trial had escalated into a national *cause célèbre*
– becoming, as the media itself proudly boasted, 'the story
that took the Gulf War off the front pages'.[3] Or did it?

What has remained of interest about this trial was the
extraordinary media coverage it precipitated. This often
contradictory coverage, both vied with and complemented

the speculative excesses that seemed to characterize media presentations of the 'Mother of all Battles' – the conflict between the West and the Middle East. As the media's Gulf War ground to a slow sales death, Tracey Wigginton's trial beckoned mirage-like to a dehydrated journalism lost in the sands of 'Operation Desert Storm'.

Indeed, for the gleefully moralizing media, this story – or, more importantly, the scandalous revelations that marked the subsequent trial of Wigginton's co-accused, Lisa Ptaschinski (aged twenty-four, Wigginton's lover), Kim Jervis and Tracey Waugh (both twenty-three, also lovers) – seemed like a dream come true. These three women had accompanied Tracey Wigginton on the night of the killing in October 1989. It was claimed that they had combed inner-city streets in Wigginton's green Holden Commodore, listening to the strains of the Prince tune 'Batdance' whilst searching for a suitable victim.

The women were alleged to have participated in luring the severely drunken Edward Baldock to his death with the promise of sex. Baldock's naked body was discovered the next morning on the banks of the Brisbane River, with Tracey Wigginton's Commonwealth Bank automatic 'teller' card tucked in his shoe beneath his neatly folded clothes.[4] He had been repeatedly stabbed in the neck with two knives. Wigginton's friends pleaded not guilty to the charges, their defence claiming that at the time of the murder they were paralysed by Wigginton's hypnotic influence.

The claims of a criminal or 'unnatural' intensity to Tracey Wigginton's relationships are all the more astounding given the short time she had known the women before their arrests. Lisa Ptaschinski, for instance, had met Wigginton for the first time in the week leading up to the murder. Apparently, 'these two large women fell in love after sharing the kick of an asthma inhaler' – not so surprising, given that the pair had hardly time to draw breath before embarking on their affair.[5] According to Lisa, their brief and 'consuming' passion proved so intense that she had been moved to cut her own wrists in order to wine and dine Tracey with blood. Ptaschinski had been introduced to Wigginton by her longtime friend Kim Jervis.

Jervis and Tracey Waugh had befriended Wigginton during the few weeks before Baldock's death. They all apparently belonged to a loosely defined Brisbane sub-culture known as the Swampies. Swampies celebrated Gothic sensibilities, Acid House music, Doc Martens, black hair dye and, most insidiously of all, 'nocturnal lifestyles'.[6] To complete the picture, they frequently sported tattoos featuring religious and occult motifs. Swampies, it seems, made good 'suckers' – easily enticed into Wigginton's 'sinister plot'.

The defence representing Wigginton's three friends alleged throughout their trial that Wigginton drank pig and goat blood, had 'special' powers, wore nothing but black, avoided sunlight 'at all costs' and did not like to look in mirrors. They claimed that the women felt that Baldock's death was necessary for Wigginton to feed, and that after the murder she looked as if 'she had just finished a three-course meal'. All three women testified to the police of their unwavering belief in Wigginton's satanic powers and vampiric hunger for human blood. From these court claims the 'lesbian vampire killer' legend was born.

'Cruel childhood turns bright bubbly girl into evil killer'

Raised in the small northern Australian coastal city of Rockhampton, Tracey Wigginton was adopted at the age of nine by her mother's own adoptive parents, George and Avril Wigginton. She suffered a brutal upbringing, claiming to have been sexually abused by her grandfather for four years and regularly punished by her grandmother, who reputedly flogged her with an ironing cord whilst screaming over and over that men were 'dirty bastards'.[7] It seems that George, a self-made millionaire, was something of a 'womanizer', and as testament to his demonstrated capacity for social (if not for sexual) mobility, the city named a street after him. George's fortune was based on a prosperous earth-moving business supported by generous government contracts.[8] Avril's hatred for her husband was matched only by her adoration for a clutch of spoiled pet chihuahuas upon which she lavished all her affections – usually in the form of copious amounts of fresh steak. Tracey was not to be so lavished until George and Avril's death in her late adolescence, when she became the recipient of a (quickly spent) inheritance.

Tracey entered adolescence in rebellious style. Treated to an exclusive girls' grammar school education where she 'played the organ and did ballroom dancing', she was soon expelled for allegedly 'molesting other girls'.[9] Later, she was enrolled at a Catholic convent school but eventually abandoned her education until just before her arrest. The importance of these formative years was not lost on the ever-vigilant media, and they devoted some of their finest writing to them:

> Quick to spot the nascent depravity that was to later turn her into a killer, the school expelled her for molesting other girls, thereby saving its pupils from the reign of terror Tracey initiated at the nearby Range Catholic School where she was sent instead.
>
> In the quiet cloisters and under the massive old trees of this haven of learning, Tracey Avril Wigginton was honing the aggressive lesbianism that climaxed eight years later when she plunged a knife into the neck of her male victim and drank his blood from the gaping hole.[10]

As if in answer to the media's hyperventilating flashbacks, Tracey's mother, Rhonda Hopkins, could still find plenty of (de)captivating highlights from these years to reminisce about: 'I remember one time when we had a sick chook and someone told Tracey to chop its head off and put it out of its misery, she couldn't do it. She did not drink blood.' According to the media, such admirable restraint with animals was not repeated with humans, and Tracey's infamous later comment, uttered under hypnosis, was widely misquoted: 'I'd like to slice the top off someone's head and say, "Think, let me see you think".'[11]

Surprisingly, some reports about Tracey's life were presented in a more sympathetic fashion. One news report titled 'Killer was a hurt child' went so far as to declare: 'Tracey Avril Wigginton's trial was the family nightmare come true'.[12] The shock value of a report such as this is supposed to lie in the unlikely combination of the terms 'family' and 'nightmare'. But in the media's ever-frequent invocations of 'vampirism', these terms may be seen as by no means mutually exclusive.

Media reports, like so many vampire fictions, show Wigginton's family life to be a battle for 'nourishment'. The themes of incest and illegitimacy that inform the media's picture of Tracey's family history are reminiscent of traditional vampire tales. A vampire's 'children', for example, are her 'victims of (blood)lust', and in the light of this implied incest, vampires are believed to breed sideways – by association, from victim to victim – like diseases and, some would say, homosexuals and other 'criminals'. Their behaviour, like Tracey's, is deemed to elicit the full horror of non-productive sexual behaviour. Hence the excitement with which the media uncovered a hitherto neglected aspect of Tracey's desire. Tracey Wigginton had wanted to be a mother:

> Blood-drinking killer Tracey Avril Wigginton, who thinks she is a vampire, once sought out a man to make her pregnant so that she and her lesbian lover could have a child.[13]

Even Tracey's approach to motherhood confirms for the media her predatory and perverse inclinations. In performing a most public of heterosexual acts – sexual intercourse, apparently taking place in front of about six friends – Tracey's insincerity betrays her suitability for the domestic, private life she wishes to lead. The reports go on to describe Tracey's subsequent miscarriage with a smug flourish – as if nature and common sense have won out. And with nature and common sense against her, there would be no metaphorical miscarriage in the courtroom.

'Tale of horror plays to a packed house'

The trial of Wigginton's co-accused friends effectively amounted to a 'trial by association' of the four women. Rather than directly examining the event of Baldock's murder *per se*, the court entertained a climate of speculation and accusation in which the personal relationships between the accused women and Wigginton became the central issue. As the weeks of personal testimony and anecdote about Tracey Wigginton passed into print, it seemed all the more clear to an audience of increasingly horrified feminists that Wigginton's guilt did not stop at the death of Edward Baldock (by this time a minor figure in the proceedings). Instead, a legal and thus public validity was bestowed on psychiatric conjecture and sexual innuendo as the court, and the media constructed their (dis)respective pictures of a group of women perfectly capable of random murder. The accused women themselves did not take the stand in court – their testimonial 'evidence' being presented entirely in the form of videotaped police interviews recorded within days of their arrest over a year earlier.

From the media's point of view it was this second set of court hearings that had everything – death, sex, the supernatural, family scandal and – not to be forgotten – credit cards: all the necessary ingredients for a good long media 'stakeout'. The allegations of incest, lesbianism, vampirism, bloodlust and satanism that stirred the courtroom provided the press with what seemed the perfect contrast, the 'light relief', to the comparatively serious-but-dull machinations of mass violence in the Middle East – or were they in the same vein after all? Popular media reports of the women's trial are often difficult to distinguish from 'quality' or 'serious' journalism and criticism.

Both mainstream and critical discussions of the case have been dominated by a common emphasis on discourses of 'victimization', despite the overt subject of their contemplation – women who kill. And although these discourses often differ in terms of their specified intent, they are not so fundamentally different at the level of content. One possible reason for this similarity is the limited amount of information and commentary available to feminists who want to discuss Wigginton's crime.

It is from the popular media's images of a violent woman (or four violent women) that many feminists have tried to account for and explain the events, with little success. Despite their few attempts at pop psychology and family welfare-speak, Wigginton today remains in many ways the fly-by-night figure of the media's worst imaginings. Official psychiatric reports, for example, are unavailable for public review, court records are restricted to family members, and direct interviews with Wigginton herself are vetted as 'unlikely' to eventuate. And even these careful barricades were themselves made the subject of legal and media scrutiny during the trial.

The media's televised disclosure of confidential videotape recordings showing psychiatric interviews with a hypnotized Wigginton provoked more than a successful legal challenge from her lawyers. Loud public discussion vacillated between the left-of-centre Queensland government's arguments for both a prisoner's rights to doctor –patient privacy (and the consequent issue of copyright breaches) and the media's claims for an 'overwhelming public interest' in the case. The victory for Wigginton's privacy was a joy for only the most ethical and (perhaps paradoxically) most postmodern of feminists. In the absence of any 'real' Tracey Wigginton beyond her mediated familial, legal and psychiatric selves, sympathetic feminists following the case around Australia were hard pressed to issue alternative readings of the event. At the centre of this stormy sea of debate lay a completely silent Wigginton.

Without clear information, then, it was difficult to make a convincing case against the media that was not already reliant on its – albeit contradictory and ambivalent – presentation of the trials. It was difficult, for example, to see how feminists might reclaim Wigginton as a hero in the way Lindy Chamberlain had been. Could she be another media martyr – a latter-day Joan of Arc unfairly tried and convicted by sensationalist press attention? Unlikely, given that she had pleaded guilty and chose to defer any personal explanations in apparent acceptance of the facts of her crime.

Sympathy for the victims of authority is a theme that is also common to popular descriptions of the stereotypical masculine Australian character – the unflagging Ocker admiration for (and some would say identification with) the 'underdog'. This romantic national masochism has been successfully invoked by left and right alike and is invariably linked to overt masculine mateship rituals. It is also, however, a theme that some Australian feminists, with the necessary (surgical) alterations, have also found appealing – contributing to their successful claims for affirmative action legislation designed to recognize a socially 'victimized' population of underprivileged women.

In this sense, could Wigginton be seen as an avenging victim – a 'good' murderer lashing back at social and familial persecution? Wigginton was, after all, an incest survivor, and the murder of Baldock might be viewed allegorically as a misdirected attack on her/the Father. Such a metaphorical reading of the crime could even be directly linked to the public Oedipal drama that was then unfolding in contemporary Queensland politics. Baldock's murder, for instance, might be read as a modern fatal fable, embellished by the collapse of the seemingly interminable and ultra-conservative Queensland government which had been presided over for more than a decade by a proverbially ugly stepfather, patriarchal peanut farmer Joh Bjelke-Peterson.[14] 'Queens'land, despite the suggestive place name, enjoyed the ignominious reputation of being Australia's most politically reactionary and corrupt state. With a similar climate and agricultural style to the 'Deep South' of the USA, Queensland was popularly known throughout the rest of Australia as the State where only the gay community and the bananas remained straight.

Similarly, another reading of the case might applaud a more contemporary, psychoanalytically informed feminist description of the trial – that of Wigginton-as-hysteric, a woman not just on the edge but completely beyond the pale, her aberrant actions outside the bounds of Reason (and perhaps, therefore, contemplation). Wigginton would represent the abject 'other' – everything that a heterosexist patriarchy and thus Baldock, the legal system, the media, and so on, are not. Wigginton's silence could be read symbolically as an (unconscious) decision not to participate in these institutions. [15]

But this romanticized image only echoes and fixes the popular positioning and ultimate silencing of women who kill. And it is a theme that the media itself took up with great gusto – delving with undisguised delight into conflicting assessments of Wigginton's mental health and so-called 'personality disorders' in order to reiterate the limits of 'agreeable' behaviour for women.

The image of female victimization and suffering is a powerful and seductive trope for feminist celebration. Given its importance to many feminist understandings of women's historical and social difference, it is little wonder that analyses of a violent female protagonist like Wigginton proved difficult to sustain. But what is even more astonishing is how the mainstream media in Australia excelled in liberally distributing discourses of victimization throughout its reports of the case. At any given moment Baldock, the co-accused, Wigginton herself – not to mention the 'general public' – were characterized as possible or probable victims.

In general, however, the media's attention to the idea of women killers as victims rather than as perpetrators differed from feminist accounts in its overriding search for some definitive explanation or cause that might justify the 'ends' of Wigginton's violence. How was it that the 'bright-eyed baby eventually grew into a killer who sought out the company of depraved women'?[16] What exactly were 'the forces which shaped her dark destiny'?[17] And thus, how might other men avoid the unpalatable fate of Edward Baldock? The media's search for causes was also frequently conflated with the search for cures, and the consequent 'medicalization' of its probings pointed to the pathological nature of the women at the centre of the case. Media narratives became teleological attempts at correction. After all, what can't be cured must be endured!

The case presents a welter of questions and dilemmas for possible criticism as well. For example, Tracey Wigginton's crime and the trial of her co-accused friends raised awkward questions for Australian feminists who rely on understandings or knowledge of the personal and more specifically personal suffering, at the expense of a discussion of what sort of politics we really want. These were dilemmas that themselves resisted familiar or clear understandings of our own difference(s). Ultimately, for feminists, the Wigginton coverage begged the question: how can critical feminisms challenge the popular image of women's difference (however violent we may or may not be) in both Australian politics and media?

What is of interest about the case and the way it was represented in Australia were the ways in which familiar and even common-sense social and political divisions became difficult to distinguish. For example, in its various representations of the 'victim', in its ambivalent use of the 'vampire' allegory and its attention to the pathology of women's violence, the mainstream media more often than not occupied the shifting terrain of their sometime staunchest critics – despite the media's repeated rendering of the Wigginton case as for the most part an erotic, exotic aberration.

'Unwitting victim brought "vampire" murderer undone'

On this point the media do have statistics on their side. In the fiscal year 1990–91, for instance, although 58 per cent of all homicide victims in Australia were male, only 10 per cent of offenders were female. Of the possible victim/offender combinations, only 7 per cent of the total number of homicides featured a female offender and a male victim.[18]

Edward Baldock's statistically anomalous demise makes him seem all the more a victim – not just of the four women who murdered him, but of 'Lady Luck' herself. Baldock is the media's favourite sufferer: the 'innocent' victim:

> It was a sad and undignified death for a blameless family man. His murderers did not know him and bore him no grudge but they were utterly callous towards him. They were four women, and they 'needed' a victim. They found Edward Baldock, drunk but harmless. He suffered a brutal attack at their hands.[19]

Baldock's status as an 'innocent' is further suggested by his blithe belief in the women's sexual promises, despite the obvious unlikelihood that they should be made at all. What might initially be seen as an evident 'moral' weakness on the part of the 'blameless family man' is quickly transformed into a vulnerability. His lack of judgement on the night for example, is easily excused: 'With a blood alcohol of more than 0.3 – six times the legal driving limit – the little ginger-haired man probably hardly knew he had been stripped naked.'[20] It is Baldock's innocent incapacitation that inexorably leads him to his deadly decapitation.

The media's attempts to position Baldock as the luckless victim are evident in their parallel comparisons of the events on that fateful night – Baldock's regular evening of 'beer and darts' at a 'proudly Scottish and clannish drinking hole enjoyed by men' in clear contrast to the 'champagne-sipping girls plotting a killing' at a 'dingy hangout frequented by lesbians'.[21] The approved politics of pub culture (as opposed to 'sub'cultures) in Australia has never been so persuasively put.

Baldock's virtual canonization by the media, however, renders him about as characterless as he is powerless – an anaemic element in an otherwise colourful account of this rare encounter between riven Australian genders and sexualities. So in its description of the preamble to murder, the media try to show that their pallid victim also had his heroic moments:

> On that fatal night Baldock may have been too drunk to drive, or even to perform sexually, but alcohol did not drive away the habits of a lifetime. He was a fastidious man and, even on the beach, he folded his clothes fussily, checking that nothing had fallen out of his pockets.[22]

Baldock's death, however, was more than just a case of 'old habits die hard'. In the media's speculative reconstruction of the fatal events, it is Baldock's habitual fastidiousness and fear of theft that save him from immemorial ignominy.

In purportedly hiding a bank keycard in his shoe, the fomerly benign Baldock ends up playing a significant role in determining the fate of his attackers. It is this clue that causes Wigginton to return to the scene of the crime more than once, and ultimately reveals her identity to the police.

> 'He, by putting it up into his shoe, helped us solve his murder', said Senior Sergeant Pat Glancy, who led the murder probe. 'It was just an unbelievable clue.'[23]

In both the police and media scenarios, Wigginton and her companions can be seen not so much as active perpetrators but rather as the victims of Edward Baldock's joyless 'last laugh'. Even posthumously, Baldock is clearly identified by the media as, in the final analysis, one of 'us' – an active, investigative, 'probing' protagonist – rather than one of 'them'. But just who were 'they'?

'Accused "under vampire's spell"'

The idea of women as victims was a key issue for the trial defence and media incarnations of Ptaschinski, Jervis and Waugh. The three women were largely represented not so much in terms of their participation in the event of Edward Baldock's death as in terms of the extent to which they were under the influence of Tracey Wigginton herself. They were literally being judged in relation to their perceived passivity, or lack of it. The problem was really the extent to which *they* should be understood as the real victims of Tracey Wigginton – rather than Baldock who, after all, was under the influence only of those more socially approved 'spirits'. This portrayal of the women as unwitting, if not unwilling, participants in the murder has the advantage of upholding traditional associations between women and passivity. In order to preserve the cultural correlatives – masculine/active, feminine/passive – the media, for example, must depict those women who stray as either reluctant protagonists or 'masculinized' women.

In fact, the media presentation of the *'lesbian* vampire' makes no sense at all if Edward Baldock is viewed as Wigginton's object-choice – the erotic victim of vampiric desire surrendering in a fatal moment of (heterosexual) delirium to Tracey's kiss. The 'lesbian' in 'lesbian vampire' is no slip of the media tongue. By entwining the two terms the media's apparent preoccupation with the event of murder becomes inextricably linked to their more evident interest in the nature of the relationship between Tracey Wigginton and her companions. The media invited their readers to enjoin in livid tabloid style – if it seems hard enough to believe that one woman might (and in fact did) kill a man, try four!

Popular (heterosexual) fantasies of power and surrender, at first disrupted by the death of a man at the hands of 'women young enough to be his daughters', were further disturbed by the intimate interaction of the four women.[24] These actively violent women could be reinstated to their 'proper' places in a passive/active division of relationships only with a little effort and some contradiction: a (re)positioning which both the media and the trial defence employed in their representations of them.

The defence's various depictions of the relationship between Tracey Wigginton and her friends seemed to fit neatly on to the idea of the victim as being at the receiving end of a simple one-way distribution of power and powerlessness. Consider Tracey Waugh's videotaped evidence, reported under the screeching banner 'Killer was devil's wife with power to control minds': 'Tracey has mind power. She has a hold on you. She is like a magnet. You can't stop yourself doing what she tells you to do.'[25] Waugh, the only defendant aquitted by the jury, was described to the court by her lawyer as 'a coward who was vulnerable to Wigginton's manipulations'.[26] The key to Waugh's successful defence might well have been its argument that Waugh believed herself to be Wigginton's 'reserve victim' – to be killed in the event that blood could not be found elsewhere.[27]

Alternatively, Kim Jervis's defence relied on the idea of disbelief as the central factor for her participation. Her barrister presented her to the court as 'a young lady of good character who collects dolls and Garfield cats' who had been 'sucked in'. For good measure he added: 'Wigginton wrote the script, Wigginton wrote the story and she conscripted an extra, my client . . . Wigginton gave Kim Jervis the chance to step from the audience on to the stage so she could take part in it.'[28] Jervis, the 'gullible victim', was found guilty and sentenced to eighteen years despite the fact that she was not a direct protagonist in Baldock's murder – choosing to remain in the car with Tracey Waugh throughout.

Tracey Wigginton's lover, Lisa Ptaschinski, was characterized less specifically, as someone with a history of emotional instability who was not aware of the consequences of her actions and genuinely believed Wigginton to be a vampire. Lisa was shown to be a 'willing victim' of her well-intentioned attempts to please Wigginton. She described her relationship with Wigginton to a psychiatrist in the following terms: 'She had a strong attraction, I don't know what, it's normally very unusual for anyone to push me around. She dominated me more than anyone has in my life.'[29] Ptaschinski, an active participant in Baldock's death, was sentenced to life imprisonment.

But more surprisingly, in an intricate twist of metaphor, Tracey Wigginton herself was characterized by the media as a victim of sorts – an undernourished vampire driven by her insatiable desire 'to feed'. Wigginton was the 'voracious victim':

> In a taped interview with police, Jervis said the four
> women had planned to kill someone two nights
> before Baldock's murder to feed Wigginton. She said
> Wigginton had claimed she needed blood to survive
> and could not eat solid food . . . Ptaschinski said
> Wigginton was like a shark in a feeding frenzy because
> of her cravings for blood.[30]

> Mr. Baldock, drunk after a night at a hotel, was
> murdered by Tracey Wigginton to feed her blood lust.
> Wigginton, who her friends claimed could not eat
> solid food, gorged herself on Mr. Baldock's blood after
> stabbing him in the neck.[31]

In these accounts, both victim and vampire alike are seen
to be driven by forces beyond their control. Baldock,
Ptaschinski, Jervis and Waugh are in some ways regarded
as blameless for surrendering to the vampire's will. But
ultimately, even the female vampire is more a victim to
her 'blood lust' than 'master' of her actions.

Later magazine coverage reversed the whole scenario
even further, casting Wigginton herself as the defenceless
victim of her friends' legal strategies:

> The story of the 'lesbian vampire' is really the sad story
> of Tracey Wigginton, abandoned by her fellow criminals,
> who denied their own roles in the plot, leaving her to
> face a murder charge alone.[32]

This treatment is further supported by the fact that
Wigginton herself has never publicly claimed to be a
vampire or to have drunk blood. And given that she
did not give evidence in either trial, the public and press
speculation over her motives and identity have remained
largely unchallenged. We can only wonder, then, as to the
precise point of the vampire/victim allegories for the media
and the defence alike.

'Vampire's sick sex secret'

'Vampire killer' Tracey Wigginton was obsessed with
a sickening desire to perform oral sex on her lesbian
lovers while they were menstruating.[33]

The allegories of vampiric victimization have implications
that extend far beyond explaining Wigginton's act of
violence and hypnotic hold over her peers. It is hard
not to see how these descriptions delineated the terms
of the women's sexual preference as well.

Vampire folklore has a long-established tradition of
polymorphous sexualities that allows a certain eroticiz-
ation of protagonist and victim alike. The terms of the
media's vampire allegory suggest that the women's lesbianism couldn't be resisted – any more than the vampire's kiss. In describing the milieu in which Wigginton
moved, one journal noted, in a typical metaphorical leap:
'It was a scene Tracey Wigginton found irresistible as
a hunting ground for homosexual young women who
liked to flirt with the occult'.[34] Violence and sexuality
are shown to be 'intimately' linked under the cloak of
vampirism – testimony to common-sense stereotypes of
passive/active distinctions and appropriate behaviour for
women. Much as they would *like* to be a heterosexual and (re)productive member of society (the unwritten assumption here, of course, that heterosexuality is
really the only appealing/sensible option), lesbians are
the hapless victims of their own sordid desires for each
other. Homosexuality becomes a sort of socially transmit-
ted disease – a form of sexual self-immolation. Except
that according to classical vampire legend, good vampires never bite the dust – they just get longer in the
tooth.

The effect of the vampire metaphor for a reading of
lesbianism in this murder case involves the ordering of
the women's relationships into conventional and familiar

hierarchies. This 'disciplinary' activity is especially evident in the media's prurient interest in Tracey Wigginton's sexuality. It was reported, for instance, that she 'allowed a lover called Jamie to belt her with a strap and she wore a specially-made collar with a lock on it to signify her "slave" relationship to a "master"'.[35] What is not mentioned is that this relationship was only referred to by Wigginton under hypnosis in the voice of a personality known as 'Bobby'.[36]

Descriptions of Wigginton's affair with Ptaschinski follow a similar theme:

> The relationship was fuelled by Wigginton's aggressive, dominant personality and Ptaschinski's vulnerable infatuation . . . There is nothing particularly unusual in this kind of dominant submissive relationship.[37]

It is the fact of the hierarchy that is important in the description of the sadomasochistic relationships. It is the unequal interaction of dominant and submissive, or active and passive positions that matters in the relationship – not necessarily the specific identity of its members, the potential parody of the characterizations or the possible eroticism of the actions. Similarly, the reports that Tracey's lover Lisa Ptaschinski, 'on four occasions, cut open her wrists and let Wigginton suck her blood to keep in Wigginton's "good books"' are seen to characterize lesbian relationships as negotiations of power and domination rather than pleasure.[38]

This division of Wigginton's sexuality into sadistic and masochistic elements, along with the media's emphasis on the horror or bestiality of vampiric pleasure, could be seen as an attempt to provide a possible crossing point between homosexuality and heterosexuality. Lesbianism can be superimposed on to the social division between masculinity (as active) and femininity (as passive). Wigginton's sexuality as described by the media might then be indirectly linked with – or 'explained' by

– the reports of her experiences of incest, for instance: 'explained' not in the sense that her lesbianism is the eventual consequence of a heterosexuality out of order, but rather in the sense that her experience of incestuous sexuality was similarly one of control and contention. So, by suggesting that conflict or violence subsumes eroticism and pleasure, the media may unknowingly depict sexual desire as a political struggle for dominance.

This probably unintentional politicization of Wigginton's relationships – sexual and familial – serves most often to affirm conservative rather than liberatory narratives of social control. The media's ambivalent vampire/victim positioning of Tracey Wigginton in particular seems to express the legitimacy of – or necessity for – institutions of discipline and order: the police, the criminal justice system, the media themselves, and so on. Hence the curious reports of the prosecuting police:

> Homicide Squad Det. Snr-Constable Nick Austin was one of the six arresting officers . . . 'She had her story already made up and only admitted things she knew we knew. It did not worry us but she could unnerve weaker people; a typical psychopathic personality' . . . Det. Sgt Burton had only brief but uncomfortable meetings with Wigginton. He scoffs at suggestions that she had hypnotic powers, except upon much weaker associates. But he was impressed with the strength of her personality, a voice which – using two or three words at a time – suggested a commanding presence from which feminism [*sic* – presumably he means femininity] by its very nature was excluded.[39]

This last quotation in particular, set amongst newspaper headlines such as 'Vampire killer had Hitler-like influence', suggests that power ('commanding presence') is somehow equated with masculinity (or at least the exclusion of femininity).[40] Such an understanding of sexual difference and its unquestioned relationship to other social assumptions about passivity and power implies that those who fall outside these 'consensual' cultural maps – masculine/active, feminine/passive – are somehow deceiving us, 'performing' their gender badly. Gender is paradoxically characterized as a natural state and an arbitrary attribute.

Tracey Wigginton is clearly depicted as an aberrant *woman*, but one who has betrayed her real difference by 'acting' out of character, 'acting' like a man. For example, the man she chose to father her child claimed that in the time he knew her:

> she appeared distinctly different to him at various times. Sometimes she acted in an aggressively masculine manner. The time sexual intercourse had taken place, she was quite feminine.[41]

Gender performance is directly linked here to sexual performance, and if we're on the subject of the equivalence of gender and sex, then we shouldn't forget that for the tabloid press cars will probably form some part of the equation:

> At that time [1987 – on meeting her lover Donna] Wigginton rode a motorcycle and took her lover on the pillion. She always exceeded the speed limit. But when Wigginton slipped behind the wheel of the 'loving couple's' Commodore car, her character changed completely – to that of the helpless female who always drove cautiously and never exceeded the speed limit.[42]

In these quotations Wigginton is literally characterized as 'gender mobile. Gender – or, more specifically, Wigginton's gender – is identified as an unstable symptom – completely context-bound. The evident difference displayed when Wigginton gets off her motorbike and slides behind the wheel of her iconic Holden Commodore – the 'all-Australian family car' – reveals her behaviour to be gender-(d)riven. And it also shows her to be a woman who is by no means beholden to fixed gender distinctions. Women like Wigginton wear their femininity on the surface, like a cloak – to be exchanged according to whim, the cover of its folds simultaneously revealing and concealing the interior beneath.

'But the surface of Tracey's life then was as deceptive as the calmness which cloaks it now'[43]

The presentation of women and femininity as a question, above all else, of masquerade – of appearances and possible falsehoods – has the effect of maintaining 'the masculine' as something fixed: the measure against which the 'feminine' is assessed. Women who play at being masculine for a while, by taking on particular activities (or even by merely being active), will remain only pale imitations – 'bad' copies of men, or just plain 'bad'.

In this context, Tracey Wigginton's apparently inexplicable violence was shown to correspond to her physical masculinity/lack of femininity. It seems, for example, that it was not just Tracey's actions that carried weight. Frequent references linked her crimes to unflattering descriptions of her body size: as 'a 180 cm tall, 110 kg woman with huge buttocks and thighs':[44]

> Tracey Wigginton had a personality to match her 17-stone frame – big. She was deeply committed to all her causes: lesbianism, occultism and devil-worship. Before long she had coerced her friends from the Valley to kill for her.[45]

> Physically the butch in Tracey was beginning to appear – short, spikey hair, predominantly black outfits, studded leather. On one occasion she returned to Range College [her former high school] in an army uniform offering 'to smarten the kids up'.[46]

The social currency or 'recognizability' of stereotypes

gives these descriptions of criminal masculinity a certain 'common-sense' authority. These quotations suggest that in relation to Wigginton's gender, changes on the surface – 'the butch in Tracey was beginning to appear' – reflect changes in nature. But how does this make sense in the context of the previous descriptions of women's duplicitous uses of gender? On the one hand, there is seen to be an arbitrary relationship between appearances on the surface and their hidden underside – a relation of masquerade and all manner of conceivable deceptions between exterior and interior. On the other, women who kill will visibly reveal their identities – their bodies acting as unwitting symptoms or keys to their interior inclinations.

Both explanations of the woman's gender can be reconciled only if we assume, along with the media, that it is the very nature of women to be unstable or unfixed. In both senses, then, the prosecuting attorney could warn the jury 'not to be fooled by Tracey Waugh's "chameleon-type camouflage" in appearing well-groomed [and] dressed up'.[47] If Tracey Waugh endeavours to display the feminine social graces, it can be suggested that she is hiding something more – it is, after all, only a display, a picture:

> Waugh, the most attractive of the three, sat demurely
> with her wide brown eyes downcast. Looking the
> picture of innocence, she prompted the prosecutor to
> remark that she looked 'like a 16-year-old schoolgirl'.[48]

Equally, however, proof of the women's aberrance is signalled by the fact that they no longer cared about appearances. Reports emphasize the symptomatic role of clothing and ornamentation such as tattoos which, despite their elaborateness, signify a lack of concern for convention. Even in court, they can't quite get it right:

> The women showed little emotion during the trial and

rarely spoke among themselves, sitting stoney-faced in the dock, occasionally sipping water. The three dressed neatly and appeared each day well groomed but without make-up.[49]

Damned if you do (wear make-up) and damned if you don't. Nevertheless, prison life had its curative moments for Lisa Ptaschinski: 'Her hair hung in black, shoulder-length curls sharply contrasting with the cropped style she wore at the time of her arrest.'[50] Similarly, whilst Wigginton's well-publicized disregard for mirrors was initially useful in implying that her supposed vampirism was a recognizable feature of her everyday behaviour, it actually had more suggestive power as further evidence of a defiant attitude to social demands for female narcissism. By not reflecting (on) herself, Wigginton protests her positioning as a subject for speculation, in any of its various forms. This apparently impaired or aberrant attitude to her own image becomes a factor that is itself symptomatic of the trouble to come.[51]

The media's fascination with the women's façade is a motif that characterized the case at a number of levels. In general it shows women who kill to be treacherous examples of femininity – betraying their gender in moments of destruction rather than (pro)creation. Violent women such as Tracey Wigginton are portrayed as cunning – plotting their secret crimes in advance and hiding them behind impassive faces. But curiously, their faces are also what gives them away. Despite their concealed intentions, their calculated cunning, an element of their carefully constructed image will always remain awry. Away from the mirror and behind her sunglasses, Tracey might avoid the possibility of insight, but her eyes will still act as a window to the soul:

The dark eyes of Tracey Avril Wigginton, man-killer and lesbian lover, are now but an unpleasant, sometimes

chilling memory for most of those who knew her.
There are few if any people they can intimidate any
longer. And the blood-lust behind them which led to
the slaughter of a harmless drunk . . . is likely to be
confined behind bars for many years to come.[52]

A consultant psychiatrist examining Lisa Ptaschinski was
told that Wigginton had the 'ability to make people disappear except for their eyes',[53] and according to Tracey
Waugh, 'Wigginton was a devil worshipper who could
disappear, leaving only her "cat's eyes" visible'.[54] A former
student at Tracey's school was cited as remembering: 'I'd
always stay clear of her – she had that strange evil
look'.[55]

These quotations throw up a number of ambiguities in
their assessments of Wigginton's 'look'. It is unclear, for
instance, whether they are invoked in order to suggest
that Tracey's appearance was unconventional or if it was
in fact her way of looking itself – her point of view – that
was aberrant. Nevertheless, the metaphors of visibility
and invisibility that sit in uneasy proximity in these
accusations seem to suggest that it is the eyes that act
as a 'sight' of power. Surfaces are merely symptomatic,
and the depths of a person's character, their most invisible
secrets and essences, will be uncovered only by the most
penetrating of gazes – a gaze that Wigginton herself had
(illegally) come to possess: '"When she looked at you it
was almost as if you didn't exist," says Det Sgt Glenn
Burton of South Brisbane CIB. "It was a stare that went
right through you".'[56]

The eyes, as some anthropologists and all good horror
films have suggested, occupy an anxious position in the
social delineation of the body. They, like other body
orifices, allow possible passage between 'inside' and 'outside', a place at which we engage with the external world
and through which we equally reveal our internal life.
Neither solid nor liquid, the eyes are a permeable barrier

between a person's interior state and exterior context. They are the symptom *par excellence* – a point of observation and an observation point. In Ptaschinski and Waugh's curious testimonies, the eyes sit in unsettling suspense – on a borderline – between definition and indeterminacy. Like a vampire, Wigginton, a woman and a lesbian, can change shape at will in her attempts to defy detection and definition. It is this very potential to formlessness, as the media would have it, that suggests an additional assault on an ordered and disciplined set of social structures.

In seeming defence of this orderly understanding of society, the media made frequent reference to official psychiatric reports that referred to Wigginton's disrupted exterior life in the encompassing terms of an inner disarray. Rather than suggest that Baldock was killed by a cunning but singularly minded criminal, the press attributed to Wigginton a secret inner life more active than most.

'The four faces of multiple terror'

Before her trial Tracey underwent two weeks of psychiatric examination at the request of the Queensland Mental Health Tribunal to determine whether or not she should appear in court. In over twenty-six hours of hypnosis, she was questioned by prominent psychologists and psychiatrists who determined that Tracey suffered from a 'multiple personality disorder' and was legally insane when she committed the murder. The Mental Health Tribunal, comprising a Supreme Court Judge and two doctors, considered this and other evidence before declaring that Tracey was in fact responsible for her actions on the night of Baldock's death, and that she fully understood their consequences.

Under hypnosis Wigginton was alleged to have revealed four main personalities to those examining her:

Bobby: contemptuous, callous and cynical, the murderous side of her personality.

Big Tracey: anxious and depressed, distressed by the
  murder, a good personality believed by psychiatrists
  to have left Wigginton's bank card at the scene of
  the crime.
Young or Little Tracey: childlike and naive, who represented Wigginton's childhood days; and lastly
The Observer: detached, calm and rational, who acted
  as a record of the thoughts and actions of Wigginton's
  other personalities.

Medical examiners also speculated as to the existence of a
further personality: Avril, a terrifying presence appearing
to control Bobby 'by causing a screaming in her head'.[57]
 In the wake of these official announcements, the 'four
faces' of Tracey Wigginton came to be seen by the media as
the actual protagonists in the drama of Baldock's murder.
The three other women involved in his death were quietly
sidelined in much the same way as Baldock had been
earlier on in the proceedings. As before, Tracey Wigginton
could be 'blamed' as the key figure in the killing of Baldock.
Nevertheless, she is also depicted in a manner that, once
again, positions her as a 'victim'. This time, however, she
is the victim of her own undoing:

Vampire killer Tracey Wigginton deliberately dobbed
herself in, claims a psychiatrist who helped unlock
her twisted mind . . . Dr. Quinn, from Lismore,
NSW, said he was convinced that a good personality
within Wigginton plotted against the evil personality,
Bobby.[58]

Popular women's magazines such as *New Idea* (note the
singular), in which the above quotation appears, flaunted
the 'multiple personality' stories. The distinction drawn
between mind and body in many women's magazines
preserves a view of the world in which proper women are

primarily defined in relation to their bodies – as mothers, brides, het desperadoes in search of a man, victims of medical trauma, and so on. And so if women are to be granted a mind of their own, there are no prizes for being excessive. For instance, the magazine quotes one of Tracey's examining psychiatrists who expresses his fear that 'Wigginton, or at least one of her alter personalities, could kill again'. He warns: 'she could commit suicide (one of her personalities would actually kill another)'.[59]

The media's contradictory portrait of Wigginton as both perpetrator and victim is given its final realization. In view of her multiple personalities, Tracey can be revealed in the last instance as her own victim. Able to switch personalities in a single bound, Tracey is attributed a pathological formlessness – an incoherent relation between the common-sense association one body/one mind. A polymorphous personality of vampiric proportions?

All, however, is not lost. Even though women such as Tracey Wigginton cannot be taken at face value, it is still possible for some members of the community to see through their feeble attempts at disguise, recognizing the telltale signs. In this sense the media, the police and other institutions such as psychiatry played a central role in uncovering the nature of the crime, and at the same time the 'true' nature of the criminals. As in the most riveting of suspense novels, Tracey's story is structured to suggest that the ending cannot be anticipated. On the other hand, the descriptions of the characters, the use of conspicuous stereotypes, suggest the opposite. They are the clues (and the red herrings):

> Edward Baldock's time to die was approaching fast. Wigginton cut her hair and dyed it a colour known as 'Midnight Black'. Homicide Squad Det. Snr. Constable Nick Austin was one of the arresting officers. In about six hours of interrogation, he said, Wigginton remained 'a very calculating woman'.[60]

We can scarcely imagine how much calculation it required to choose the hair colour!

In the media's treatment of the Wigginton story, women (lesbians, criminals) possess the unique capacity to appear to be what they are not. There is no *necessary* indication or neon warning sign that identifies a woman killer from appearances alone. In the logic of these reports, a 'true identity' hidden behind the veil of deception and appearances will only eventually be uncovered. As Mary Anne Doane noted in a slightly different context, women can paradoxically be seen to be both 'enigmatic, but still decipherable'. It is in the unfolding of these 'essentially essential' investigative medical, police or media narratives that the double (or, in Wigginton's case, multiple) life of the female criminal will be unveiled.

'The murder no one could believe'

> The trauma of the Gulf war has been cynically portrayed by the television networks as some unfolding dramatic production, creating an entirely new standard of bad taste.
>
>   (Mr Dawkins, Federal Education Minister[61])

> The story has forced the Gulf war off the front pages in Brisbane. Television news producers were at first wary, thinking that the public simply would not believe it but as the case proceeded, all the networks, and the national current affairs shows were reporting each sensational development.[62]

The media-Wigginton, appropriately cloaked (for an alleged vampire) in a mysterious past – and with a possibly darker future – is the only Wigginton most members of the reading public are likely to encounter. This is the Wigginton of national debate, the Wigginton whose private motivations and personal relationships fuelled front-page speculation in even the most respected Australian newspapers. Broadsheet 'quality' dailies such as Melbourne's *The Age*, the *Sydney Morning Herald* and the national newspaper *The Australian* leapt like leeches into the mêlée, clamouring along with the tabloids to deliver every latest sensational stab-in-the-dark.

This sudden united front amongst the press is all the more remarkable given the conditions of newspaper enterprise in Australia. In a society where major media ownership is more concentrated than most, newspapers in Australia cherish (and market) differences of 'standard' and 'quality' – glossing over the samenesses produced by syndication or other monopoly (pre)occupations. This was also a time of heightened competition for the major players. A recessed market had led to the amalgamation, for instance, of the afternoon and morning editions of particular newspapers and the introduction of additional weekend issues for broadsheet newspapers vying with tabloids for the lucrative Sunday trade. Much of the Wigginton coverage was syndicated (with minor changes) through the national dailies; as a result, staff by-lines were often conspicuous by their absence. Somewhere in this anxious relationship between proprietorship and propriety, the Wigginton coverage presented implicit narratives of national as well as gendered and sexual apprehension.

Overtly, however, the anxiety or question for the media seemed to be: How could an incredulous reading public be expected to swallow such bad-tasting journalism? How could it all be contemplated as 'actual' rather than improbable? Or – to look at it from the other vantage point – the question asked by the discerning reader was invariably: How could the Australian media give lip service to vampires?

The implicit assumption of many media reports of the case seemed to suggest, as if in answer to these queries, that if the public could believe a woman would actually kill a man at random, then it was capable of believing anything. The coverage certainly relished the ambivalent pleasures of incredulity – ambivalent, because there is a potential danger for the media in brazenly encouraging the public to suspend its disbelief. Many of the newspapers covering the case, for instance, would usually rely on the management of appeals to credibility for the force of their legitimacy. To actively engage in wild speculation and obvious opinion might produce an adverse reaction to the conviction of other news coverage – unless, of course, you are prepared to credit the average reader with the same polymorphous qualities demonstrated to such deadly effect by Tracey Wigginton herself. It is not clear, however, that the coverage of Tracey Wigginton's crime was particularly distinct from the nature of news reportage in general at that time. The heavily censored media reports of the Gulf War, for example, were also marked by a speculative excess. In both cases a conventionally accepted relation between fact and fiction was no longer clear, and interpretation of the possible rather than the 'actual' had the status of a media *modus operandi*. The 'speculative' and the 'facts' seemed to be eminently interchangeable.

During the Gulf War, for example, in place of unclear or unavailable information, the media installed widespread 'opinion' dressed in authoritative tones. Retired army personnel became hot media property. Journalists themselves became personalities and participants – US reporters in the Gulf were even encouraged to wear uniforms. Representatives of relevant institutions became instant authorities: academics, environmentalists, munitions manufacturers, and so on.

In order for the media to remain within the terms of its own self-appointed and dubious choices (the opinion or the facts) they engaged in some adroit manoeuvres of their own, shifting emphasis away from the distinction between what was known (the facts) and what remained unknown (opinion of the possible) by privileging the act of interpretation itself. In this way the media could have their cakewalk and eat it too. We see the same fancy footwork in the case of Tracey Wigginton's media manifestations. As the media three-step with the possible, they also flirt with the impossible – (bat)dancing 'with the devil in the pale moonlight'. Or to sum up by quoting another well-worn dance track: if you're going to trip the light fantastic (the emphasis here being on 'fantastic'), 'better the devil you know'.

In this sense we can understand Rhonda Hopkins's observations about the unwritten connections between her daughter's so-called 'vampirism' and the 'logic' of the media itself:

> All I want to get across to people is that she is not an evil person at all. She is not a vampire and she did not drink blood . . . Tracey is a murderer but she is still a person and she still has rights . . . It would do a lot to restore Tracey's faith in human nature if she saw the truth printed.[63]

Rhonda Hopkins's plea can be read not so much as a 'humanist' condemnation of the media's misrepresentations of her daughter, but rather as an exposé of the binary structures the media value so highly. The media's 'common-sense' distinctions (between masculine/feminine, active/passive, vampire/victim, and so on), even set against a vivid landscape of imaginative indiscretions, form the basis of their appeals to impartiality and authority. For Rhonda Hopkins, however, the opposition 'human/murderer' is by no means mutually exclusive. It is yet another example of the shifting sands on which the media's interpretative probity rests, and possibly falls.

Threading together the various aspects of Tracey Wigginton's identity such as gender, sexuality and criminality within the terms of the anomalous itself (vampirism), the media's metaphoric flights of fancy create unforeseen connections and questions. Under close scrutiny,

125

the media's dichotomous and value-laden view of the world, rather than clarifying social distinctions, seems more likely to produce unexpected alliances, ambivalences and paradoxes. In attempting to depict violent women such as Tracey Wigginton as somehow outside the ordinary bounds of human behaviour, the media have momentarily revealed their own pathology.

Acknowledgements

Thanks to: Kim Fisher, Amanda George, Amree Hewitt, Jeanette Hoorn, Greg Langley, Trish Luker, Jude McCullogh and Vivienne Wiles.

A decade of deadly dolls

*Hollywood and
the woman killer*

Christine Holmlund

Hollywood has long been fascinated by women who kill. In the last ten years, however, deadly dolls have filled the screen. Willingly, even gleefully, they pick up the rocket launcher, the gun, the knife, the fork. Unlike the 1940s *film noir femme fatale*, moreover, these dolls often wield their weapons right up close, although like the *femme fatale* they usually get the job done quickly and cleanly, without relishing the spectacle of bloody, protracted, or humiliating death as modern male screen killers do.

Many 1970s films, it is true, also featured female killers, but their murders were almost always motivated as self-defence or revenge, as in *I Spit on Your Grave* (Meir Zarchi: 1978). For the most part these 'innocent' killers were confined to a single genre: the thriller. American films from 1981 to 1991, in contrast, widen the range of possible genres and expand the list of possible motivations. Today women kill as central characters, not just sidekicks, in films which mix elements from comedy, science fiction, horror and melodrama, as well as the thriller.

Of course, regardless of genre, several films still promote female violence as self-defence or revenge for rape and/or abuse: *Ms. 45* (Abel Ferrara: 1981), *Sudden Impact* (Clint Eastwood: 1983), *Alley Cat* (Eduardo Palmos: 1984), *Jagged Edge* (Richard Marquand: 1985), *Nuts* (Martin Ritt: 1987), *The Accused* (Jonathan Kaplan: 1988), *The Handmaid's Tale* (Volker Schlondorff: 1990), *Mortal Thoughts* (Alan

Rudolph: 1991), *Thelma and Louise* (Ridley Scott: 1991) and *Switch* (Blake Edwards: 1991) are all examples. But now killing in the line of duty and/or as a professional has become a popular justification, invoked by films as diverse as *Prizzi's Honor* (John Huston: 1985), *The Grifters* (Stephen Frears: 1990), *Blue Steel* (Kathryn Bigelow: 1990) and *Silence of the Lambs* (Jonathan Demme: 1991). Killing to protect biological or adoptive family members is also prevalent – witness the popularity of *Aliens* (James Cameron: 1986), *Fatal Attraction* (Adrian Lyne: 1987), *Surf Nazis Must Die* (Peter George: 1987) and *Terminator 2: Judgment Day* (James Cameron: 1991). And while Hollywood's visions of female killers as seductive, greedy vamps (*The Hunger* [Tony Scott: 1983] and *Black Widow* [Bob Rafelson: 1986]) or corrupted innocents (*Heathers* [Michael Lehman: 1989]) are familiar and hence understandable, how do we digest the female cannibals of *Eating Raoul* (Paul Bartel: 1982) and *Parents* (Bob Balaban: 1989), especially pre-Jeffrey Dahmer's spring 1992 conviction for murdering and cannibalizing several young men and boys in Milwaukee, Wisconsin?

Although they are in part a response to feminist gains, these deadly dolls are not necessarily a cause for feminist jubilation. Their average age (eighteen to thirty-nine) alone corresponds to what women who kill in real life look like. Otherwise, with the sole exception of *Surf Nazis Must Die*, the murderesses in these films are, to a woman, white, lithe and lovely, because Hollywood sees female violence as erotic and defines 'erotic' within narrow parameters. In real life, most women kill family members or people they know; in movies women may kill in close-up, but they do not usually kill people who are close to them.[1] Of the twenty-plus deadly doll films made in the last decade, only *Thelma and Louise* shows an attempted date rape, and only *Mortal Thoughts* suggests that battery might be the reason behind the central murder, only to reveal that revenge for rape was actually at issue and it was the wife's friend, not the wife, 'who done it'. No film confronts spousal homicide to the extent television has done since the 1984 docudrama *The Burning Bed*.

When these celluloid female murderers are compared with the biggest male killers of the last decade, Sylvester Stallone, Arnold Schwarzenegger and Freddy, Hollywood's queasiness about deadly dolls becomes even more obvious. Unlike Rambo or the Terminator, most of these women can claim no kill counts. Unlike male horror heroes like Freddy, they are not mindless or deranged either. *Terminator 2*'s resourceful, muscular, lean, mean warrior mother (Linda Hamilton) can kill only in the most passive of ways, although she knows she must terminate the Terminator to save herself, her son, and the entire world from destruction. Essentially it is up to Arnold himself to commit suicide: he steps on to the lift and presses the button which lowers him into a vat of molten steel to be – for ever? – destroyed.[2] The narrative of *Nuts* painstakingly establishes that its heroine is sane, not 'nuts': call girl Claudia Draper (Barbra Streisand) killed the 'john' who abused her in self-defence, not – as her upper-class family would have it – because she was crazy.

Today's mainstream movies worry so much about why women kill that they often provide female assassins with multiple motives for murder: in *Sudden Impact* Jennifer Spencer (Sondra Locke) kills to revenge her own and her sister's gang rapes; in *Silence of the Lambs*, Clarice Starling (Jodi Foster) kills both in self-defence and as a professional. That many films legitimate murders which save the family is no coincidence, for in Hollywood it is axiomatic that the family, like capitalism, is sacrosanct. Of all these films, only the independent spoof *Eating Raoul* pokes fun at making money by chronicling a husband and wife's serial murders of perverts for profit.

In comparing the heroines of these films with Rambo, the Terminator and Freddy I am not, of course, arguing that we will be closer to equality when Hollywood portrays both women and men as brutal murderers, although I am neither morally nor politically opposed to seeing women fight and kill. Nor am I condemning these films for being 'unrealistic' by juxtaposing deadly dolls against real women killers. Neither cinema nor society is transparently 'true' or 'objective'. In the USA today, controversy envelops established notions of what constitutes femininity and masculinity, sexuality and violence just about anywhere you care to look. Analysing how popular films portray women killers is particularly important, however, because Hollywood's representations of murdering molls influence greatly how we look at and treat ourselves and each other. As Teresa de Lauretis argues, at any given point in time, a 'standard frame of visibility' determines 'what can be seen, and eroticized' in both cinema and society. Yet this frame, which de Lauretis calls 'representability', can and does change (de Lauretis, 1990: 12). What is portrayed and what is perceived shift over time, according to who is looking, at whom, when and where.

In order to understand how a decade of deadly doll films has helped to translate and create what counts as 'representability', I compare six of the more typical and popular of these films – *Black Widow, Aliens, Fatal Attraction, Blue Steel, Mortal Thoughts* and *Thelma and Louise* – in the central section of this essay. Two shorter sections precede and follow this core section of textual analyses. The first briefly surveys the discussions around women who murder, with the double aim of underlining how much myths permeate 'objective' statistical data, and of pointing out where perceptions of women killers have changed in the last decade. The third section touches on the critical reception the six films received in order to explore what women and men are finding to love and to hate in these movies, and why.

Finally, I turn to the central issues which these films and their critics displace and avoid. Again I compare this decade's deadly dolls with earlier film *femmes fatales*, and with current male killers. I believe that it is these suppressed and silenced issues which most mark deadly doll films as of an era, and position them as such influential players in contemporary arguments about women in general and female killers in particular, as social and cinematic subjects.

Contested figures: real-life women who kill

The increase in the number of deadly doll films, especially in the last five years, fuels and responds to popular belief that more women are killing today than ever before. Criminologists themselves acknowledge how prevalent is the idea 'that a "new", more violent and aggressive female criminal has emerged in our society . . . over the last decade' (Flowers, 1987: 86). Yet, they maintain, although the *number* of murders committed by women has indeed risen, the *percentage* of women killers has not changed significantly because the population has also increased.[3] Elsewhere data indicate that in the USA even the total number of women killing men decreased rather sharply – by 25 per cent – in the last few years,[4] while other data suggest that the percentage of women killers has been fairly stable throughout history: about 10–15 per cent of all homicides.[5]

All researchers agree, however, on one aspect of female homicide: women usually kill men with whom they are or have been involved. Many of these murders are what psychologists refer to as 'victim-precipitated', the product of what Lenore Walker calls the 'Cycle of Violence': a history of repeated and often – though not always – escalating abuse of the woman, and sometimes her children as well. The severity of isolation and variety of physical and mental abuse women endure before they kill emerge with sickening clarity from most contemporary studies. Foster, Veale and Fogel's interviews with twelve North Carolina women imprisoned for homicide may be taken as typical. One woman told them:

In the beginning I could go out by myself, but after a

while, he went with me everywhere. He would drive me
to the beauty shop and wait, to the laundry and grocery
store. We had no telephone, no mail box. We had two
cars, but I had no [car] keys.

Another said: 'He would hit me upside the head for
burning the chicken. I had cuts on my head and bruises
under my eyes. He would put cigarettes out on my arms.'
Still a third described her most frightening experience as
follows:

He had a shoe and he beat me constantly for fifteen or
twenty minutes. I thought that I was going to die, I was
bleeding all over. I thought that it would never stop – he
just kept going – it was never this constant before. He
was so jealous. (Foster, Veale and Fogel, 1989: 276–7)

Women like these murdered their partners only because
they felt they could do nothing else. Without adequate
resources to draw on, leaving was not a real option. Moreover, although many did leave temporarily, 'the abusers'
threats to kill . . . made it seem virtually impossible to leave
safely' (Foster, Veale and Fogel, 1989: 282).[6]
Yet while psychologists and criminologists generally
agree today that abuse plays a key role in triggering
female homicide, their consensus is recent, a product of
changes in professional and popular attitudes towards
battered women. In the 1920s, women who remained
in abusive relationships were viewed as unintelligent or
even mentally retarded. In the 1940s they were labelled
masochistic. In the 1970s and 1980s, thanks to feminist
pressure on the legal system, social services and mass
media, they were more likely to be seen as victims, isolated
and deprived of economic and educational resources,
terrorized by repeated beatings into what Walker calls
'learned helplessness'.[7] Today battery, like rape, is commonly discussed in terms of power, not sexuality. As a

result, American juries may be more likely to acquit battered women who kill, seeing their acts as self-defence. Ten years ago, battered women had to plead not guilty by reason of insanity to avoid a murder conviction.

The changes in society's perceptions and treatment of women who kill, however, are neither simple nor complete. Psychologists and criminologists still quarrel over the profile of the typical female killer. Many insist that battery of women is a universal phenomenon, occurring in roughly the same percentages cross-class, cross-race and cross-culture. They maintain that battered women who kill are indistinguishable from battered women who don't kill.[8] Most studies indicate, however, that a higher proportion of African-American than white women are arrested and convicted for murder.[9] Poor, uneducated women of all races have higher arrest and conviction rates.[10] Are the high percentages of Black and poor women who are apprehended and convicted for murder and manslaughter the result of a bias in law enforcement? What connections exist among sex, race, social class and education and the number of women killers? The FBI Uniform Crime Reports, like Hollywood's deadly doll films, do not record class or education levels, and they report sex and race separately. As Flowers argues, these are 'unfortunate omission[s] when one considers the biases and assumptions so pervasive in official interpretations of criminality' (Flowers, 1987: 75).

Paradoxically, conservatives in the USA now urge equal treatment under the law, charging that the legal system discriminates in favour of women criminals. At the same time, of course, they deplore the changes in women's roles and suggest that these changes are responsible for increasing female violence and for making women's crimes look more like men's crimes. In fact the opposite is true: as a group, women continue to be economically, educationally and politically disadvantaged in comparison to men. And most women criminals still commit small-scale property crimes, not crimes of violence,[11] although they often receive harsher sentences than men do, and face worse prison conditions.[12]

It makes no sense, then, to claim women are gaining equality simply because the number of female homicides has risen, especially since male violence against women has increased dramatically in the last two decades. Indeed, it is quite possible that, as Walker and Jones maintain:

> During periods when women were more vociferously demanding their rights, those who killed men were punished more severely than they might have been during relatively 'tamer' times . . . [T]he percentage of homicides does not rise; rather the number of women punished by our justice system fluctuates, according to the social norms and perceived vociferousness of women's rights groups at the time. (Walker, 1989: 259)[13]

The picture of female murderers which emerges from sociological and psychological studies is thus both complicated and contested, intimately and intricately tied to popular debates about gender, race and class. Conspicuously absent from the debates around real-life women who kill, however, is any framing of violence as sensual or erotic. Hollywood, in contrast, as I will now show, always considers the display of female bodies to be more important than the portrayal of female violence, and sometimes even links criminality with marginal sexuality, warning that women who kill are lesbians.

Up from the sheets and into the streets: Hollywood harpies in the home and the heavens

Black Widow, Aliens, Fatal Attraction, Blue Steel, Mortal Thoughts and *Thelma and Louise* echo and extend professional and popular debates over why women kill and what this might conceivably mean for society. As big-budget Hollywood films concerned to recoup production costs and garner profits, they consciously market their messages, tailoring them to suit the broadest possible audience. To this end, all six films try to combine different genres, which means that all offer overlapping and at times contradictory motives for each murder. *Black Widow* melds *film noir* with the detective film; *Aliens* mixes together the war film, science fiction and horror; *Fatal Attraction* flips from melodrama to horror to thriller; *Blue Steel* is both action adventure cop film and romantic thriller; *Mortal Thoughts* jumbles *film noir* and thriller conventions; and *Thelma and Louise* blends comedy, the road movie, romance and the female buddy film (popularized recently in films like *Beaches* [Garry Marshall: 1988] and *Fried Green Tomatoes* [Jon Avart: 1991).

Each film includes at least one murder, but often only as the starting premiss or end point of narrative lines otherwise structured around romance, sexuality, conquest and violence – for all six movies are really more obsessed with the changing shape and status of heterosexual femininity than with homicide. Most translate this obsession visually, paying hyper-attention to costume and make-up and offering lingering and/or shock close-ups of soft and hard bodies. Since all feature at least two women characters, it is easy to measure the shape of femininity: one has only to compare. Each film underlines how very important measurement is, using body size, costumes, hairstyles, make-up, even murder weapons, not just as indices of eroticism but also as clues which help to explain why women murder.

These clues do not necessarily, however, resolve the discomfort generated by violent women. Indeed, except for *Aliens*, all the films in some way portray women who kill and/or work as anomalies, and all at some point insist that women without men are incomplete.[14] Five (*Black Widow, Fatal Attraction, Aliens, Blue Steel* and *Thelma and Louise*) visually code working women as masculine through costume, make-up and casting, even though these masculinized women kill in only three (*Aliens, Blue Steel* and *Thelma and Louise*). Four (*Black Widow, Fatal Attraction, Aliens* and *Blue Steel*) oppose masculinized women to more traditionally feminine women.

Mortal Thoughts alone adopts a different strategy, positioning both its female leads as ultra-feminine dolls on a par with the mannequins in Joyce's (Glenne Headly) hair salon, the Clip 'n' Dye. Miniskirts, tight pants and sweaters show off their perfect bodies, while artful make-up and stylish hairdos frame their flawless faces. The film opens after the murders of their husbands. Flashbacks recreate the story Cynthia (Demi Moore) tells during her interrogation in a police station. She frames her childhood friend Joyce for the murder of Joyce's husband Jimmy (Bruce Willis), but legitimates it as self-defence against battery. Cynthia admits that she helped Joyce to cover up this murder, but then claims that Joyce also killed her husband Arthur (John Pankow) because he knew too much. Just as all seems explained, Cynthia's story changes. A second set of flashbacks rearranges roles and actors, making Cynthia responsible for Jimmy's murder, though now justifying it as self-defence against rape. Joyce is still held responsible for Arthur's death, although the possibility emerges that this murder was not just a cover-up but a swap, arranged because the two wanted to be together, without men.

Black Widow and *Fatal Attraction*, in contrast, distinguish as well as double their two leading female characters. Both assign the androgynous name of Alex to the more masculine of the pair. The Alex of *Black Widow* (Debra Winger) is a frumpy workaholic who wears little make-up, likes baggy sweaters, and rather ineptly carries a gun: much to the amusement of her male co-workers at the Justice Department, she gets caught in an airport weapons detector. Awkward with men, she becomes obsessed with a *femme fatale* con artist (Theresa Russell) who adopts a series of disguises, backgrounds and names (Catherine, Marielle, Margaret and Renee) in order to marry, then murder, three wealthy men for their money. When the two finally meet, Alex is openly envious, even self-deprecating, telling Catherine wistfully, 'We spent most of the day in the pool: you come out looking like that and I look like this . . . Can I borrow your hair?' In response Catherine lends Alex her hairdresser and one of her dresses, and gradually transforms her into a 'real' woman. The two start to think alike, and even share the same lover. The final shot shows off Alex's successful 'sex' change: dressed in a tight-fitting blue flowered sundress, she walks out of a courthouse past an admiring group of male reporters, leaving Catherine behind bars.

Fatal Attraction pits Alex (Glenn Close) against Beth (Anne Archer) from the start, though both are glamorous. Alex likes leather, padded shoulders, snaky perms and black eyeliner; Beth likes soft tailored pants, cocktail dresses, loose curls and black underwear. Alex has a job; Beth has no job. Alex feels keenly the fact that she is single, childless, parentless, friendless and carless; Beth, on the other hand, is happily married, with a cute young daughter, doting parents, loving friends, a beautiful house and a roomy station wagon. Shortly after the movie begins, Alex seduces Beth's husband, Dan (Michael Douglas), then tells him she is pregnant. Spurned, her anger escalates from harassment to property crime to kidnapping to physical attacks. When Beth finally shoots Alex, her murder is doubly justified as self-defence and protection of the family. Yet although Alex becomes utterly diabolical as the movie progresses, she and Beth are briefly shown as doubles near the end of the film: dressed in white, they appear side by side in a steamy bathroom mirror.

Aliens and *Blue Steel* assert more strongly that women who kill are almost men. As scientist, Marine and cop, respectively, Ripley (Sigourney Weaver), Vasquez (Jenette Goldstein) and Megan (Jamie Lee Curtis) hold traditionally male jobs where they have the right to carry big guns. Their muscular bodies, androgynous costumes, short hair and lack of make-up further mark them as masculine. *Aliens* sends Ripley back into space with a group of Marines to uncover why human colonizers on another planet died. Once there Vasquez, not Ripley, leads patrols through the womblike labyrinthine tunnels of the alien planet and ultimately offers her life for comrades and country. At one point, her effortless execution of overhand chin-ups prompts a 'real' man to ask, 'Hey, Vasquez, have you ever been mistaken for a man?' 'No, have you?' she replies, undercutting his masculinity without establishing her own femininity.

Ripley's close-cropped curls, boyish face, flight jacket, boots, big guns and baggy pants make her look somewhat masculine, too. At one point she even dons a huge 'eco-skeleton' which enables her to perform manual labour. But in her case these masculine outer 'bodies' are juxtaposed against an inner 'feminine' one. Repeated shots of Ripley in her underwear offer reassurance that she is still very much a woman, as do the hints of a romantic involvement with the handsomest male Marine (Michael Biehn) and the stress on her maternal instincts (she adopts the colony's sole survivor, a little girl named Newt). When Ripley finally kills her arch-rival, an alien insect mother with hundreds of eggs, her original motives have multiplied: she blasts the alien into oblivion as a professional, as a mother, in revenge and in self-defence.

Like *Aliens*, *Blue Steel* views masculinity as outerwear and femininity as underwear, with the female face and body cast as fundamentally androgynous. Jamie Lee Curtis plays a rookie cop, Megan Turner, who drills multiple holes in a grocery store robber on her first assignment. Psycho stockbroker Eugene Hunt (Ron Silver) watches in fascination, then flees with the robber's gun. Obsessed with violent women, he courts Megan, all the while murdering men and women in her name. When he kills her best friend (Elizabeth Pena), Megan vows vengeance.

Slender but muscular, Megan looks fine in police uniforms obviously designed for men. Out of uniform she usually opts for masculine clothing as well: unlike her voluptuous Latina friend who loves low-cut blouses and short skirts, Megan prefers loose-fitting pants, jackets and hi-top sneakers. Yet an early sequence lingers on the lacy bra which lurks under her tight police shirt, and positions her and her gun as well as erotic, blue-lit objects. No wonder Megan's friends, family, co-workers and casual acquaintances can't understand her choice of profession and counsel her to find a man, settle down, and have children. Finally Megan takes their advice, sleeping first with Eugene, then with her superior and double, Lieutenant Nick Mann (Clancy Brown), another long-faced blond like herself who loves police work. Eugene is so jealous that he stalks, then rapes, Megan, adding psychological terror, revenge and self-defence to the long list of reasons why she finally kills him.

Thelma and Louise links murder and masculinity, too, although unlike *Fatal Attraction*, *Aliens* and *Blue Steel* it sometimes allows its heroines to be happy without men. Shortly after the film begins, Louise (Susan Sarandon) shoots a cowboy named Harlan (Timothy Carhart) who is about to rape her friend Thelma (Geena Davis). Defence seems the obvious motive, but the situation is complicated because Louise kills Harlan after he insults her, not while he is on top of Thelma. Fearing that no one will believe the murder was justified, the two women flee across a country filled with phallic symbols such as shiny tanker trucks and strutting Marlboro men. They shed the accoutrements of femininity as they go. Louise trades her jewellery for a beat-up hat and throws her lipstick in the dust. Thelma switches from frilly blouses and bikinis to T-shirts with motorcycle insignia. From an afterthought, tossed into the car after three suitcases full of clothes, a butterfly net and a fishing pole, Thelma's gun becomes a crucial part of her attire. Meanwhile, a third motive for the murder emerges: seeing Thelma's victimization triggered Louise's long-dormant anger over her own rape years earlier. By the time the two stop their car in the Arizona desert, they are as sweaty, dusty, nonchalant and hardened as any pair of male outlaws would be. They have even reversed roles: where once Louise protected the spoiled and childish Thelma, now Thelma provides for the scared and exhausted Louise.

In no other film is a female bond more consistently present. The two women look at each other constantly, in shot/reverse shots and two-shots. Often the camera pans slowly from one to the other as they laugh, joke and cry in the front seat of Louise's car. Thelma, especially, begins to equate independence with female space and marriage with jail. 'There's no going back,' she tells Louise, 'something inside of me has crossed over.' Somewhat more reluctantly, Louise refuses her beau, Jimmy (Michael Madsen), choosing freedom with Thelma instead. When they are at last cornered by cops at the edge of the Grand Canyon, the two friends have squared off against so many violent and immature men that their final handclasp, kiss, and plunge into space become eminently logical and discreetly lesbian.

But all the films, not just *Thelma and Louise*, at some point acknowledge female friendship, and half insinuate that these female friends are lovers. Such positive treatment of female pairs represents a significant shift from earlier movies about women killers. In classic *film noir*, if there were two female characters one was always a good girl, the other always a bad girl. The good girl stayed home and the bad girl worked. Of these films, only *Fatal Attraction* follows formula, but even it breaks with convention during one key sequence when Alex goes to visit Beth in her apartment, and the two drink tea and talk. They are having a wonderful time until Dan enters. A shaky hand-held camera translates his terrified point of view: he obviously finds the prospect of a sisterly exchange of information and trust threatening. From this moment on Alex is transformed from alluring masochistic victim to revolting sadistic villain.[15]

Black Widow takes female pairing furthest, structuring its entire narrative around the good girl's desire for the bad girl and vice versa. At one point the two eagerly practise mouth-to-mouth resuscitation. Alex's flip 'Don't take this the wrong way' only underlines the possibility of lesbian desire. Later, at her wedding, Catherine kisses Alex. Still later, betrayed by Alex, she clutches Alex's handkerchief to her face and kisses it sadly. Yet an undercurrent of violence and alienation underlies these expressions of affection and permeates the film's point-of-view structures: before they meet, Catherine spies on Alex and Alex spies on Catherine; after they meet, their looks at each other are shown in shot/reverse shots, emphasizing separation and distance rather than connection and proximity.

In *Mortal Thoughts*, in contrast, although Cynthia tells the story, looking is largely a male, not a female, privilege: men ogle the two women constantly, and the interrogating officer (Harvey Keitel) scrutinizes Cynthia and records her voice and image on video. Lesbian references are present in *Mortal Thoughts*, but less overtly so than in *Black Widow*. Opening and closing clips from home movies of Joyce and Cynthia – first as babies, then as children, and finally as adolescents – underscore the intimacy and duration of their bond, and in the course of the film Cynthia and her husband both suggest that she and Joyce might be lovers.

Male violence permeates many of these films, yet the only violence which is denounced is that perpetrated by strangers and/or working-class characters. *Fatal Attraction*, for example, both legitimates Dan's manhandling of Alex as part of his passion,[16] and rationalizes it as a necessary defence against a monster. Not coincidentally, Dan is an upper-middle-class lawyer. *Blue Steel* and *Mortal Thoughts*, on the other hand, show and condemn male abuse of women, but confine battery to the working-class family or position it outside the family altogether. As *Blue Steel* begins we hear, then see, a domestic quarrel between a couple in a rather run-down apartment. Later Megan discovers that violence pervades her own blue-collar family: her father beats her mother. Megan's own abuse and rape come at the hands of a wealthy stranger. *Mortal Thoughts* consistently documents Jimmy's abuse of Joyce, but only Cynthia ever tries to intervene. Everyone else regards violence as an integral part of working-class marriage. Nor is Jimmy the only abusive man in the film. On their way to the hospital with Jimmy's body in the back of the hairdressing shop van, Cynthia and Joyce stop for a moment to decide what to do. As soon as they turn the engine off, a carload of drunken men zooms up, threatening them just as Jimmy had. Yet in all these films, a remnant of romance lingers around rape because the rapists are cast as attractive and virile, because their victims are all young and beautiful, and because all the crimes take place at night.[17]

All six films thereby promote heterosexual sex. As an extra added attraction, they also portray female violence as sexy. *Black Widow* is far more obsessed with heterosexuality than with homosexuality, treating its audiences to a love scene in front of the fire between a naked Catherine and her third husband; a love scene in a swimming pool between Catherine and Paul (Sami Frey), both of whom are naked; and to foreplay between Alex and Paul. Dan and Alex spend a good part of the first half of *Fatal Attraction* grinding in the elevator and thumping on the sink. For Eugene in *Blue Steel*, Megan with her gun is a wet dream come true. Fondling first her breasts, then her revolver, he rhapsodizes: 'I think you're the most beautiful woman

I've ever seen in my life . . . Take out your gun and hold
it.' Even Thelma and Louise take a break from travelling
to conduct torrid and fairly lengthy affairs in sleazy hotel
rooms.

In every film, shadowy lighting, sharp camera angles,
probing camera movements, rapid editing and relentless
soundtracks weave an erotic aura around the murders most
fail to show. *Black Widow* lovingly details Catherine's prep-
arations for poisoning, emphasizing her well-manicured
hands, sleek legs and exquisite face. Then it elides the
deaths, implying that her male victims don't suffer by
simply jumping to the next sequence. *Aliens* and *Blue Steel*
draw out the deaths of the alien insect queen and Eugene,
but again without showing any pain or agony. And why
should audiences care if an insect or a psycho killer dies?
Why not focus instead on the dishevelled, panting but still
beautiful female killer, and relish the (sexual) frenzy of the
hunt? Louise and Beth offer quicker, cleaner versions of the
same scenario: each breathlessly dispatches Harlan and
Alex respectively. Only *Mortal Thoughts*'s Jimmy seems to
suffer, bleeding profusely and repeatedly in close-ups and
flashbacks.

How deadly, then, are these deadly dolls? How radical
and/or how reactionary are these films? *Aliens* and *Fatal
Attraction* never doubt that bad women deserve to die.
Fatal Attraction, *Blue Steel*, *Mortal Thoughts* and *Thelma
and Louise* punish powerful 'good' women as well. Beth
is lied to by Dan and stalked by Alex; Megan is terrorized
by Eugene; Jimmy makes Cynthia's life a living hell;
and Thelma's roadside pick-ups destroy both her life
and Louise's. Women on the verge of lesbianism fare
particularly badly: Thelma and Louise die; Vasquez dies;
and Cynthia, Joyce and Catherine go to jail. Nevertheless,
as the following survey of critical responses demonstrates,
reviewers from diverse backgrounds found much to like,
love and lust after in these films, even as they fixated on
female violence.

Rebels to relish or rubbish to repudiate?: Critical debates around deadly dolls

Critics of all six deadly doll films asked similar questions and confronted similar dilemmas: how to define violent women in relation to men, in relation to male violence, and in relation to feminism? Neither the gender of the individual reviewer nor the political stance of the periodical guaranteed how evaluations were made. Indeed, disagreements were often sharpest among women and men who wrote as feminists, and leftist and feminist periodicals often produced reviews which were virtually indistinguishable from those appearing in Christian magazines.

Most found the genre mixes and multiple motivations presented by these films chaotic and confusing. Many indicted them for being unrealistic, yet they usually did not comment on their most glaringly 'unrealistic' aspects: the absence or marginality of non-white characters. The thirty-plus reviews of *Thelma and Louise* I surveyed are typical. Only one, written by Manohla Dargis, mentioned a sequence where a Black Rastafarian bicyclist stumbles on a state trooper Thelma and Louise have locked in his car trunk. The bicyclist blows marijuana smoke into the trunk's airholes, then rides away. Dargis concludes: 'the American landscape has ceased to be the exclusive province of white masculinity' (Dargis, 1991: 16).

Aliens drew more attention to race, class and imperialism, because it rewrites American defeat in Vietnam as American victory in space. Nevertheless, of the over twenty reviews I looked at here, half still focused on female sexuality and motherhood to the exclusion of all else. Many critics referred to Ripley as 'Rambolina' without questioning the warlike resonances embedded in references to Rambo. A few described the film as an apology for capitalism, while a handful labelled it militarist and imperialist. Yet the Marxist weekly *The Guardian* was not among the latter group, insisting that the aliens represented 'the mindless destructiveness of nature', not 'an inferior or evil race of yellow or brown-skinned human beings' (Rapping, 1986: 24).[18]

When repeatedly prompted by a film narrative, some critics mentioned sexual preference. The lesbian sub-plot in *Black Widow* garnered the most varied reactions. The British feminist journal *Spare Rib* ignored the issue; Charles Sawyer touted the 'rapport wavering between friendship and something deeper . . . [as] the most original and fascinating thing about the movie' (Sawyer, 1987: 227); while David Ansen, David Denby, Adrian Sibley and Marina Heung concurred with Stanley Kauffmann that 'the film flirts with homoeroticism between two patently heterosexual women' (Kauffmann, 1987: 25). Pauline Kael went further, referring to the film's 'occasional near-porno texture' (Kael, 1987: 112) without commenting on its lesbian allusions; and Teresa de Lauretis angrily charged that 'the film's heavy hints at lesbianism are . . . there merely to blow the viewer's mind' (de Lauretis, 1990: 22).

Occasionally articles about *Thelma and Louise* noted how popular the movie was with lesbian audiences, but only a few critics described the female characters *as* lesbians. No one mentioned what a cult favourite Susan Sarandon has been since her role as scientist turned lesbian vampire in *The Hunger*. Very few reviewers saw Vasquez as gay or commented on the film's appeal to lesbian audiences,[19] and only one reviewer tersely mentioned *Mortal Thoughts's* whispered lesbian references.[20]

Instead, debates centred on perceived changes in femininity and the connections between gender and violence. *Fatal Attraction* and *Thelma and Louise* were among the most controversial movies of the decade. People used the words 'fatal attraction' so frequently to describe their own experiences that the term temporarily entered the national vocabulary. During the summer of 1991, the influential news magazine *Time* devoted a cover story entitled 'Gender Bender' to *Thelma and Louise*, exploring the questions everyone seemed to be asking: were these characters girls on a spree, feminist martyrs, or bitches from hell?

Most critics mentioned the male violence in the films in passing, if at all. No one objected to Dan's physical attacks on Alex; indeed, some reviewers labelled him a wimp. Several commented on the prevalence of male violence in *Blue Steel*, but only Michael Bronski noticed Megan's father's abuse of her mother. Reviewers of *Mortal Thoughts* disagreed about how they saw Jimmy, one describing him as 'a thoroughly despicable, abusive lout' (Daws, 1991: 92), another finding him intolerable but charming (Ainslee, 1991: 48), a third merely mentioning Willis's 'overblown, sweaty, naturalistic acting' (Alleva, 1991: 407). The all-pervasive male violence of *Thelma and Louise* was often played down as mere 'sexism'. Richard Schickel, for example, objected that the film shows 'all forms of sexual exploitation, great or small, [as] consequential and damaging' (Schickel, 1991: 54). And the tabloid *Daily News* even denounced the movie as 'degrading to men' because it 'justifies armed violence, manslaughter and chronic drunken driving as exercises in consciousness-raising' (Schickel, 1991: 52).

Screenwriter Callie Khouri's retort that *Thelma and Louise* 'isn't hostile to men, it's hostile to idiots' (Shapiro, 1991: 63) did little to set anyone at ease. Similarly, Adrian Lyne's incessant assertions that *Fatal Attraction* was merely a love story about 'uncontrollable passion' (Beaulieu, 1988: 76),[21] or Sigourney Weaver's disingenuous confession, 'I like to think the real message [of *Aliens*] is love' (Schickel, 1986: 58) were dismissed as self-serving simplifications not to be taken seriously.

What critics did see – and, for the most part, liked – in these films were their capable, attractive female characters. Ripley, Thelma and Louise were especially popular, though even *Fatal Attraction*'s evil Alex had her supporters.[22] A great many reviewers – and not just those who called themselves feminists – liked seeing women characters fight back. They proudly labelled *Thelma and Louise* a 'butt-kicking feminist manifesto' (Schickel, 1991: 52);[23] welcomed *Aliens* as a 'blood and guts war flick feminists can relish' (Rapping, 1986: 24); and gloated that *Fatal Attraction* reversed that 'classic female night-mare', unwanted pregnancy without option of abortion, by painting Dan's plight as:

> a huge, distressing, apparently endless consequence
> he cannot rid himself of. And all because the poor guy
> had a little fun. Hey, is life unfair or what? He even
> tries to get an abortion, but Alex is having none of it.
> Sorry fella, she says, *you can't get an abortion*! (Durbin,
> 1987: 90)

Anne Billson spoke for women spectators in general: 'Men are always behaving so badly in real life that you should never underestimate a woman's satisfaction in seeing them get their just deserts on screen . . . Men have no idea how annoying they can be' (Billson, 1991: 32).

Yet although most critics focused on 'the strength of the image of the women in the face of textual repression' (Kaplan, 1980: 5), just as audiences had done with 1940s *film noir* heroines, some found it impossible to overlook the lethal treatment meted out to these deadly dolls. They saw *Fatal Attraction* as fundamentally misogynist, and protested that *Thelma and Louise* was too hard on women. Amy Taubin complained, for example, that the latter film 'suggests that the situation of American women is dire indeed' (Taubin, 1991: p 88) while Annette Insdorf simply asked: 'when death is your only choice, how free are you?' (Schickel, 1991: p 56).

Others, and especially certain feminists, objected sharply to seeing violence attributed to women and feminism because, like *LA Times* reviewer Sheila Benson, they saw feminism as having 'to do with responsibility, equality, sensitivity, understanding – not revenge, retribution or sadistic behavior' (Schickel, 1991: 52). Some even charged that these deadly dolls were not really women at all but men in drag, because they thought of violence as *a priori* male. As *New Directions for Women* put it: '[Vasquez] prove[s] that she not only looks like a man, but that she fights like a man as well. Her maleness is the proof of her heroic capabilities. The same is true of . . . Ripley' (Prigozy, 1986: 6).[24] *Time*'s Margaret Carlson viewed Thelma and Louise in much the same way: '[they] behave like – well, men . . . [They] act out a male fantasy of life on the road, avoiding intimacy with loud music, Wild Turkey, fast driving – and a gun in the pants' (Carlson, 1991: 57).

But another set of critics seemed to believe that feminism makes more women more violent more often. They labelled deadly dolls feminists precisely *because* they were violent, then condemned them for directing their violence against men. Some even warned that a new feminist-led fascism lurked on the horizons of *Thelma and Louise*. *People Weekly* branded Ridley Scott a 'gender quisling' (Novak, 1991: 54) and the *US News and World Report* charged: 'making fun of men . . . has gotten mixed up with what I call a fascist idea that there's rebirth and spiritual revitalization in crime, particularly in violent crime' (Leo, 1991: 20). *Fatal Attraction* aroused such virulent hatred that satirist Lydia Sargent predicted it would 'set that women's lib back about 5000 years. Maybe more. Clearly you gals can't be allowed out . . . After all, what are you when you're not fulfilling your God-given roles as wives and mothers? You're either out of control or out of your clothes' (Sargent, 1988: 34).

Still other critics countered: 'Compared with most gun-toting males in the movies, Thelma and Louise are practically apostles of nonviolence' (Shapiro, 1991: 63). And Susan Sarandon insisted that charges that her character was too violent merely showed 'what a straight, white male world movies traditionally occupy. This kind of scrutiny does not happen to . . . that Schwarzenegger thing [*Total Recall*] where he shoots a woman in the head and says, "Consider that a divorce"' (Schickel, 1991: 56).[25] Many protested that it was incorrect to call Thelma and Louise, Ripley and Vasquez, Joyce and Cynthia, Megan or the two Alexes 'feminists' simply because they were assertive, independent and/or violent.[26]

Much more is at stake, however, than can be seen from the gender-based and gender-biased arguments which the films, their critics, and sociologists too, conduct around violent women. I want in conclusion, therefore, to explore the two major areas these six films and their critics distance and deny: sexual preference and racial difference.

The ultimate unthinkable: deadly dolls as lesbians and blacks

In all six films, in the majority of critical reviews, and in a portion of popular responses to real-life women who kill, a murmured fear of lesbianism lurks beneath the general discomfort with violent women, and hides behind their portrayal as man-hating feminists or as men, *tout court*. A deeper, more immobilizing terror of racial difference and possible miscegenation remains altogether unspoken, camouflaged by the brouhaha around comely white super-heroines.

The fact that most reviewers avoided such issues only highlights how volatile and frightening they are. If anything, the films' pairing of powerful women heightens the profound ambivalence today's spectators feel towards both homicide and homosexuality. The narrative condemnation of covert couples and promotion of heterosexual sex-capades do not entirely erase what a decade of misinformation about AIDS has only reactivated: the fear that male and female homosexuals alike are disease-carriers and death-dealers.

For years, mainstream films have proclaimed that lesbians are killers, vampires, even rapists: *Club de Femmes* (Jacques Deval: 1936), *Huis Clos* (Jacqueline Audry: 1954),

149

Vampire Lovers (Roy Ward Baker: 1971), *Daughters of Darkness* (Harry Kumel: 1971), *Windows* (Gordon Willis: 1980), *The Hunger* (Tony Scott: 1983) and *Sudden Impact* (Clint Eastwood: 1983) are all examples.[27] A kinder, gentler lesbian briefly appeared during the mid 1980s.[28] But although she may have muted *Black Widow*, *Aliens*, *Mortal Thoughts* and *Thelma and Louise*'s portraits of deadly dykes, more recent films, such as *Basic Instinct* (Paul Verhoeven: 1992) leave no doubt that today's film femmes are more dazzlingly deadly than ever. As Lindsy Van Gelder succinctly said: 'In many minds the leap from the butch to the butcher knife is but a tiny one' (Van Gelder, 1992: 82).

Yet at least white lesbianism is represented, however pejoratively or tentatively, in deadly doll films. The same cannot be said of the far more visible difference of race. Where violent femme films are concerned, in those limits on 'what can be seen, and eroticized' which Teresa de Lauretis calls 'representability', much less can be seen than eroticized. While several 1970s movies featured black female killers, 1980s films were more likely to associate African-American women, whether as victims, perpetrators or police, with crimes other than murder. *Jumping Jack Flash* (Penny Marshall: 1986), *Fatal Beauty* (Tom Holland: 1987), *Burglar* (Hugh Wilson: 1987), *Angel Heart* (Alan Parker: 1987), *Above the Law* (Andrew Davis: 1988) and *Homer and Eddie* (Andrei Konchalovsky: 1990) all follow this pattern. The only deadly doll film with an African-American female central character is the low-budget independent spoof *Surf Nazis Must Die*. And although she is deadly, 'Leroy's mamma' (Elinor Washington) can hardly be called a doll. A stereotypical wide-hipped big-bosomed mammy, she is a comic, not a sexual figure who, during the film's finale, commandeers a motorboat, then shoots and runs over the evil white Nazi surfer who killed her son. Not coincidentally, the only Latina who kills in these films, Vasquez, is strongly coded as lesbian.

Why are today's deadly dolls, by definition, 'all-American', read 'white'? In the 1950s, 1960s and 1970s the most popular and prolific male killers had oh-so-English names like John Wayne, James Coburn and Clint Eastwood. Most of the model male murderers today – Sylvester Stallone and Arnold Schwarzenegger, Jean-Claude Van Damme, even Mel Gibson – are ethnic or foreign. Virility, once home-grown and Anglo-American, is now imported. Deadly doll films, which overtly acknowledge that white American men are weaklings and/or nincompoops while at the same time insisting that heterosexual passion is still possible, will not – cannot – simultaneously acknowledge cross-racial alliances and relationships. In the USA today, so many people still find miscegenation unacceptable and unsuitable that miscegenation plus emasculation is, quite literally, unthinkable. No wonder even the black male Rasta biker of *Thelma and Louise* disappeared from the critics' view.

Clearly, then, there are limits to what these deadly doll films and their critics represent and perceive. The very popularity and proliferation of these movies should encourage feminists to ask how much our own visions of gender may be similarly clouded by failures to acknowledge sexuality and/or see race. Yet there have undeniably been changes in how violent women are viewed in relation to home, work and the world, in movies as in real life, and we can certainly take some satisfaction in knowing that cinema lags behind society. So far at least, we have not had to applaud Gulf War 'heroines' or boo foetus 'killers'. Movies still afford some escape from newspapers, radio and TV.

But how long can a good thing last?

Acknowledgements

Thanks to Judy Fiene, Elaine Gorman, Jon Jonakin, Peter Lehman and Dale Watermulder for their comments and suggestions.

Body talk

The sexual politics of PMT

Melissa Benn

Ask Linda Hewett what went through her head at the
moment she took a carving knife and plunged it into
the neck of the man she loves, and she replies simply:
'Don't ask me . . . ask the other woman'.

The other woman in question answered to the name
Linda Hewett, looked like her, WAS her as far as the
outside world was concerned.

'But was it really me?' she asks. 'Was it me any more
than Dr Jekyll was Mr Hyde?'

Just what turns a happy, loving woman into a knife-
wielding maniac can be summed up quite easily.

'The doctors have a technical word for it' said Linda
yesterday. 'They say I was suffering from post-natal
depression, and at the time my condition was aggravated
by pre-menstrual tension. I was in a total trance. I didn't
know what was happening. The first time I realised
what I'd done was when I was giving my statement to
the police. *I remember telling them that I had tried to kill
him because he expected me to do all the housework, look
after the kids, answer his business calls and still wander
round the house singing like Julie Andrews.* I was trying
to find logical reasons for a completely irrational act.'
(emphasis added)

(*Today*, 28 February 1987)

152

A computer expert who was sacked after she hit her head of department while suffering from Pre Menstrual Tension was unfairly dismissed, an industrial tribunal ruled yesterday.

Yvonne Tibbles, 34, of Swindon, a software support assistant, was sacked from the electronics firm Fujitsu after hitting Mike Slaughter. When during a row over a report she had been working on, Mr Slaughter told her to stop 'copping out' of her responsibilities, she screamed and swore at him, and told him never to say that again.

The tribunal was told that she then hit him around the head and threw a waste paper bin across the room. She said that at the time of the incident she had been suffering from PMT *and the attack followed two and a half years of sexist abuse and being continually checked on by Mr Slaughter.* (emphasis added)

(*The Independent*, 20 March 1992)

PMT is a relatively new addition to the acronyms we use about the female body, the place of that body in the world. It is a given of my generation, the generation born into or formed through the transitions of second-wave feminism; we invoke it in a way that women of my mother's generation would not dare and those of my grandmother's generation would not dream of. This is more than just a refreshing public openness, a new naming. PMT has become something of an obsession in our culture: you can hardly open up a woman's magazine or a tabloid newspaper without reading of some trouble connected with it, some healthy way to banish or minimize it. In this, it has become part of a bundle of media tag words that supposedly describe the new woman and her world.

But what is it exactly?

I believe that any writer on PMT must come clean from the start and answer the seemingly simple question – does it exist? – before asking the more complicated question of what we should do in the light of that acknowledged existence. My own answer is: yes, clearly, yes. The empirical evidence is overwhelming: some kind of mental/physical change assails many women in many forms at some point in their menstrual cycle. In Tennessee Williams's play *Cat on a Hot Tin Roof*, Brick, the alcoholic son, describes the 'click' in his head that tells him that the drink is finally having an effect; from that moment on, he will be lost in a welcome drink-sodden blur. Many women might recognize an analogous hormonal shift, a moment or patch of time when the body/thoughts 'click' into some state more impossible than possible; the reverse of integration.

But immediately, we must be careful. Immediately, we must begin to make distinctions between the places in which it is appropriate or safe to make such admissions and those where it is not. I may profit (privately, as it were) from the lessons of PMT; its sudden overwhelming welter of irritations may tell me what or whom I am tolerating at other times in my life that I need not tolerate after all. Or the gloss of crisis that PMT can frequently put on daily life may hint at something deeper, the beginning of a recognition of more threatening elements that lurk beneath the apparently ordinary surface of things. But what would any of this often ironic self-realization mean should I be planted in a witness box and asked to explain myself in relation to a crime? What would an understanding of the wellsprings of my own irritability (or creativity, for that matter) mean should it form part of an application to be a surgeon or an airline pilot?

It is somewhere within this tangle of questions that the public difficulty of PMT begins.

The problem goes wider still. It is my argument that the invocation of PMT too frequently allows both men and women to escape from the truth of a story that simultaneously exists within them and stands before them. Both Linda Hewett and Yvonne Tibbles seem to speak at a double level of the reasons why they acted violently: Hewett in particular describes as 'illogical' the explanation she gave to the police in the aftermath of the stabbing: that she acted in response to her husband's unreasonable expectations of her as a wife and as a mother. But was it illogical? Can we talk of emotions in terms of logic anyway? And is she herself not denying what she knows?

Such apparent confusions of motive and meaning are extraordinarily common in cases where PMT is invoked as the ultimate explanation of a violent act. It is striking how often even the briefest press report on a murder or attempted murder case involving PMT hints at the dim shape of a human-sexual-political story lurking just beneath the surface – a story not so much of individual biological malfunction as of unhappy, unfulfilled, deceiving human relationships, strained to breaking point.

What follows is an attempt to insert the beginnings of those missing tales.

Murder one

There is nothing new in menstruation, its presence or absence, being viewed as disability. The nineteenth-century conception of middle-class femininity was dependent on the preservation of the idea of biologically induced weakness, at least for the middle-class woman, and the denial of her autonomous agency. The feminist criminologist Susan Edwards has detailed instances from the mid nineteenth century where crimes from murder to shoplifting were ascribed to problems of menstruation and attendant lack of psychic 'control'.[1] The medicalization of pre-menstrual tension – work initiated in the 1930s – is clearly a part-continuation of those perceptions.

Since the 1950s the main public proponent of PMT – or pre-menstrual syndrome, as she calls it – has been Dr Katherina Dalton, an endocrinologist (a specialist in hormones) who has pursued the subject with an extraordinary single-mindedness. Dalton has written several books and countless papers on the subject, appeared on radio and television, and – as I describe below – appeared in several legal cases as an expert witness.

The essence of Dalton's argument is that PMS is a form of biochemical disturbance manifested in range of physical and mental symptoms, of which the prime psychological ones are depression and anxiety, and characterized by the appearance of these symptoms in the pre-menstrual period and their disappearance afterwards. In Dalton's view, PMS is caused by a lack of progesterone: her own treatment in severe cases involves the administration of the synthetic version of the hormone through injection, pills or pessaries. In less severe cases, she suggests non-hormonal treatment.

Dalton's analysis of the aetiology and treatment of PMT is not undisputed in the medical world: several researchers have questioned the link she draws between PMT and progesterone levels.[2] Others have questioned the connections she unproblematically draws between aggression levels and PMT. Despite these opposing views, Dalton's analysis and arguments have attained an almost unchallenged status in lore *and* law. From the late 1970s onwards, she became a key witness – and her PMS argument, a key argument – in a number of cases where women were accused of serious violence. In 1978 Nicola Owen, a chronic arsonist, appeared in court on a charge of arson. Before sentence, medical reports were prepared on her by Dalton, who argued that Owen suffered from 'a classic case of PMS'. As a result of this argument, mitigation succeeded and Owen was placed on probation. In 1980, barmaid Sandie Craddock – later known under the name of Smith, when she again appears in PMT case law – stabbed a fellow barmaid to death. Although Craddock had a long history of violent behaviour and previous convictions, medical evidence put forward by Dalton at the trial suggested that she was suffering from PMT. The case was put back to allow preparation of a medical report and treatment with progesterone, during which her behaviour was said to have improved dramatically. The Recorder, James Miskin, subsequently accepted her plea of guilty of manslaughter due to diminished responsibility and imposed a probation order with the condition of continued medical treatment. In 1981 Christina English, whose case I look at in greater detail below, also successfully pleaded guilty to manslaughter on grounds of diminished responsibility, having run her lover down in her car. Again, after Dalton gave evidence, Justice Purchas accepted that the offence had been committed in 'wholly exceptional circumstances' in the light of evidence that 'at the time of the offence she was suffering from PMT'. English received a conditional discharge and a twelve-month driving disqualification.

In 1981, the day after English walked out of Norwich Crown Court, a free woman, Sandie Craddock, now known as Smith, was charged at the Old Bailey with two offences of threatening to kill a police officer and one offence of possessing an offensive weapon. Smith's violent conduct was explained by a reduction in her progesterone therapy at the time of the offence. Dalton told the court that a return to previous levels would render her 'safe and benign'. Keith Evans, Smith/Craddock's lawyer, tried to deny criminal liability altogether on the grounds that PMT was a 'disease'. Craddock was convicted, but was sentenced only to a three-year probation order. Going to appeal, Keith Evans (who held to a strong personal belief that PMT is a kind of illness) attempted to argue that PMT was a 'substantive defence' to crime on grounds of 'automatism': in other words, that the faculty of independently originating action was reduced to the point where the person in question was not in full possession of her faculties.

The appeal was rejected. In explaining the basis of its judgement, the Court of Appeal declared:

There is no question of automatism providing a defence

in this case. It is quite clear from the doctor's evidence that this woman knew exactly what she was doing, intended to do it, but was led into doing it because the dark side of her nature appeared as a result of being unable to control the impulse which she would not have allowed to dominate her normally due to the lack of progesterone. If we acceded to Mr Evans's submission we would find this picture. After she had stabbed the barmaid, the appellant would be entitled to come before the court and seek an acquittal because she would be able to say that as a result of a lack of a necessary hormone, she lost control of herself and that she is not morally guilty. As a result of that, she would be acquitted and discharged with all the consequent risks to society. There would be no control over her by society through the courts and she would continue to be a danger to all around her.[3]

Despite the caution of this judgement, there have been many criminal cases since where the PMT argument has successfully been argued, either as a substantive defence or in mitigation. It has also been argued in adoption and wardship proceedings, and in cases involving child-battering.

Feminist first answers

The feminist critique of the 'PMT defence' reached a peak in the early 1980s, around the time of English and Smith/Craddock. It was a powerful counter-argument, surprisingly shared and elaborated by radical, socialist and liberal feminists, albeit in quite different language. For them, PMT slotted only too neatly into the stereotyped mad/bad split that has reigned for so long in public perceptions of women and crime.

Interviewed in the *Sunday Times* in 1985, feminist criminologist Susan Edwards argued that PMT, with postnatal depression and menopause, were used as a 'handy scape-goat . . . to shroud other pressures to which both women and men are subject; poverty, unemployment, single parenthood, bad housing, loneliness'. She said: 'If women go on colluding with the thinking that they are the victims of their own biology, how can they complain when their biological functions, and how they respond to them, are put forward as grounds for discrimination when it comes to education, opportunities and job prospects?'[4]

Sophie Laws, writing in the radical feminist *Women's Studies International Forum* in 1983, went even further. She declared that PMT is

> at its root a political construct – a part of patriarchal ideology. Many feminists have supported the idea of PMT and have promoted its acceptance by the medical profession but have feared that it might be 'used against women'. I now think that we have been mistaken. PMT, constructed as a medical problem, is an idea through which women may be divided and controlled . . . the advertisement used in medical journals for Cyclogest (natural progesterone) also illustrates this splitting of women. The photograph shows two versions of one woman: one in a black round necked tee shirt with untidy hair and a sad expression, the second with a shining smile, shining hair and a white V neck blouse.[5]

Hilary Allen, writing in the Marxist–feminist journal *m/f* in 1984, disputed the oversimplistic connection between PMT and female violence. This, she argued, neglected the complex links between biology, medicine, social action and the law which the PMT defence inevitably evoked. Writing about the application of such arguments to Sandie Craddock/Smith's case, Allen argues:

> We are asked to believe that that [Craddock/Smith's] hormonal state not only made her behaviour possible,

but made it inevitable. She had no option but to behave as she did; biological state led to mental state led to social action in a single mechanical movement of causality, in which no other factors intervened. Against the tempting simplicity of this formulation it is only necessary to counterpose the evidence of empiricism itself. Although it is easy to demonstrate that everywhere biological states provide the necessary conditions for particular human behaviour, their failure to provide sufficient conditions has repeatedly been demonstrated. Even such minimal units of 'biologically programmed' behaviour as the reflex action are subject to external variables . . . similarly, a number of now classic psychological experiments have demonstrated that hormonal states may modify but never determine behaviour . . . In the context of this insufficiency of biology in the explanation of individual behaviour, the attribution of a woman's criminal behaviour to her hormonal state offers at best only a misleading scientificity to the evaluation of her conduct and *obscures the whole political nexus of social factors which structure and influence the behaviour of human actors.* (emphasis added)[6]

Female anger and bad faith: reinterpreting English

Interestingly, Allen's argument anticipates a welcome shift in thinking about PMT in recent years: away from worries about women's biology or the effect of PMT on their job prospects (I am exaggerating slightly) to a more socially based exploration of the reason for women's crimes. Both feminist and public discussion is increasingly directed at the notion of 'provocation' – a defence long available to men who murder their spouses, but not, until recently, to women who have done the same.

The case of Christine English is most interesting when looked at in this way.

The brief facts are these: English, aged thirty-seven, a mother of two, had been the lover of Barry Kitson for three years. It was a difficult relationship: Kitson was an alcoholic, and on the night of the murder he had been taunting her about another woman. The couple had a quarrel in their shared flat in Colchester, after which Kitson stormed off to the nearby 'Live and Let Live' pub, where he drank heavily. After English had come to pick him up, they again argued on the drive home. She had tried to persuade him to give up drink – an old quarrel between them – but he 'lashed out' at her with his fists, got out of the car and stormed out into the darkness, telling her: 'I hate you and never want to see you again'. As she was driving away, English, in a paroxysm of fury, drove the car at high speed towards Kitson, crushing him against a telegraph pole until his leg was almost severed. She then ran into the street, screaming: 'Please God, tell me it's not true. God, tell me it didn't happen.' Kitson died in hospital fifteen days later.

At the trial, Dalton argued that English suffered severely from PMT; the fact that she had not eaten for nine hours had 'brought on severe depression and [made her] confused, aggressive and irritable'. Dalton said: 'We are talking about something beyond the range of what women would normally suffer. It is a disease of the body which has an effect on the mind.' As long as she ate sensibly in the future, English would not suffer the severe symptoms, Dalton claimed. English's defence lawyer, James Rant QC, argued that the dead man's drinking had 'destroyed the relationship, caused his death and almost destroyed Mrs English'. But it was the PMT argument that seemed to have the most effect. English was convicted of manslaughter on the grounds of diminished responsibility, conditionally discharged for a year, and given a driving ban for the same time.[7]

But Susan Edwards and others have argued that English would be an ideal case for reinterpretation as a form of provocation. In the long term, Kitson was violent, abusive; in the short term, he had taunted her about another woman. In comparable cases where men had murdered their wives, provocation was successfully argued – for example, in the case of Stephen Midlane, tried for the murder of his wife Sandra in 1989, where the judge accepted evidence of Sandra's infidelity as a major contributory factor to Midlane's claim of provocation.

So why were such arguments not used in the case of English?

The answer is: provocation as a legal defence is rarely available to women. As Sue Lees argues in an interesting essay on provocation, 'Naggers, Whores and Women's Libbers', the availability of this defence to men depends on a view of women's sexual and familial 'duty' to those men. The defence is then argued on the basis of the victim's liability, through failure of her duty: 'No such licence to kill is given to women who stand trial for male murder since the basis of the defence rests on the idea that a "reasonable man" can be provoked into killing by insubordination. In other words, the woman provokes her own death.' In an analogy with rape trials, it is often the woman who is on trial – even where she is the victim, even where she is dead. Lees concludes:

> The acts of men and women are subject to a different
> set of legal expectations and standards. As we have seen
> in most cases where provocation is alleged by men, it
> is the character of the victim, if a woman, rather than
> the defendant, who is up for trial. Where the victim is
> a man, allegations about his sexual infidelity would just
> not be taken seriously and it is doubtful whether they
> would even be made.[8]

Just as the defence of provocation symbolizes acceptance of the cultural necessity of male anger, the defence of PMT signifies the cultural denial of the possibility of serious female anger. Sue Lees says:

> The law in regard to murder legitimates male anger
> through the defence of provocation. To be driven beyond
> his senses. But a woman who expresses anger is mad
> not reasonable. That is why PMT is so vital – it rests
> on the idea that if women are angry they are driven by
> their hormones. That's reasonable. But if they're angry
> because someone has let them down, then they're mad.

The PMT axis – Dalton, and her allies in the courts and popular press – locate female anger as an unnatural bodily state that passes with the flow of blood. Dalton is perfectly straightforward in her analysis of women's anger: housewives who get irritated at domestic tasks or their husbands or their children are angry because of the time of the month, not because of anything within the dynamic of those relationships – certainly not because of disappointment or frustration. Of one case, Dalton wrote: '[When the PMS has ended] she is once more her usual sweet-tempered and placid self or she may be filled with guilt and remorse at the problems her actions have caused. One woman said, "I wish others would realise it wasn't the true me who caused all this".'

Thus, we have an explanation of women's anger that places it both deep within themselves and curiously outside their control: it has the function of splitting women, literally in two; setting up two creatures (the placid and the angry) who would not even recognize each other should they meet. More crudely, it provides an explanation that does not threaten existing social arrangements. This is the classic objection of feminists who see 'the whole political nexus of social factors which structure and influence the behaviour of social actors' – in this case, women.

But doesn't the function of PMT go even deeper than that? Is it not both a symbolic and literal mechanism by which women can explain and escape the consequences of their own actions? There is a purely opportunistic side to this. If I were on a charge of murder and knew that I had a better chance of a conditional discharge on grounds of manslaughter (as opposed to a life sentence, the mandatory punishment for murder) if I pleaded this way or that, I doubt that I would think twice about introducing PMT into the argument.

The courts are, of course, wary of such opportunism, as reflected in the 1982 Court of Appeal judgement: the elderly judges imagining thousands of screaming women flocking to the courts with their ready-made excuse. But this kind of opportunism is, ironically, more understandable than the bad faith inherent in the more authentic usage of PMT as an explanation of anger. I use the term 'bad faith' deliberately, for the PMT phenomenon is so easily explained in traditional existentialist terms as best expressed in Simone de Beauvoir's *The Second Sex*, still the classic exposition of rational feminist existentialism. De Beauvoir's meditation on the 'Young Woman' growing up, and the different place of force in the formation of the male and female psyche, is particularly relevant here:

> In the adult world no doubt brute force plays no great
> part in normal times; but nevertheless it haunts that
> world; many kinds of masculine behaviour spring
> from a root of possible violence; on every street corner
> squabbles threaten; usually they flicker out; but for
> a man to feel in his fists his will to self-affirmation
> is enough to reassure him of his sovereignty. Against
> any insult, any attempt to reduce him to the status of
> object, the male has recourse to his fists, to exposure of
> himself to blows; he does not let himself be transcended
> by others, he is himself at the heart of his subjectivity.
> Violence is the authentic proof of each one's loyalty to
> himself, to his passions, to his own will; radically to
> deny this will is to deny oneself any objective truth, it

is to wall oneself up in an abstract subjectivity; anger
or revolt that does not get into the muscles remains a
figment of the imagination. It is a profound frustration
not to be able to register one's feelings upon the face of
the world.[9]

Where de Beauvoir is herself unmodern is in her failure
fully to recognize that women too feel anger and violence,
just as men do: their problem lies in internal and external
restraints on its expression. So we must ask: by what
means do women 'register their feelings upon the face
of the world'? A majority still express their anger through
such classic vehicles as depression (a turning of anger
inward) or 'nagging' – the stretching out of anger to a
thinner but none the less poisonous substance. Women
rarely put up a straight dirty fight.

But when they do, why must it be explained away?
Christine English ran from the car, crying 'God, tell me
it didn't happen!' And in a sense the court told her that it
didn't happen: *she* didn't do it, her hormones did. Thus she
became witness to some other part of herself, expressing
anger and fury to the point of serious violence.

Looked at in this context, PMT represents the ultimate
denial of agency. It is as if the woman has gone right to 'the
heart of her subjectivity', only then to retreat. By emptying
the heart out of her action, it disempowers her, returning
her (paradoxically) to a state of 'abstract subjectivity',
witness to some other part of herself who acts so strangely.
Hence the constant use of the essentially unintegrated
language of Jekyll and Hyde, 'myself' and 'otherness' that
permeates the conservative politics of PMT.

The ordinary extraordinary truth: Anna Reynolds

Different questions about the relationship between PMT and
agency are raised by the case of Anna Reynolds, who in 1986,
when she was still a teenager, killed her mother, striking her

over the head in her sleep with a series of hammer blows. Reynolds was initially convicted of murder, but on appeal – thanks once again to evidence introduced by Dr Dalton – was found to be suffering from a combination of pre-menstrual tension and postnatal depression, and the conviction was changed to manslaughter on the grounds of diminished responsibility. Press photos on the day of Reynolds's release show a seemingly fatally withdrawn young-old woman, hair falling over her face, looking down at the ground.

Reading the court shorthand-writers' notes on the Reynolds appeal judgement evokes confusion about the complex relationship between crime, law, the body and the truth. The facts of the case seem fairly well established. Anna Reynolds came home one night from work, had an argument with her mother, went to bed. Feeling disturbed in the middle of the night, Reynolds came into her mother's room to sleep on a camp bed. Plagued by a 'funny feeling', she then got up, saw a hammer and struck her mother a repeated number of blows on the head: afterwards, she made a rather half-hearted attempt to rearrange the room to make it look as if it was a burglary, an explanation which she abandoned soon after she reached the police station.

With none of the facts in dispute and her guilt admitted, both the trial and the appeal were concerned to establish how much Reynolds was in control of her actions at the moment of the crime. There was a confusing mass of evidence as to whether she was suffering from a depressive illness, when it had come on, how long it had lasted: eventually, the jury concluded that she was not suffering from such an illness – at least, not at the time of the killing – and convicted her of murder.

But Dalton introduced new evidence at the appeal: she told the court that after a set of tests on Reynolds while she was in Holloway prison, she had found the presence of SHBG (Sex Hormone Binding Globule Estimate) in her blood which indicated the existence of pre-menstrual tension – a result fully accepted by the judges in their summation of the evidence. Taking this in tandem with the clear evidence of postnatal depression (Reynolds had given birth to a baby only weeks before she killed her mother), the prosecutor for the Crown and the Court of Appeal accepted a changed plea of manslaughter on grounds of diminished responsibility.

There is little doubt that at the time of the murder Reynolds was suffering from pre-menstrual tension, combined with postnatal depression, allied to other physiological factors brought on by depression, such as lack of food and sleep. But is that why she killed her mother?

Perhaps this is a naive question. For what I am trying to do is in part to transfer the discipline and depth of the psychoanalytic explanation (or the complex emotional truths of a certain kind of novel) to the courtroom. Are they incompatible truths that will not tally? Probably not. Courts of law are concerned with the moment of murder; they focus on it frequently, obsessively: what state the defendant was in, what physiological/medical phenomena motivated her or him. Hence the crucial nature of medical evidence, the marvel of a doctor who can come to court and utter unambiguous words to the effect 'that at the point of criminal action, the defendant had the presence of SHBG in her blood. That is why she did it' (I am parodying).

Interestingly, Reynolds casts doubt on such simplifications in her own autobiography, *Tightrope*.[10] Not only is this an extraordinarily writerly and subtle account; it also clearly roots the cause of her mother's murder in something far more complex than her bodily state on the night in question. In effect, it traces the bleak course of her childhood, her relationship with her parents and with the outside world, which culminated in the desperate action of murder.

Anna was frequently lonely, if not unloved. An only child, she lost her father when she was eleven. He had died soon after an argument between them and she had always blamed herself for his death. In her teens, she suffered severe depression, twice trying to commit suicide and spending time in a mental hospital. Always terrified of poverty, Anna sometimes held two jobs – working in a warehouse and as a freelance journalist – while also studying for her exams. She is clear that the birth and subsequent adoption of her child, while she was only in her late teens – a pregnancy which was (incredibly) concealed from her mother, with whom she was living – was what led her to 'break'. That, and the long history of alternate silence and loud recrimination that marked her relationship with her mother. (An interesting discrepancy arises here between descriptions given by Reynolds at different times of her relationship with her mother: in a *Woman's Own* article written after her release, Reynolds claims that when she finally told her mother about the birth of the baby, her mother refused to discuss the matter with her, provoking Anna to enter an 'unreal state'.[11] But the court transcript states: 'In the event, when the mother was told, after the birth had taken place, it was said that she took it very well.')[12]

On the PMT factor, *Tightrope* is muted. Anna mentions first hearing Dr Dalton on a 'Woman's Hour' discussion about her own case. She says little of Dalton's post-trial visit (to record her levels of progesterone) or of the effect injection of the drug has had on her. At the time when she was beginning to take progesterone, she sums up the many-faceted aspects of her story: 'sceptical as I had been at the first mention of the PMT idea, I had to admit that for years I felt strange around period time. *The trouble was that, with so many valid reasons for being and feeling strange, it was difficult to identify another*' (emphasis added).

If Reynolds herself does not make the mistake of over-determining the cause of her own crime, this cannot be said about certain sections of the popular press. In July 1988, *Woman's Own* ran an interview with Reynolds. The cover line screamed: 'How Her Hormones Turned this Woman into a Killer', while the inside story ran: 'Anna Reynolds went to prison for murdering her mother. Then doctors discovered the reasons why'. In the light of the subtlety of *Tightrope*, the interview makes for schlock reading.

Modern times

PMT became one of the more fashionable phenomena of the late 1980s, particularly in the mass-circulation media. Up-market tabloids like *Today* and the *Daily Express* took on the issue with centre-spread fervour. A typical piece (from the 1980s) would be illustrated with a large colour picture of a blonde/brunette in her early thirties in boxed-out shoulders and striped butcher's apron, looking down in horror at a cup smashed in hormonal madness, New Man looking on in kind forgiveness. True-life stories are recounted with serious glee: men forced to seek refuge in the car or garden shed from knife- and saucepan-wielding wives; mothers so frustrated that they resort to the appalling depths of kicking their own children's toys.

Whatever the slant – men should be nicer to women; women should be nicer to men – these reports have one thing in common: they all represent PMT as Alien 3, invader and disrupter of the neat life Ms/Mrs X has made for herself in the middle echelons of a working-girl existence. Murder, suicide; hatred of work, children, parents; irritation at the dog, the kitchen floor; love of chocolate, a craving for rest: all are reducible to the biochemical alone, the Dalton thesis *par excellence*. In the last decade, PMT has merged with the most banal of body, therapy and green politics to become one of those sensible things sensible women know about themselves. It is also big business, with sales of hormonal and nutritional supplements soaring.

But what sense are we to make of this vaunting of PMT? In part, it is a collision of the imperatives of 1970s feminism with the needs of modern (1990s) femininity. 1970s feminism heralded a new openness about the body politic: matters of the womb, bladder, breast; pleasure and diseases; all were discussed with a new frankness which has filtered from the *Guardian* through to the tabloids. In the 1980s, femininity borrowed from feminism some of its seriousness about work and sex. It also set impossible standards for women, who were now supposed to do – and enjoy – it all: work, consumption, friends and family.

Nevertheless, should something nag at the New Woman, should something seem dissatisfying – even terrorizing – about this all-capable self, PMT provides not only an explanation but also a kind of resolution. For if PMT is about anything, it is about routine. Once you pinpoint your own bad temper as cyclical rather than organic, there is nothing easier or more efficient than to plan around it. You can even shop and cook for it. It is yet one more reason to exercise, eat fresh vegetables, go to bed early. Write it up on the kitchen wall, in the Filofax. Put this way, it becomes one more item on the all-capable modern woman's agenda: *Make space for hating humanity, Tues/Wed/Thurs.*

A more materialist analysis of women's position would argue that PMT's prominence in the last decade was a reflection of women's fragility in the labour market at a time of rising unemployment, particularly in the early 1980s.[13] In a direct analogy with the postwar period – when women were discouraged from paid work and urged back to the family – women's biological weakness is stressed when the state needs them not to work. (In this context, it is interesting to see that Dalton began writing about PMT in 1949, just before the most conservative of decades for women, the 1950s: indeed, she still writes and argues in a quintessentially 1950s language). Certainly, over the last decade, PMT has served to remind women of their essential fragility; to suggest, perhaps, that full-time entrance into the labour market requires something of them – continuous unchanging commitment – which they may not be capable of nor care to give.

As we move towards the middle of a new decade, however, the messages are again changing. New economic times make women central to the labour market as never before – albeit in low-paid, part-time jobs. Social and financial support for working mothers has again become politically respectable. Will women's biological weakness continue to be stressed in the same way as before? I doubt it. One tiny indicator of the shift – or, at the very least, the whimsicality – of media trends came in a *Daily Express* article at the end of 1989. Yet another pre-menstrual centre spread, but this one heralded the arrival of pre-menstrual joy, that time of the month when women discover fresh bursts of energy, 'especially for sex and for housework'!

There are also wider, politically based changes. As I write this (in early spring 1992) the question of women claiming provocation as a defence to crimes of violence has become the focus of greater public discussion. Women's groups and MPs are increasingly protesting the hypocrisy and injustice of men walking free after murdering their wives (claiming provocation by 'nagging' wives) while women who have spent years enduring violence and abuse from their husbands are sent down for life. There have been parliamentary attempts – for example, Jack Ashley's 1991 Ten Minute Rule Bill – to widen the definition of provocation to include women's experience of domestic violence. The Bill unfortunately fell because Parliament was dissolved. Sara Thornton, who killed her violent husband, is currently serving a life sentence. She claims provocation, and public debate is raging on the questions raised by her story.

What such activity signals is the beginning of a shift in public understanding of the true causes of women's crime. If it is understood that women kill not from inherent biological instability but in angry reaction to cruelty or neglect or abuse, the use of the PMT defence may correspondingly fade. Legal and public attention will then shift from the unstable workings of the ever-mysterious female body to the mysterious workings of the ever-unstable social world.

Pleading for time

*Justice for battered
women who kill*

Lorraine Radford

On the evening of 8 May 1989, Kiranjit Ahluwalia threw petrol at her violent husband Deepak and set fire to him. Deepak died a week later from the effects of the burns, which covered 40 per cent of his body. At Lewes Crown Court, Kiranjit, who was silent throughout her trial, was found guilty of murder and sentenced to life imprisonment.

Feminists and local people began to campaign for her immediate release, arguing that the real crime was the domestic violence she had suffered during her ten-year marriage. Kiranjit had been subjected to forced sex, frequent beatings and mental cruelty from her husband. Evidence of these beatings – nail marks around her throat and bruising on her face and wrists – had been verified in court by friends, work associates and her GP. Yet her trial judge, Judge Leonard, claimed that the violence she had experienced was 'not of the highest severity'. It could not be used to explain her inability to 'simply walk out' of her unhappy relationship, rather than resort to murder.

The law governing murder and manslaughter recognizes that in some circumstances people may feel 'driven' to kill. Murder is distinguished from manslaughter by a 'malicious intent' to kill or to cause serious injury to the victim.[1] In the absence of malicious intent to kill, a 'partial' defence against the murder charge may be available to a defendant. Thus, if the offender had killed another person but had been provoked into doing so,[2] or was suffering from an abnormality of mind that would diminish responsibility,[3] or had been acting in pursuance of a suicide pact,[4] a finding of manslaughter can be substituted for a murder charge.[5] Murder in the UK carries a mandatory life sentence, while manslaughter may result in variable terms or sometimes no imprisonment at all. Someone who kills in self-defence is justified in the use of force, and is innocent.

Self-defence, diminished responsibility and provocation are the three most common defences to murder put forward in UK courts by spouse-killers. These defences must be assessed by juries in relation to the individual facts of the case, taking into account the following general principles:

1. *Self-defence*: To argue self-defence successfully, the act of fatal violence must be *necessary*, a *response* to and *proportional* to an *immediate, life-threatening attack*. The defendant must have been in *imminent danger* of losing her/his life. Force can be legitimate only if it is the only option available to deter the attacker and enable escape,[6] – hence the importance attached to 'simply walking out'. Self-defence is judged according to the standards of the 'reasonable man' and the circumstances in which he found himself at the time. Juries are expected to consider whether, in the same situation, taking into account the relative age, vulnerability and characteristics of the accused, they would 'do as he did'.[7]

2. *Diminished responsibility*: involves assessing a medical concept of abnormality of mind and a legal concept, mental responsibility for the crime. The defendant must show first that s/he was suffering from an abnormality of mind arising from an injury, a sickness or a developmental problem and, secondly, that this substantially impaired her/his

responsibility at the time of the killing. Expert witnesses usually establish the aetiology of the abnormality of mind – thus a psychiatrist may argue that a mental illness such as schizophrenia caused the defendant's impulses to kill. But it is the jury which decides whether or not the impairment was substantial enough to affect the responsibility for murder.[8]

3. *Provocation*: Provocation was defined in the leading judgement on R.v. Duffy (1949) as:

> Some act or series of acts done by the dead man to the accused which would cause and actually causes in the accused a sudden and temporary loss of self control, rendering the accused so subject to a passion as to make him for the moment not master of his mind.[9]

Like self-defence, the loss of self-control is assessed according to the standard of the reasonable man. There are two elements to a successful plea of provocation: (a) the provocation must have resulted in the defendant's *sudden* and *temporary* loss of control; (b) the provocation must have been sufficient to cause a *reasonable person* to lose control. The likelihood that the defendant had lost self-control declines with a lapse of time between the provocation and the fatal response. With a lapse of time, the defendant may have formed the malicious intent to murder. A killing motivated by revenge or a sudden passion of anger is inconsistent with provocation, since 'the conscious formulation of a desire for revenge means that a person has had time to think, to reflect, and that would negative [*sic*] a sudden temporary loss of self control'.[10]

On the night of the killing, Deepak Ahluwalia had tried to break his wife's legs, hit her and threatened to burn her face with the iron. At 3 a.m. Kiranjit went downstairs and fetched half a bucket of petrol from a lean-to store outside her kitchen, lit a candle from the gas cooker and picked up a long thin stick, which she carried upstairs. She set the candle down and poured petrol over the bed near where her husband lay. Deepak woke up. Kiranjit dipped the long stick in the petrol, lit it from the candle and threw it into the room. The petrol vapour ignited in a fireball, consuming Deepak in flames and burning Kiranjit on the arm. In his summing-up at the murder trial, Judge Leonard suggested that if Kiranjit was able to walk up and down the stairs to fetch the petrol, the candle and the stick, she may have been thinking clearly and in control of her actions. Taking the time to collect together the equipment needed to kill her husband might be an indication of her malicious intent to commit murder.

Feminists have argued that the notions of 'victim precipitation' which underline defences to murder weight the law in favour of violent men.[11] Women are dealt with more harshly as victims and as offenders, while wife-killers are treated with relative leniency.[12] Battered women who kill are treated with undue harshness by the criminal courts because of the failure to give consideration to the circumstances which lead them to kill. The 1949 Duffy case illustrates the point. The 'he' who was possibly 'not master of his mind' was in fact Mrs Duffy, a woman who had suffered frequent domestic battery from her husband. Deciding she could take the abuse no longer, Mrs Duffy tried to leave, but her husband prevented her from taking her child. After another brutal assault, Mrs Duffy axed and clubbed her husband to death while he lay in bed. At her trial in Manchester Assizes in 1949, the night's events and a long history of violence were put forward as evidence of provocation, but Mrs Duffy was found guilty of murder. At her appeal, Judge Devlin explained the relevance of a history of abuse to the provocation defence as follows:

> A long course of cruel conduct may be more blame-
> worthy than a sudden act provoking retaliation, but you

are not concerned with blame attaching to the dead man
. . . It does not matter how cruel he was, how much or
how little he was to blame, except in so far as it resulted
in the final act of the appellant.[13]

Mrs Duffy's plea of provocation failed because she had
not acted immediately in response to her husband's brutal
assault. She had waited until he had fallen asleep. In light
of the evidence before the court that Mrs Duffy, in a state
of fear, had been trying to leave, the significance attached
to revenge by Judge Devlin seems incredible. In a short
space of time Mrs Duffy's motives were assumed to have
switched from those of a woman frightened for her life to
those of the vigilante seeking revenge.

Provocation as defined by the Duffy standard and Section 3 of the Homicide Act 1957 is clearly based upon a
belief that a person will 'cool off' between or after assaults
rather than slowly boil towards a loss of self-control. The
time allowed for 'cooling off' is limited owing to fears that
an intent to murder may be formed. In the case of Ibrams
and Gregory in 1982, two young men who killed their
sexual abuser to deter a threatened further attack were
found guilty of murder because there was a time lapse
of five days between the last assault and their response.[14]
In recent cases involving battered women, which I will
discuss below, the time delay has been much shorter.
Even the briefest lapse of time is assumed to give the
person under threat the chance to walk away from her
aggressor, to go and get help or, alternatively, coolly to
form the decision to kill.

It has been argued that the sudden response to provocation does not apply to the circumstances of perpetual
fear and desperation in which battered women kill.[15]
A woman who lives with her abuser may not, in fact,
respond immediately in the 'heat of the moment'.[16] She
may, like Mrs Duffy and Kiranjit Ahluwalia, wait until he
falls asleep.

Why do battered women kill?

Many survivors of domestic violence have said that they previously considered killing their partners.[17] In her book *When Battered Women Kill*, Angela Browne found seven variables common to battered women who put this thought into action:

1. frequent assault;
2. severe injury;
3. frequent forced sexual intercourse or other sexual acts by the man;
4. the abuser's frequent intoxication;
5. the abuser's habitual use of illegal drugs;
6. the abuser's threats to kill; and
7. the woman's past threats or attempts to commit suicide.[18]

Five of these variables could be shown to exist in Kiranjit's case.

The topsy turvy justice of patriarchal law puts women on trial for their own victimization. Thus the three key questions asked in courts of battered women who kill emphasize women's own responsibility for prolonged victimization.

Why don't battered women leave their abusers? Why are they abused so many times? And why, when they kill, do they suddenly strike back with fatal effect? These are the three key questions asked in the courts of battered women who kill. Anyone who has the slightest experience of a divorce should be well aware that it is not easy to 'just walk out' of a relationship. Poor welfare provision and limited economic opportunities for women compound the difficulties of leaving violent men.[19] Breaking free from a possessive man, like Deepak Ahluwalia, who musters up relatives' support to enforce ties to hearth, home or family honour is infinitely more difficult. To ask why battered women don't leave is to ask the wrong question;

instead, we should ask what and who prevents them from doing so.

A vast amount of research, much based upon survivors' accounts, has shown beyond doubt that battered women do try to leave time and again. Many succeed and become survivors, while others find themselves forced back into an abusive relationship by fear of losing their children, lack of alternatives (usually accommodation), or inadequate protection.[20] Kiranjit Ahluwalia had tried to leave Deepak to get away from his beatings, but *he had run after her and fetched her back.* She had no relatives she could turn to for help – her own parents were in India, and her in-laws invoked the izzat (family honour) to ensure her domestic imprisonment. Like many abused women, Kiranjit had turned to the law for protection. After Deepak had held a knife to her throat, she had been given an injunction, but this had little effect on his subsequent behaviour. After this, she may well have seen her options for escape shrinking.

The question 'Why don't battered women leave?' also rests upon the naive assumption that leaving will end the violence.[21] Research into survivors' experiences shows that up to a third of the women who leave violent men suffer abuse after the separation.[22] In theory, women who suffer domestic violence should receive equal protection from the criminal law of assault and from a variety of legal sanctions and injunctions, some specifically devised for the protection of battered women. Special provisions for battered women – as in the Domestic Violence and Matrimonial Proceedings Act 1976 and the Domestic Proceedings and Magistrates' Court Act 1978 – are, however, of little use if they are not enforced by the police or the courts.[23] Even within the much-publicized Domestic Violence Units, battered women are not guaranteed protection from abuse. In May 1991 Jayanti Patel killed his second wife Vanda whilst being 'conciliated' within a domestic violence unit at Stoke Newington Police Station. Patel had also previously been convicted of violent assaults and stabbing his former wife.

Research into the lives of women in prison shows a link between the past experience of sexual and physical violence and the commission of violent crime.[24] Criminological studies show variations in male and female offending behaviour: women who kill are more likely to have a history of suicide attempts; men who kill often have criminal records for violent assault; women more commonly kill using a knife or a weapon, in a domestic setting; while men use knives, their hands, fists, feet to strangle their victims or to batter or kick them to death.[25]

Domestic homicides committed by women tend to be defensive and victim-precipitated. Typically, battered women who kill do so in response to an attack or following a threat from the abuser to harm another, usually a child. Some kill whilst the abuser sleeps after an attack, convinced that it will continue when he awakens. They kill because they feel there is simply no other way out. After previous failed attempts, they lose hope of escaping. The violence, tension and fear reach a point where death seems inevitable: a choice between suicide and homicide. Housing departments, social welfare agencies and law enforcers who adopt policies of non-intervention and return women to violent relationships thereby give abusers implicit support. If they refuse to become involved, both the woman and the abuser may believe that it is impossible for a victim of abuse to break free from a violent relationship. There is nothing to stop an abuser, armed with this realization, from stepping up the level of violence or repeating the violence in another relationship.

In Leeds in 1983, Julie Stead was stabbed to death after numerous attempts to get the police to enforce the domestic violence injunctions granted by the courts to protect her from her abusive lover. Seven years later, while on parole from imprisonment for her manslaughter, her killer Keith Ward murdered again. At the trial for this second domestic killing, Ward (unsuccessfully) argued a case of provocation almost exactly the same as that used in the previous hearing.[26]

There is no evidence to suggest that men kill their wives or lovers in order to defend themselves from further assaults after years of battery and abuse. On the contrary: all the available research suggests that wife-killers *worldwide* kill for the same reasons that men batter women – to control their behaviour, or as a response to sexual jealousy or possessiveness.[27] The power of this possessiveness is apparent in the 'if I can't have you, nobody can' justification commonly adopted by men who kill their wives, their children and sometimes themselves as well. An abusive man may track down his wife like prey, pursuing her from refuge to refuge and area to area for a number of years.[28] In the context of the reluctance of the police and judiciary to enforce the law, it could be argued that men have been allowed to get away with murder.

'Getting away with' murder?

For women currently in prison for killing violent men, the injustice is painfully obvious. Sara Thornton killed her possessive, violent and alcoholic husband in June 1989. Malcolm Thornton, an ex-policeman, had repeatedly battered Sara during their ten-month marriage. She had turned to the Church, her doctor and the law for assistance. Malcolm Thornton had been charged with a serious assault on Sara, but, despite this, his abusive behaviour had increased in severity and frequency in the week before his death, culminating in his threat to kill Sara and her daughter. On the night of the killing, Sara walked away from a row into the kitchen to calm herself. Looking around for something to protect herself with in case Malcolm became violent, she picked up a carving knife and sharpened it. She returned to the living-room, where her husband lay drunk on the sofa. He repeated his threat to kill her, warning her that he would do it whilst she slept. Sara replied that he would not have the chance, as she would get him first. Malcolm invited her to try. Sara slowly brought the knife down towards her husband and plunged it into his stomach, killing him.

At Birmingham Crown Court in February 1990 Sara Thornton was found guilty of murder. An appeal was held in 1991: it was argued that the provocation Sara had received from her violent husband had not been adequately explained to the jury. On 29 July 1991, Sara lost her appeal against the charge of murder. Two days later, again in Birmingham Crown Court, Joseph McGrail received a suspended term of imprisonment for the manslaughter of his alcoholic and verbally abusive wife. On hearing about McGrail's comparatively lenient treatment, Sara Thornton began a hunger strike which lasted for several weeks.

An alliance of women's groups had joined forces that spring to campaign for the reform of the English law of homicide. The Women's Campaign for Justice united groups which had been monitoring abusive men who kill with the supporters who had been striving to secure the release of three women recently imprisoned for life for killing violent men: Kiranjit Ahluwalia, Sara Thornton and Amelia Rossiter. As part of these groups' concerted effort courts were filled with abused women's supporters, sitting in judgement of the judiciary. There was a mass demonstration in London and women organized fortnightly pickets of the Home Office. Petitions containing thousands of signatures were collected and handed in to the Home Office. Late in 1991, MP Jack Ashley introduced a Private Member's Bill which aimed to change the wording of the law of homicide. The Bill failed to reach its second reading, as Parliament was dissolved, but interest in the issues remained. Talking to Sue Lawley on BBC Radio Four's 'Desert Island Discs' programme on 25 May 1992, the newly appointed Lord Chief Justice Taylor said that the law of provocation would soon be reviewed. In the so called 'post feminist era', women's energetic initiatives, direct actions and loving support had succeeded in bringing about a review of legal policy.

The notion that the law may discriminate against battered women who kill runs counter to the ordained belief that women offenders are treated equally or even with 'chivalry'. The belief that any offender, male, female or juvenile, could be dealt with chivalrously within the British system of criminal 'justice' is hard to accept. Feminists have pointed out that debates about 'leniency' and 'chivalry' have to be examined in the context of Britain's punitive sentencing practices, and must be based upon adequate empirical research.[29] There is still no adequate research into domestic homicide in the UK; thus debates about differential treatment take place against a backdrop of partial understanding.

Aware of this problem, the initial negative response of the Home Office rested upon the 'we need more research' red herring.

Battered women who kill are a statistical rarity. Between 1982 and 1989, the numbers indicted ranged between 4 and 14 a year, compared with 80 to 109 cases a year involving men who were indicted for killing their wives, ex-wives or lovers.[30] Women are much more likely to be victims of violent crimes than offenders.[31] Women who break the law are just 3.5 per cent of those imprisoned for crimes of violence against the person,[32] yet 40 per cent of all homicide victims are female.[33] On average two women a week are killed by their husbands or lovers. Wife and lover killings account for 45 per cent of the homicides on female victims (103 in 1989), compared with 7 per cent of the homicides on male victims (26 in 1989).[34]

In response to the furore aroused by Sara Thornton's and Kiranjit Ahluwalia's trials, Home Office Minister John Patten commissioned research into the outcome of

domestic homicide trials. Shortly before a huge demonstration organized by supporters, *The Guardian* published
a report on the Home Office findings under the headline
'Provocation Plea Success For Women':

> It is understood that the Home Office believes its
> information counters claims that the law is prejudiced
> against women.[35]

These figures do show that between 1982 and 1989 women
were more frequently convicted of manslaughter when
charged with murder than were men. Between 61 and
94 per cent of women's murder charges a year resulted
in findings of manslaughter, compared with 48 to 69
per cent of men's murder cases.[36] When they were convicted for manslaughter, men received longer terms of
imprisonment. Seventy per cent were sentenced to imprisonment between 1986 and 1989 compared with 45 per
cent of women similarly convicted (the average lengths
of sentences were 59 months and 33 months respectively,
excluding life terms).[37]

The figures suggest that women can and do use the
provocation defence with some 'success'. It is not true that
most women plead diminished responsibility whilst most
men plead provocation.[38]

Although diminished responsibility has been applied to
defend the actions of abused women such as June Scotland,
Joan Calladine and Celia Ripley – willing to argue that
they were 'sick at the time' – diminished responsibility
is more frequently successfully pleaded by men. Section
2 manslaughter convictions accounted for 31.5 per cent of
men's domestic homicide convictions between 1982 and
1989, compared with 20 per cent of women's.[39]

Proportionately more women than men charged with
spouse murder successfully plead provocation. Between
1982 and 1989 approximately 39.5 per cent (70) of women's

spousal homicide convictions were for manslaughter on the grounds of provocation compared with 30 per cent (225) of men's.[40] Women have been able to convince juries of provocation in, for example, cases such as Gillian Philpott's, involving sexual jealousy and infidelity. On New Year's Eve 1989, Gillian Philpott strangled her husband with a dressing-gown cord after he had grabbed her round the neck during a row about his affair with her twin sister. Gillian Philpott later tried to commit suicide by driving over Beachy Head. She successfully argued provocation and was imprisoned for two years for manslaughter.

The Home Office findings do not, however, counter the claims of injustice made by abused women and their sympathizers. Statistics can cover a variety of untruths and encourage inappropriate conclusions. Statistics do not show the different experiences of men and women, rich and poor, black and white. One could conclude that the innocent get a good deal as fewer of them end up in prison than do the guilty. There is no way of learning from the *figures* the circumstances underlying men's and women's claims of diminished responsibility and provocation. We would need to know the circumstances leading up to the pleas of provocation and diminished responsibility to make conclusive empirical claims about discriminatory practice. Reported cases of provocation and diminished responsibility currently show that when the circumstances leading up to homicidal acts are examined, justice for battered women who kill is at the very best inconsistent. In December 1991 at Plymouth Crown Court, Pamela Sainsbury was put on probation for two years for killing the man described in court as 'a violent, jealous psychopath'. Sainsbury successfully argued a case based upon her diminished responsibility for a sudden, impulsive act of homicide. Sara Thornton's plea of diminished responsibility, however, was rejected at her original trial. Men such as Joseph McGrail and Rajinder Bisla defended themselves from murder charges by arguing either provocation or diminished responsibility due to women's interminable 'nagging'. Yet a few moments' gap between a woman's response to an act of violence from a habitually aggressive man is taken as proof of her desire for revenge.

The Home Office may have leapt too readily from the finding that women are able to argue provocation successfully to the conclusion that this defence is relevant and accessible to the circumstances of *abuse victims*. With the Royal Commission on Criminal Procedure currently reviewing miscarriages of justice in Britain, there is an urgent need for thorough investigation of the treatment of both battered women and battering men who kill.

Victimization as defence in the USA

There are striking similarities between Kiranjit's acts and those of Francine Hughes, an American woman whose life history became the subject of the film *The Burning Bed*. After years of abuse, Hughes poured petrol over her husband's bed whilst he slept, and set fire to him. Hughes had the charge of murder against her dismissed because of 'temporary insanity', but her case became a *cause célèbre* for feminists. In 1978, the Women's Self-Defence Law Project was formed and defence lawyer Elizabeth Schneider began to establish landmark defences to murder which took into account the circumstances in which abused women kill.[41]

The problems which battered women face in retreating and escaping from a situation of 'imminent danger' were acknowledged by American courts from 1977 onwards. Cases were won which recognized that a man involved in a street fight and a woman in fear of an attack from her abuser might respond differently when acting as a 'reasonable man'. Beginning with appeals where women had defended themselves against rapists, a series of cases relaxed the imminent danger and proportional force principles, thereby allowing women room to argue self-defence when they had performed a 'pre-emptive' strike to ward off an anticipated attack.

Several hours after she was attacked, Inez Garcia shot and killed the man who had helped to rape her. Her attackers had said they would assault her again when they next met. At her trial in 1977 it was argued that because of this threat it was reasonable for Garcia to think that she was in imminent danger when she later met one of her attackers, even though he had not repeated his threat immediately before she shot him. In the same year Yvonne Wanrow won an appeal against a murder verdict for killing the man whom she believed to be a rapist and child molester. Wanrow's vulnerability as a five-foot-four-inches-tall woman threatened by a six-foot-two-inches-tall man was taken into consideration by the court in assessing her case for self-defence. In this case the proportional force rule was amended to take into account the possibility that it might be reasonable for Wanrow to have used a weapon against this unarmed but patently much stronger man.[42]

Interpretation of the law of homicide in the USA varies from state to state, but subsequent cases in the American courts have extended these principles in some areas to cover the circumstances in which battered women kill. This means that past experience of victimization and knowledge of the abuser's usual pattern of behaviour can be considered when looking at defensive killings, especially those involving a pre-emptive strike against a delayed threatened attack.[43] A history of victimization is not sufficient ground by itself in American law to establish a case of self-defence. It is pertinent to the time when the killing occurred only if it formed the basis of the woman's belief that she was in imminent danger of severe bodily harm or death. Whether or not her belief was reasonable, therefore, depends upon the experience she can prove she has gained on the basis of her partner's past behaviour. Courts thus assess a woman's perception of imminent danger not in relation to the standards of a 'reasonable man', but as a 'reasonable battered woman'. Her perceptions of danger and the possibility of escape are judged with reference to her past victimization and its effects upon her physical and psychological well-being. Self-defence cases involving battered women in the American courts tend to centre upon the woman's state of mind at the time of the killing. The prosecution aims to show that the defendant was not really an abuse victim, whilst the defence counters with the claim that she was.

The battered woman's syndrome was developed in the late 1970s from insights offered by the American psychologist Lenore Walker's therapeutic work with survivors of domestic abuse.[44] The syndrome allows expert witnesses to explain how a woman believed she was in imminent danger even if the circumstances of the killing do not involve the kind of immediate threat traditionally seen within the scope of self-defence. The expert witness's role is to furnish the court with scientific evidence which is probably outside the experience and knowledge of the jury.

A recent case from the American courts, Vermont v. Grace (1992), illustrates the problems raised by the battered woman's syndrome.[45] The case involved Christine Grace, who had been a sexually abused child. At the age of fifteen she met Chicci Bazette; three years later she became his common-law wife. Bazette was a heavy drinker who became violent when he was drunk. He threatened to kill himself if Christine ever walked out. On the night of the killing, after a bout of drinking, Chicci hit Christine's head against a wall, pushed her backwards on to the floor, got on top of her and grabbed her by the neck. He then released his grip and let her get up. Christine picked up a knife and killed Chicci by stabbing him in the back and neck. In court she pleaded not guilty to murder on account of self-defence. It was argued by the prosecution that the few seconds which it took Christine Grace to stand up gave her sufficient time to form the intent to murder.

Elizabeth Novotney, the prosecuting lawyer, said that Christine Grace had killed in *anger*, not fear. Presumably a victim is unable to experience anger as well as fear. Grace was not a 'typical' battered woman unable to escape from a tortuous relationship. She had no broken bones or permanent injuries, and she had never been rendered unconscious. Bruising comprised her worst documented injuries and she had reciprocated by bruising her abuser in return.

Angela Browne, expert witness at the trial, gave information to the court on how Christine's case fitted the battered woman's syndrome. She described a three-phase cycle of violence which occurred in the early days of the relationship, tying Christine Grace to a state of passivity and dependence upon Chicci Bazette. Phase one of the cycle is characterized by *tension building*. The abuser instigates minor incidents of physical or emotional violence that escalate. In response, the abused tries to manage the tension by adapting her behaviour to appease or conciliate – by, for example, keeping the children quiet. In phase two of the cycle the tension escalates into the man's use of *violence*. The abuser seems out of control, so the abused tries to escape or to survive attack by reacting passively. *Denial* is central to the cycle. The abused person pretends either that the violence did not happen or that it will never happen again. The final phase is the *honeymoon* phase where the abuser is sorry, apologetic and lovingly contrite. So cruelty and kindness alternate, causing confusion in the mind of the victim and maintaining her emotional dependence upon her abuser. One day he may tell her she is useless and cannot survive without him. On the next, following a violent episode, he will plead forgiveness, beg her to stay and say that he cannot survive without her.[46]

Christine Grace's defence rested upon the argument that her perceptions of the imminent danger of Chicci Bazette killing her were reasonable given his actions that night and her past experience of his behaviour. Christine's past experience of sexual abuse as a child made her 'more prone' to the passivity and helplessness associated with the battered woman syndrome. She felt trapped within the relationship and there was no other way in which she could deter the imminent assault. Killing in this case was portrayed by the defence as an act of despair. Although Christine 'walked free' after her trial, her plea of self-defence was not accepted. Her passivity as a victim was made to appear so extreme that the jury were unable to accept that she could have found it in her to retaliate at all. They found her guilty of involuntary manslaughter and put her on probation for an indefinite period.

A survivor of sexual abuse may well have limited options for family support as an alternative to a violent relationship, but it does not necessarily follow that she will be more prone to passivity – certainly not to the extent that her actions become 'involuntary'. The battered woman's syndrome leans uncomfortably towards 'violence-prone' explanations for women's victimization.[47] The feminist battered women's movement has, however, been concerned to dispel the myth that abused women are weak, damaged or less intelligent individuals, unable to 'walk out' because they need someone to tell them what to do.

Feminist supporters such as Lenore Walker argue that the advantage of the syndrome is that it takes into account the effects of violence upon women as well as the social constraints which keep them in violent relationships.[48] Yet as Christine Grace's experience suggests, the feminist intent behind the cycle of violence theory may not necessarily be taken as the most significant factor in courts of law, where the emphasis is upon disproving revenge or anger, not examining the lack of opportunity to retreat. In court, defence lawyers tread a precarious route between explaining the effects of violence upon victims and blaming a 'violence-prone' woman for her own demise.

The syndrome is a gender-specific, double-edged defence with a tendency to fuel images of abused women
as sick or passive, mentally impaired and unable to
help themselves. Not only is men's violent behaviour
marginalized and women's medicalized, but the idea of
self-defence becomes incredible. How can a woman fight
back at all in such a state of passivity and paralysing fear?
How can she ever resist his almost hypnotic control over
her actions? The defence can be used just as readily *against*
women, defining as non-victims those who actively resist
violent abuse throughout their relationships.[49] The history
of appeals by battered women in the USA shows that this
does happen. As abused women 'got off' murder charges,
the misogynists' backlash devised its own campaign to halt
a wife's 'license to kill'.[50]

Moral dilemmas have been posed by cases where
abused women, possibly suffering from the 'battered
woman's syndrome', may also have been involved in
cruelty towards a child. Debate on a woman's 'duty to
protect' her children from abuse in situations where she
is not able to protect herself has produced a new twist in
the tail of the victim-blaming beast. Hedda Nassbaum, for
example, a middle-class professional publisher, was locked
in a room and persistently abused by her common-law husband Joel Steinberg. Feminists in the USA were accused of
an unwavering dogma for supporting Hedda Nassbaum's
claim that she had been unable to protect her illegally
adopted daughter Lisa from Steinberg's fatal blows.[51]

As a result of cases like these, feminists in the UK have
resisted creating gender-specific defences which could
pathologize battered women who kill at the same time
as liberating abusive mothers and excusing their violence
towards children. A woman's sense of desperation and
anger towards an abusive man is different from that which
she may direct towards her children. Women are in fundamentally different power relationships with their children. Mothering may indeed rest upon the exploitation of

women's labour in the home, women may feel oppressed and trapped by their children, but small children are unable to intimidate their mothers with violence.

Time for change

While expert evidence in the USA is a highly lucrative business, the UK courts have been far more sceptical of its value to the defence. Recently, however, the barrister Helena Kennedy and Sandra Horley, director of Chiswick Family Refuge, have introduced expert testimony in trials involving battered women in England and Wales.

In January 1992, Sandra Horley was called as the expert witness in the trial of twenty-one-year-old Sally Emery for failing to protect her eleven-month-old daughter Chanel from the fatal blow delivered by her abusive partner Brian Hedman. Sally had experienced severe violence in her relationship with Hedman, including being throttled and raped by him on the day she left hospital after childbirth. Short of leaving him, Sally Emery did all she could to avoid Brian Hedman's violence, and took steps to protect her child such as taking Chanel out of the room to prevent him getting annoyed with her. Sandra Horley testified in court for the defence to explain why Sally was not able to 'simply walk out' or otherwise intervene to protect her child from murder. She pointed out that Sally had become totally isolated and dependent on her abuser, unable to protect herself or her child. Sally was jailed for four years, but after appeal in November 1992 she was released.

The use of expert testimony in Sally Emery's trial was a precedent for the British courts, although it is too soon to tell whether this will become a routine feature of cases involving domestic battery or homicide. In 1992, to support her plea of diminished responsibility, June Scotland successfully made use of expert testimony to show the effects of fear, battery and sexual assault upon her state of mind when she killed her husband seven years previously. In contrast to the trial of Kiranjit Ahluwalia, the pre-planning in June Scotland's case was taken as an indication of her fear, rather than as a desire for 'revenge'. June Scotland bought several travel sickness pills, dosed her husband with over fifty of them and mixed some Valium into his dinner. When he complained of feeling drowsy, she pretended to phone the doctor. She then battered him to death and, with the help of her teenage daughter, wrapped his head in a plastic bag, ready for burying two days later. Thomas Scotland's body was found seven years later when a neighbour moved the garden fence. In court, Dr Nigel Eastman, consultant forensic psychiatrist at St George's Hospital, London, testified that June Scotland was unable to leave her violent husband and that she was suffering from a depressive illness at the time of the killing. The illness made her overreactive to her impulses and more likely to act in an apparently 'calculating' way.

Supporters argue that it is possible for expert testimony to be used to bring justice for victims of abuse who kill without resort to the passivity or 'violence-prone' assumptions found in the American battered woman's syndrome. Nevertheless, moves to amend the law of homicide in England and Wales have centred more upon provocation, because this involves assessing an understandable response rather than an offender's temporary sickness. Diminished responsibility has been a popular defence for abused women but, like the battered woman's syndrome, it can sometimes work to the detriment of the defence. A finding of diminished responsibility may result in a woman's long-term medical or psychiatric treatment, yet provocation could happen to any reasonable person. With a provocation defence it is more likely to be the deceased's behaviour which is pathologized.

The Ashley Bill proposed dropping the requirement for

a *sudden* loss of self-control established by the Duffy case. This move was based on a critique of the quick-response, heat-of-the-moment requirement, and an awareness that provocation can have a slow-boiling effect. By dropping the word 'sudden', the amendment aimed to take into account the fact that victims of abuse may need to wait for the opportunity to defend themselves against attack. Consideration of a time-delayed response to provocation could affect children and male victims of abuse who kill as well. Unlike the battered woman's syndrome, the defence would be open to any victim of provocation regardless of gender.

Allowing for a slow-boiling provocation would not by itself remedy the current inequalities and inconsistencies in homicide cases. Removal of the requirement might also have a liberatory effect upon battering men who kill. Sexually possessive men such as Peter Davies,[52] who literally pester women to death, might be able to claim – as he tried to – that they suffered cumulative provocation.

To guard against this, the Women's Campaign for Justice has recommended that guidelines be created for the judiciary outlining the evidence required to establish a defence of provocation. Evidence of a history of abuse and threats to violence, corroborated by witnesses' testimony for the deceased, would thus lend weight (or not) to accounts of the events before the killing. Infidelity and allegations about sexual capacity/virility would at the same time lose their historically privileged positions in the law of provocation. Juries assessing a loss of self-control would need to distinguish in greater detail between provocation based mainly on 'passion' (infidelity, jealousy, improper suggestions) and provocation based on victimization and abuse. In the past, judgements in criminal cases have spread confusion about the difference between 'passion', anger and victimization when considering provocation. In the Duffy case, anger was clearly seen as an inappropriate response for a plea of provocation by an abused woman. Yet a man's anger and subsequent use of fatal violence in response to another's sexual innuendo or to a wife's adultery have been acceptable.[53]

In a submission to the Royal Commission on Criminal Justice, the well-established campaigning group Rights of Women recommended formalizing this distinction between passion and abuse-based provocation by creating an entirely new defence to murder. This would take into account women's and children's experiences of abuse and domestic battery and the likelihood of a delayed response to threats or acts of abuse. The proposed new defence, self-preservation, would be a partial defence similar to those of provocation and diminished responsibility, recognizing that homicide is not a justifiable solution to marital violence or abuse. The defence would be open to any person who:

ii. kills a partner or someone in a familial or familiar intimate relationship who
iii. has subjected them to continuing sexual and/or physical abuse and intimidation combined with psychological abuse to the extent that they
iv. honestly believe that they have reached a point in which there is no future, no protection and no safety from the abuse and believe it is a question of only one of them being able to survive.[54]

The defence would also cover someone acting to prevent abuse to a child, a sibling or a parent.

Self-preservation would recognize the link between abuse and homicide, although it would not necessarily evade the question of why a woman did not 'simply' walk out. Indeed, Rights of Women argue that the defence of self-preservation would require some proof of victimization, corroborated or based on the testimony of the victim alone. But here, too, there would be no guarantee that juries would select the criteria for defining a 'true victim' in accordance with feminist principles. To secure justice in law, women have traditionally had to earn it by conforming to prescribed standards of behaviour and life-history scripts written for them by professionals and medical experts within and behind the scenes of the courtroom.[55] Legal and popular discourses separate 'true' woman victims of domestic violence from the not really battered, undeserving viragos.[56] The deserving victims are the upper middle class man's ideal bride, a Frankenstein creation of Mary Poppins, Mrs Beeton and Barbie, 'good mothers', 'good wives', 'good housekeepers', 'good' heterosexual servicers, who try, against all odds, to make a go of the marriage. Viragos generally fight back and are thus not really battered.

The pursuit of more 'accurate' and expert-orientated methods to separate 'true victims' from 'true offenders' fails to consider the possibility that battered women who kill and are found guilty of murder do not conform to expectations of victim-initiated behaviour. Kiranjit Ahluwalia had put forward an explanation for her actions which appeared to rest upon a mixture of *both* desperation *and* anger. In this way she ran counter to expectations about how a victim should behave. She had argued to her defence lawyer that her attempts to leave were constrained by her husband's violence and control, and by the izzat. Yet she also confessed to the police that when she threw petrol on the bed near her husband and ignited it, she wanted not only to stop him from further abuse or from running after her, but to inflict some pain to show him how it felt. Judicial sympathy for the human fallibility of provoked men is not afforded so generously to battered women. Any glimmer of anger on the woman's part is held up as the most significant 'evidence' of a revenge-motivated attack and 'proof' that the woman did not need to escape from a violent relationship at all. Anger for women who kill seems not to be legitimate at all. As Melissa Benn points out in Chapter 6 of this book, women who plead defences to homicide based on pre-menstrual syndrome locate anger within an unnatural bodily state.

Judges and lawyers are always ready to note how the law is made to take 'human frailty' into account. Self-preservation could be the start in redefining homicide to take into account the impact of domestic battery and sexual abuse on the lives of women and children. It is no accident that concern over the cruelty meted out to battered women who kill has surfaced in both the USA and the UK in times when both nations have stepped up their punitive regimes of imprisonment (or execution). The number of women lifers in prison has quadrupled in the past twenty years. Recent figures indicate that there are over 2,600 lifers inside.[57] Debates about law reform and justice proliferate in punitive periods in the development of criminal justice.

The campaign to bring battered women justice in law in the UK has a difficult future filled with contradictions. There is a host of supporters waiting in the wings, hoping to ride on the bandwagon of alliances towards a destination of uneasy compromise.

Amelia Rossiter was released from imprisonment on appeal, having successfully argued a case of provocation based on her husband's violence. The issue of provocation had not even been raised in her original trial. Her release was welcomed by all concerned by the injustices to battered women who kill. Shortly after her release, the Lord Chief Justice allowed Kiranjit Ahluwalia to apply for a re-trial of her case, to look into the evidence of diminished responsibility omitted from the original hearing. Kiranjit's plea of guilty to manslaughter in circumstances of diminished responsibility was accepted by the Court of Appeal in September 1992 and she also was freed. At the time of writing, Sara Thornton is still in prison, as are other battered women who have killed. Bail was refused, as was her appeal for a review of provocation. Any future reviewers of the law would do well to bear in mind the meaning of the word justice – humane, fair and consistent treatment of offenders and victims, which does not discriminate on the basis of race, sex, class or age.

Rocking the cradle

*Mothers who kill
their children*

Allison Morris and
Ania Wilczynski[1]

Should we treat you as a wicked person responsible
for her actions . . . or as someone who was sick?
(Justice Owen in R. v. Ricketts,
May 1989, Central Criminal Court, London,
observed by Ania Wilczynski)

A pregnant woman makes an allegation of indecent assault
against her gynaecologist. Other women come forward to
confirm her experience. During the investigation of these
complaints, the gynaecologist kills himself. His pregnant
widow subsequently has a miscarriage and loses not only
her child but her womb: literally and metaphorically her
'motherhood'. Some months later, she becomes the nanny
for the children of the woman who made the initial complaint against her husband. The scene is set for revenge
– a typical enough theme in Hollywood movies. What
makes *The Hand That Rocks the Cradle* different is that
motherhood, or its loss, is not just the rationale underlying
the revenge but the mechanism through which the revenge
is taken.[2] Motherhood is presented to the cinema audience
as the essence of womanhood. It is women's ultimate
fulfilment and true destiny.

We have become quite used to these ideas. To be
a 'woman' or a 'mother' carries with it certain social
expectations: to want to have children; to love them

immediately, dearly and always; to put their interests first at all times; to enjoy every aspect of childcare and domestic responsibilities; and to be ever smiling, ever cheerful, all-perfect. And all of this, of course, comes 'naturally'. We may know that these are myths, but at the same time it is a hard message to ignore. We grow up with it; we read about it in manuals and magazines; we see it in adverts and movies; and we hear experts 'confirm' it. These ideas are deeply rooted, and widely held. Their origins are complex but draw on Judaeo-Christian beliefs, notions of biological determinism, political ideologies and patriarchy.[3]

Part of these ideas – or, more precisely, stereotypes – is women's supposed passivity, submissiveness, asexuality and gentleness; women are either born or socialized (for example, by parents, schools and the media) to conform and to be non-violent. We are always surprised, therefore, when women feature in crime, especially violent crime, and even more surprised when the victim is that desired object: her child.

Criminologists are no less puzzled by violent women than the rest of us. In offering explanations, they too have tended to rely primarily on stereotypical images. Violent women are usually presented by them as 'evil' – they have chosen to act in a way which contradicts traditional views of women; as 'masculine' – they are not 'really' women; as 'sad' – they could not cope with social pressures; or as 'mad' – they did not really know what they were doing. Feminists too seem puzzled about how they should respond to women's violence. They have in fact written very little about violent women, in contrast with the vast literature on men's violence against women. Where feminists do address women's violence, they seem unsure whether it betrays or supports feminist causes. Some present violent women as victims of men's oppression (for example, battered women who kill their abusive partners); others present them as violating core values of feminism such as non-aggression, care and nurturance (for example, women who abuse or neglect their children). This puzzlement among both criminological and feminist writers is nowhere more apparent than when a mother kills her child. How could she do it?

Although the incidence of mothers killing their children is comparatively rare, we believe that attempts to understand its occurrence raise issues which touch the lives of *all* women. In the words of American criminologist Ann Jones 'the story of women who kill is the story of women'. Like her, we see direct connections between the social circumstances of many mothers, society's expectations of mothers, and maternal child-killing. In many ways, mothers who kill their children can be seen to be responding rationally – an understandable response to particular sets of situations. But this is not necessarily the way in which the criminal justice system sees it. It has drawn rather different connections – connections derived, in essence, from the supposed irrationality and incomprehensibility of the act.

Determining numbers

According to the British Criminal Statistics published by the Home Office, the age group most at risk of death by homicide are those under one year old. Seventy-one cases of child-killing were recorded in 1989 (12 per cent of all homicides). Three-quarters of these were filicides – that is, they were killed by their parents (including step-parents and cohabitees).

For a number of reasons, however, the filicide figure – as with all criminal statistics – is likely to be an underestimate. The actual number of offences committed is unknown; we know only those offences reported to and recorded by the police. This is estimated to be only about a quarter of all crimes, though this proportion varies considerably from offence to offence.[4] Specifically with reference to filicide figures, newspapers refer from time to time to the discovery of the bodies of new-born babies; it may well be that many of these have died at their mothers' hands. There can also be considerable legal difficulties in proving filicide (for example, proving that the child was born alive), and filicides can be mis-classified as deaths which are the result of an accident, disease or 'cot death' (Sudden Infant Death Syndrome). An example of these difficulties in determining the cause of death was the death of six-week-old Glen Fletcher. Initially this was thought to have been a cot death, but it was reclassified some four years later as murder by his mother, Jacqueline Fletcher. Three and a half years later, in February 1992, this murder conviction was quashed.[5]

Moreover, the published Criminal Statistics provide information only on the number of *parents* who kill their children. It is impossible to tell the sex of the parent from this. We are able for the first time to provide information on the number of mothers and fathers known to have killed their children, and what happens to them.[6]

Over the period 1982 to 1989, there were 493 homicides in which the principal suspect was a parent. We have been able to analyse data on 474 of these. Given the low level of women's involvement in crime generally and in violent offences in particular, we might expect women to be similarly underrepresented in homicides of children by their parents. This is not so. Almost half of the child-killings attributed to parents over this period were committed by mothers. This is a startlingly high figure, since there is no other category of homicide where the proportions of female and male offenders are so equal. When women kill, they usually kill someone close to them (such as a partner or child), but even within the category of spousal killings, women constitute only around a fifth of those indicted.[7]

However, there are clear differences between mothers

and fathers who kill their children, both in the ways in which the offence is classified and in the ways in which they are sentenced. Despite the apparently similar nature of the act, few mothers are convicted of the murder of their child, and few are sentenced to imprisonment. This is in marked contrast to their treatment in some other countries. In the United States, for example, the penalty for maternal filicide is commonly a prison sentence.[8]

Murder
Murder is the unlawful killing of another person, either intentionally or knowing that death or serious harm is highly likely. The penalty is life imprisonment; there is no judicial discretion.

There were 395 parents suspected of the murder of their child between 1982 and 1989; 44 per cent were mothers. Where the victim was under the age of one, almost half the suspects were the child's mother. About a quarter of the parents of both sexes suspected of murder subsequently committed suicide. And almost a further quarter of the mothers initially suspected of murder were subsequently convicted of the lesser offence of infanticide – an offence which can be committed only by women – which gives judges the discretion to sentence the offender to any sentence up to and including life imprisonment (we discuss infanticide further below). All but two of the mothers charged with murder but convicted of infanticide were given probation orders.

A charge of murder can also be reduced to manslaughter, which again gives the judge discretion over the penalty imposed. There are a number of grounds for this. First, there is 'diminished responsibility' where, at the time of the killing, the offender was suffering from such an abnormality of mind as substantially to impair his/her mental responsibility for the crime.[9] A second ground is where there was no intention to kill or to cause serious harm. A third and less common ground (at least with respect to filicide) is provocation – a sudden and temporary loss of self-control by the offender.

More than three-quarters of those initially suspected of murder were in fact convicted of manslaughter. Just under half of these were dealt with on the basis of diminished responsibility; however, almost three times as many mothers as fathers were dealt with in this way. This disparity is reflected in the sentencing pattern too. Almost half of the mothers (though less than a third of the fathers) were given hospital orders specifying psychiatric treatment in a mental hospital (these can be with or without restrictions with respect to a release date); and more than two-fifths of the mothers (though only just over 10 per cent of the fathers) were given probation orders. Fewer than 10 per cent of the mothers were imprisoned, compared with more than half of the fathers. On the other hand, a much greater proportion of fathers than mothers were convicted in the other manslaughter categories; but even here, the same general sentencing pattern is apparent. Although half of the mothers in this category were given prison sentences, virtually all the fathers were. Conversely, a much greater proportion of the mothers were given probation.

Thus the vast majority of the mothers initially suspected of murder were later convicted of a lesser charge, and as a result the majority were given probation or hospital orders. On the other hand, about a third of the fathers were convicted of murder. Consequently, a much higher proportion of the fathers were given sentences of life imprisonment. Overall, even when the fathers were convicted of the lesser charge of manslaughter, more than half of them – though just over a quarter of the mothers – were given prison sentences.

Manslaughter
Between 1982 and 1989 there were 52 cases in which parents were initially charged with manslaughter on the basis of diminished responsibility (in addition to those

referred to above). Forty per cent were mothers. Just under half were given probation and just over half were given custodial penalties. The vast majority of the fathers, on the other hand, were given custodial penalties.

Infanticide
Over this period there were 27 homicides of children which were classified as infanticide. Infanticide refers to the killing of a child under the age of twelve months by the child's mother when the balance of her mind was disturbed because she had not fully recovered from the effect of childbirth or lactation.[10] Infanticide, therefore, is premissed on the belief that these ordinary conditions have a potentially disruptive effect on the mental state and behaviour of women. In almost half of these cases, there were no further proceedings; in addition, two mothers suspected of infanticide committed suicide. In almost all the rest of the infanticide cases, the mothers were given probation orders.

Explaining the differences

Throughout this statistical analysis, it is clear that mothers and fathers were treated differently by the criminal justice system. Mothers were less likely than fathers to be convicted of murder or to be sentenced to imprisonment, and were more likely to be given probation and psychiatric dispositions. This fits all too well with a common assumption in criminological literature that women are generally dealt with more leniently than men in the criminal justice system. They are thought to be less likely than men to be arrested, prosecuted, convicted or imprisoned.[11] This is often referred to as the 'chivalry hypothesis', since the majority of decision-makers are male and it is believed that they respond to female offenders in a 'protective' or 'paternalistic' way.

Some (including many feminist) writers, however, describe the process in quite a different way. They see the criminal justice system's treatment of women as discriminatory and sexist. In brief, they believe that women are punished for breaking not only the law but also traditional sex-role expectations.[12] They argue that certain categories of women – for example, single and divorced women, and women seen as 'bad' mothers or as 'sexually active' – are sentenced more severely than others. Such women have offended against ideals of 'femininity' and 'motherhood'.

Superficially, the criminal justice system's response to mothers who kill their children best fits the 'chivalry hypothesis'. It is clear that mothers were less likely than fathers to be convicted of murder or to be sentenced to imprisonment, and were more likely to be given probation and psychiatric dispositions. However, we do not know from these figures *why* this happens. To unravel this, we need to draw from research on responses to women's crime more generally.

Women are different: exploring pathology

Because so few women enter the criminal justice system, they have been described as 'incongruous', 'out of place', 'invisible'. Hence explanations for women's criminality are sought within the discourse of the 'pathological' and the 'irrational': menstruation, mental illness, poor socialization, broken home, and so on. Rose Pearson, for example, writing about Cardiff magistrates' court, cites the case of a woman who pleaded guilty to stealing a chequebook. Asked by the magistrates why she had done this, she replied, 'Because I was broke'. Despite this apparently rational explanation, she was remanded for psychiatric reports so that – in the magistrate's words – 'we can find out why you keep committing these offences'.

Men, on the other hand, are not out of place in courts, so

their offending is explained in different ways, within the discourse of 'normality' and 'rationality'. Their behaviour is more likely to be viewed as the product of such factors as boredom, greed, peer-group pressure or simple wickedness. These different types of explanations for women's and men's behaviour influence responses within the criminal justice system.

In 1987, Hilary Allen published her research based on an examination of psychiatric and social inquiry reports prepared for women and men convicted of serious violent offences. The reports on the female offenders almost invariably addressed their mental state, while reports on male offenders tended to focus more on their behaviour and lifestyle. This occurred not because of differences in the female and male offenders' behaviour but because the reports on the female offenders were prepared within a context which placed *women*, not just female offenders, within the discourse of the pathological. In Allen's words, it is 'as if such an unreasoning and unreasonable condition was quite a natural state of womankind'.

More generally, researchers claim that the main factor relevant to the criminal justice system's response to women is 'current problems' or 'personal circumstances', whereas for men it is the nature of their offence. This goes some way towards explaining why so many mothers who kill their children are dealt with on the basis of diminished responsibility and infanticide, and why so many are sentenced primarily to probation or orders requiring psychiatric treatment – such an act cannot be the act of a *normal* woman. She cannot have been fully responsible for her actions; she must need help or treatment.

The clearest example of this assumption of the underlying pathological nature of mothers who kill their children is the very existence of the infanticide charge. It is based on the notion that maternal child killing is due to puerperal psychosis, a relatively rare and severe mental disorder which affects one or two out of every 1,000 women within the first few weeks of childbirth. The symptoms span a number of categories of psychosis, but range from mania to delusions to acute depression; its causes are thought to be hormonal. Whether or not puerperal psychosis is actually any different from other forms of psychosis and whether or not it should, therefore, be regarded as a separate diagnostic category is a matter of considerable controversy.[13] There is certainly a *temporal* association with childbirth: the risk of psychosis is thirty-five times higher for a first-time mother in the first month of childbirth than at any other time in her life. What is clear, however, is that despite being the legal basis for a plea of infanticide, puerperal psychosis is very rarely the cause of a mother killing her child. Estimates are that this occurs in around five cases a year.

In practice, the Infanticide Act has been interpreted very liberally, both in England and in other countries with similar legislation such as Hong Kong and Australia.[14] There is certainly some flexibility in the causal connections made between the mental disturbance said to be experienced by the woman and the effects of childbirth; and it is now widely accepted that there is no relationship at all between lactation and mental disturbance. Also, the mental disturbance used to satisfy the terms of the Infanticide Act can vary considerably from puerperal psychosis to postnatal depression to no mental disturbance at all (and it is much less than required by the law in other contexts – for example, for the purpose of proving diminished responsibility). Thus studies in both England and Hong Kong have found that about half the mothers convicted of infanticide could not actually have been described as suffering from any mental disorder.[15]

An example of this is the case of Rupa, who killed her newborn child. Rupa, an eighteen-year-old girl from an ethnic minority, who had lived most of her life in her family's country of origin. She had been physically abused by both parents, had led a very sheltered and isolated existence, had had virtually no formal education and spoke little English. Her family were very religious, and Rupa was given religious instruction by a man who subsequently sexually abused her and swore her to silence. She became pregnant but did not realize this until eight months later, when her mother took her to the doctor. Rupa was aware of the shame that an illegitimate child would bring in her community, and terrified that her father would kill her if he found out. She concealed the pregnancy from everyone and delivered the child herself. The child lived only a few minutes (though there was no evidence of violence). Rupa was convicted of infanticide and given a three-year probation order, despite the fact that the psychiatrist who examined her after the child's death found that she was not mentally ill (although he believed her to be emotionally disturbed at the birth). The psychiatrist also stated that Rupa's admission to a psychiatric hospital after the offence had allowed her and her family 'the only acceptable *fiction* to enable them to cope – that she is mentally ill' (emphasis added). Describing Rupa as 'mentally ill' meant that both she and her family could be absolved of – and absolve themselves of – responsibility and blame for the act and its surrounding circumstances.

Questioning pathology

Infanticide is now used much more widely than was initially intended and, on occasions, to covertly introduce socioeconomic and other factors thought to have led to the child's death. Postnatal depression has also been linked to maternal filicide (both as a basis for infanticide and as a plea of diminished responsibility). It is said to affect about one in ten mothers; its symptoms include tearfulness, inability to cope, despondency, tension, irritability and exhaustion.

It is commonly assumed that postnatal depression has

a hormonal base, but many writers put as much emphasis on social as on individual factors, including on a lack of support, marital problems, social isolation, and the reality of motherhood which bears little relation to society's idealized view of it. We referred above to the widely held belief that women are meant to know instinctively how to care for children. In *From Here to Maternity*, Ann Oakley referred to this as the 'myth of motherhood' in which mothers are always content and children are 'wonderful repositories of nothing but joy for those who bear them and look after them'. Most mothers learn that reality is nothing like this. They are quite unprepared for the hard, selfless, exhausting and isolating work involved in looking after a child. Many become depressed.

Anne's situation was like this. She was twenty-three years old with no previous children, and had become pregnant unintentionally. Her husband did not want the child, began to reject her and made denigrating remarks about her attractiveness and weight. He provided no emotional or practical support during the pregnancy or after the child was born, and was at home only at weekends, since he worked away during the week. Anne found the birth an 'ordeal' and rejected the child immediately. However, the couple then lived for six weeks with her husband's parents, who described Anne as a 'model mother'; subsequently, they moved into a new home. Anne found it increasingly difficult to cope with the baby, housework and washing, a new house, marital problems, and isolation from her friends and family. All of this was said to have made her very anxious, particularly as her mother had always seemed able to cope. Anne tried to make a doctor's appointment but could not get one that day. Three days later, she was faced with no hot water, a pile of dirty nappies and the family wash, and a restless baby. She said that she 'felt out of control' with so much to do and no time for herself. It was then that she threw her ten-week-old baby out the window. Anne was diagnosed by two doctors as suffering from postnatal depression, charged with and convicted of infanticide, and received a probation order with a condition of psychiatric treatment.

Social and economic stresses are also prominent features in neonaticides (the killing of a baby within twenty-four hours of its birth), and these too are usually dealt with as infanticide. As in Rupa's case, these women are almost invariably young, immature, single, first-time mothers from a working-class background, and the child is usually unplanned and unwanted. They are often frightened of either social or parental reaction, particularly if the child is illegitimate. Denial of both the pregnancy and the birth are common features.[16].

Sharon became pregnant at the age of fourteen and gave birth to a baby boy at the age of fifteen. Shortly after his birth, with her boyfriend's help, she threw her baby in a river. She had been too frightened to tell her parents or anyone else about the pregnancy, in part because her sister had earlier been turned out of the house when she became pregnant. Sharon had given birth without any medical assistance and in squalid circumstances (sitting on a lavatory in the bathroom of her boyfriend's bed-sit). In a state of fear, exhaustion and panic, she wrapped the child's body up in a blanket and threw it in the river. The body was discovered three months later. Sharon subsequently pleaded guilty to infanticide. In passing sentence, the judge emphasized her immaturity, inability to cope with the pregnancy, fear of the reaction of others, and lack of preparation for the consequences of the birth. These social factors, however, had to be translated into a psychiatric condition. Hence the judge noted:

> It is clear that *the effect of giving birth* to this baby left the *balance of your mind disturbed* so as to *prevent rational judgment and decisions*.[17] (emphasis added)

Nevertheless, he went on to say that while Sharon's responsibility was greatly diminished, he did not find it removed altogether and sentenced her to twelve months in a young offenders' institution on the basis that 'the welfare of society' required it. This sentence was subsequently varied to a three-year probation order, with a condition of residence with her foster parents for the first two years. The Court of Appeal recognized that over the past ten years no cases of infanticide had resulted in custodial sentences, and there was nothing in the present case to take it outside this pattern.

One of the most common categories of filicide is what is often referred to as the 'battered baby syndrome'. In these cases, death usually results from injuries sustained in one serious assault or from a series of assaults. Most research here again points to the significance of severe social stresses. Common features are marital violence, financial and housing problems, separation from parents in childhood, current pregnancy, having other children to care for or children who were ill, and a chaotic and violent family history. Personality problems, low self-esteem, immaturity and low intelligence are also commonly noted.

Jackie, a twenty-two-year-old married woman of low IQ, assaulted her four-month-old son John, causing multiple fractures from which he died. She had three young children, one of whom had already been taken into the care of the local authority. John cried a lot and Jackie had difficulty in feeding him. Her husband worked at night, and before John's death she had asked him to leave, which he had done. Jackie said that she had had a sleepless night and had felt depressed before she assaulted John, and that she had not meant to kill him, as she loved him. Jackie pleaded guilty to infanticide and was sentenced to eighteen months' imprisonment. Her subsequent appeal against this sentence was refused on the rather unusual grounds that it would be 'in her interest to remain in prison until she had finished a course in home economics'.[18]

This case history serves as a good example not only of the stretching of infanticide beyond its statutory terms but also of a further theme which requires exploration. Implicit in the judge's statement about Jackie's sentence is the belief that her skills as a mother required some improvement. She needed to be re-formed.

Judging women

Not all mothers who kill their children are perceived sympathetically. At least some are given prison sentences, and a few are convicted of murder. Ania Wilczynski examined twenty-two English cases (collected from a variety of sources) of women who had killed their children. In these, it was clear that distinctions were drawn between 'good' and 'bad' women and, more particularly, between 'good' and 'bad' mothers.

Fourteen women were identified as essentially 'good' women and 'good' mothers for whom something had gone tragically wrong. They were given probation or hospital orders. Sara, for example, allegedly suffocated her eleven-month-old child whilst she was acutely depressed, then tried to commit suicide. She denied manslaughter, arguing that the death was a cot death, but was convicted of manslaughter on the grounds of diminished responsibility. At Sara's trial, it was stated that her child had been healthy and happy and that all who knew her regarded her as a loving and caring mother. The judge seemed to agree and gave Sara a three-year probation order, saying: 'You are in need of help and not of punishment'.[19]

Eight women in Wilczynski's sample, however, were given prison sentences. These women tended to be viewed as having acted in ways inconsistent with traditional conceptions of women's behaviour. That is to say, they were viewed as 'bad' women and 'bad' mothers – selfish, cold, neglectful, uncaring and sexually active.

In 1988, Susan Poole and her common-law spouse Frederick Scott were convicted of the manslaughter by starvation of their ten-month-old son and the wilful neglect of their two-year-old son.[20] They were given seven years' and ten years' imprisonment respectively. Susan Poole was described by the popular press as 'evil', 'callous' and 'vile', and was said to have referred to her child as 'it'. The jury were told that she sometimes left the children alone while she accompanied Frederick Scott to the pub which was a hundred yards down the road, that she had severely neglected the housework, and that although she was grossly overweight, her son had starved to death. Mr Justice Owen, at the trial in the Central Criminal Court in London, commented that she must have seen the pleading look in her son's eyes:

> When one thinks of the extraordinary maternal sacrifice and care shown by lower animals, one has to wonder at her apparent selfishness.

Yvonne Roberts, a journalist who interviewed Susan Poole after her conviction, presents her in a very different light from the popular perceptions of her. She describes her as a young, immature woman from a chaotic, abused and neglected background who in the two months before her son's death became increasingly despondent and depressed because of her deteriorating relationship with her violent and unsupportive partner, her social isolation and her feelings of being unable to cope with the care of her children. According to Roberts, when Susan Poole did go to the pub with Frederick Scott, she rarely drank more than half a lager. Susan Poole is reported as saying: 'I'd go because I was so lonely. I was on my own all day with the children, I felt I was going mad.'

At the trial, the evidence of four psychiatrists and one doctor was presented. They all believed that the combination of Susan Poole's immaturity, personality disorder and severe depressive illness would have been sufficient to impair her responsibility for her actions in at least the two months before her child's death. Although Mr Justice Owen accepted Susan Poole's plea of guilty to manslaughter on the basis of her diminished responsibility, he also seems to have regarded her as fully culpable and as, in essence, a 'bad' mother. He said: 'When all is said and done, you killed your one son and you failed properly to care for the other.'

The seven-year sentence given to Poole appears to have been more a reflection of the negative image created of Susan Poole as a mother than of the medical evidence presented. On appeal, the period of imprisonment was only reduced to five years, as was her common-law husband's.[21] Despite clear evidence of depression in Susan Poole's case, infanticide seems never to have been considered, though in many ways her situation was similar to that of at least some of the women we have described who were dealt with on this basis. It is difficult to avoid the conclusion that it was the negative portrayal of her as a *woman* and as a *mother* which was the determining factor in her treatment within the criminal justice system.

Women can also be viewed as 'bad' and 'unnatural' when they fail to protect their child from their male partner's violence. Brian Hedman, for example, was sentenced in 1992 to eight years' imprisonment for cruelty for a series of assaults on his daughter in the month before she died. His common-law wife Sally Emery was convicted of the neglect of her daughter on the grounds that she had failed to protect her. Sally Emery had also been assaulted by Brian Hedman – it is quite common to find child abuse and 'wife' abuse in the same families – and she alleged that she had been too frightened to tell anyone about her partner's abuse of the child – again a common feature in cases of 'wife' abuse. None the less, Sally Emery was sentenced to four years' imprisonment by Judge Michael Astill, who is reported to have said: 'You allowed her to die and you had much opportunity to prevent it.'[22] In other words, she was sentenced as a 'bad' mother, not as an abused woman. According to journalist Angela Phillips, who attended the trial, the jury believed that Sally Emery could and should have acted to protect her child, despite expert evidence of her abuse and its effects on her, and despite Brian Hedman's threats to kill both her and her child if she told anyone.

Conclusion

The reasons why mothers kill their children are many and varied, but what emerges clearly from this review is the unpalatable truth that 'normal' women can kill their children when they are confronted by social and economic circumstances which are severe enough. Yet the preference within the criminal justice system is to deal with these women as pathological and as warranting treatment and 'lenient'[23] sentences rather than punishment and 'severe' penalties. This in a sense may work out well for them; few can really want to see them imprisoned. But there is a cost, and it is a price which – arguably – all women pay.

First, the dominant or 'official' discourse on mothers who kill their children is rooted in the belief that *all* women are potentially mad at certain times in their lives – for example, during, before and after menstruation, child-birth, lactation and the menopause. Given the amount of time that women spend in one or other of these 'ordinary states', common sense is enough to reject such claims as generalizations. But despite this, they still provide a basis for the 'ordinary states' of womanhood to be subject to medical and psychiatric gaze, and for the stereotypical beliefs which surround such states to be perpetuated and used against women. Women, for example, should not be placed in positions of responsibility, allowed to fly aeroplanes, or whatever, just in case . . .

Second, dominant or 'official' discourse on mothers who kill their children is also rooted in the belief that *all* women are 'natural' mothers. We referred above to Ann Oakley's notion of the 'myth of motherhood', but there is a further point to be made here. Current conceptions of 'motherhood' were born (we have used these terms deliberately to indicate that they were created, not natural), and hence given meaning, within a particular social structure: patriarchy. Thus women's violence towards their children has to be understood in that context. Given the social and economic power men still hold, women's consequent powerlessness and their specific sense of failure as mothers when they experience difficulty in 'doing what comes naturally', it is perhaps not surprising that the targets for women's violence are those who are even less powerful than they are: their children. And perhaps, rather than reacting with surprise and incomprehension when we learn of a mother who has killed her child, we should ask why this does not happen more often.

Treating women's filicide as pathological diverts attention from the social conditions which are conducive to its occurrence: poverty, inordinate childcare responsibilities, social isolation, lack of support, the myths surrounding motherhood and cultural standards of 'good' (i.e. perfect) mothers. This is why Australian criminologist Jocelynne Scutt described infanticide legislation as a 'band-aid measure' which avoids the need to address the structural reasons for women's filicide. However, as feminist lawyer Katherine O'Donovan has rightly noted, 'to admit that social or economic circumstances, or motherhood, may cause crime is to open a hitherto tightly closed box'. It is debatable how sympathetic judges – and, indeed, the public – would be to a woman whose case was not packaged in wrappings which indicated either that she was 'disturbed' at the time of the offence or that she was essentially a 'good' mother who had made a tragic mistake. In this context, treating the majority of women's filicide in these ways is a pragmatic means to a non-punitive end.

But there remains a group of women who cannot present themselves as 'disturbed' or 'good', or are not perceived in such ways. Women and mothers who 'step out of line' or 'let the side down' are penalized accordingly. They run the risk of punitive sanctions. This cannot be right or fair, since objectively the situations, background and mental state of at least some of these women appear to be not dissimilar from those of the women who are dealt with 'sympathetically'.

The dichotomy between 'good' and 'bad' women and 'good' and 'bad' mothers serves as a means of patrolling, controlling and reinforcing the boundaries of behaviour considered 'appropriate' for *all* women and mothers. The response of the criminal justice system to mothers who kill their children is an extreme example of this moral tale.

'Angels of death'

The Lainz
Hospital murders

Bettina Heidkamp

Mosaic

Again she vomits when she gets home from work. Waltraud Wagner is exhausted. She waters the plants in the flat she shares with her sister Ilse, sinks into a chair and falls asleep in front of the television.

Thirty-year-old Waltraud Wagner is an assistant nurse. She lives in Vienna and works in Lainz city hospital in a Vienna suburb. Today is the second day in a five-day shift cycle: first day 7 a.m. to 5 p.m., second day 5.45 a.m. to 7 p.m., third day night shift 6.45 p.m. to 7 a.m., fourth day sleeping day, fifth day off – if she does not stand in for a missing colleague, which she quite often does. She usually starts at least an hour early and leaves late to be able to cope with the enormous amount of work. This has been her daily routine for twelve years.

Waltraud Wagner was born in Hagenberg, a small village in Lower Austria. She grew up on a small farm with her four brothers and one sister and looked after the house while her mother worked in the fields. When she was six Wagner had to repeat her first year at primary school because of her extreme short-sightedness. At twelve she was caring for her grandmother, who was crippled by open sores on her legs. From that point on her nursing career was mapped out. She failed her exam in anatomy after two years at a nursing-care boarding school and left without a diploma, but owing to a shortage of nurses in Austria she managed to get a job in Lainz city hospital as an assistant nurse soon after she moved to Vienna in 1975.

At Vienna District Court on 29 March 1991, former assistant nurses Waltraud Wagner (aged thirty-two), Irene Leidolf (twenty-nine), Maria Gruber (twenty-eight) and Stefaniya Mayer (fifty-one) are convicted of killing twenty elderly and feeble patients with lethal drug overdoses or by forcing water into their lungs. Vienna's courtroom is packed. A spellbound audience listens to the jury's chairwoman droning through the yes-and-nos to 250 questions relating to the various charges. After seventeen hours of deliberation, the jury announces its long-awaited verdict. The tension mounts to a climax as presiding judge Peter Straub rises to pronounce sentence: 'Waltraud Wagner is therefore sentenced to life imprisonment' – she starts and slumps over – 'Irene Leidolf to life imprisonment, Maria Gruber to fifteen years' imprisonment, Stefaniya Mayer to twenty years' imprisonment.' Mayer collapses.

Wagner and Mayer are carried out of the courtroom and the session is interrupted for twenty minutes. Cameras click, people queue outside the doors to catch a glimpse of the women the press had described as 'bloodhound bitches let loose', 'death angels', 'witches', 'raging devils' and 'hurricanes of death'.

The verdict concluded a sensational trial, accompanied by widespread public hysteria about the circumstances surrounding the murders in Lainz. Triggered off by an agitated media in April 1989, when the women were arrested, the case had held the public in thrall ever since, arousing heated discussions among the medical profession, in the Austrian health system, and even in Parliament. Over a period of seven years, from 1983 to 1989, these four women killed people whose welfare was entrusted to them: elderly and dying patients in the four wards of the Department for Internal Medicine in Lainz hospital. To this day, the real number of victims remains unknown. Public prosecutor Karl Ernst Kloyber suspected up to 400 killings; Irene Leidolf claimed that Waltraud Wagner had killed 100 patients – an accusation she later withdrew.

The Lainz murder case, extreme and horrific as it is, is hard to grasp in its totality. Probably hundreds of – mostly nameless – victims, people in the most defenceless position, were killed in a public place, in an environment which symbolized safety and trust. The murderers were women who seem ordinary to us, workers who day in, day out, did their job, had children and went on holidays like everybody else. How could murder have become banal, normal? The case seemed to illustrate that murder cannot be consigned to the unknown, dark margins of society; that it is not simply 'evil' or 'mad' people who are capable of killing.

Without a full account from the women themselves, a privileged insight into their consciences, it is impossible either to rationalise their actions or fully to answer the questions which so fascinated the public: What motivated four nurses to kill their patients? What kind of dynamic could have existed between them to lead them to conspire in the killings? Instead, I have attempted to assemble the pieces of a mosaic.

The events at Lainz hospital are by no means unique. The number of hospital killings appears to have increased over the last fifteen years. In 1976 a male nurse in what was then West Germany was convicted of murdering two patients and of attempted murder in four other cases. He was sentenced to life imprisonment. The following year a forty-one-year-old male nurse in an old people's home in the Netherlands confessed to 'having released five feeble, elderly patients from suffering', and was given an eighteen-year prison sentence. In 1983 a director of a rest home in Norway received a sentence of twenty-one years in prison after confessing to poisoning twenty-two patients. The same year, Genene Jones, an assistant nurse from Texas, was sentenced to 159 years' imprisonment for murdering a fifteen-month-old child. She is suspected of involvement in many more babies' deaths. And in November 1991, twenty-three-year-old children's ward nurse Beverly Allitt from Lincolnshire, England, was charged with the murder of four children.[1] These cases have led to detailed discussions on euthanasia and on the workings of the health systems in the countries where they took place. At Lainz, as in most other hospital killings, euthanasia was cited as the motive, but in this case at least, the defence of compassion seems both inadequate and highly dubious.

The fact that these killings took place in a hospital raises several questions: How does modern society treat elderly people, and how does it cope (or not cope) with death? And how significant is the structure of the nursing profession and the fact of its dominance by women?

With its 1,300 beds, Lainz hospital, situated in a south-western suburb of Vienna, is one of the city's biggest. Pavilion V, one of the eight pavilions scattered across a large, well-tended park, is the final resting place for elderly people, for hopeless cases. Ward D in particular is a death ward – dying, not healing, determines daily routine. More than 50 per cent of the patients are over seventy-five; some have had several strokes, some are confused; many of them are in a coma, emaciated and covered in bedsores. Some scream, some merely whimper; their dirty nappies stink. Doctors, nurses, patients and their relatives alike await death. Pavilion V is the one Department for Internal Medicine in a Vienna hospital which is not allowed to close its doors to casualties, even when it is full. It is open for alcoholics who are brought in during the night, for elderly people who wait for a free bed in a rest home, and for elderly people who are shoved away by their relatives just before Christmas or the summer holidays. Ward D is continually overcrowded. There are too few staff to cope with the official maximum capacity of twenty-nine beds, let alone for the constant overcrowding when up to forty patients cram the ward. This leads to chaos: with its broad corridors packed with extra beds, Ward D resembles a military hospital; the nurses have difficulties in manoeuvring the trolleys.

Around Easter 1988 Dorah Ferrada Avendano, assistant nurse in Ward D, confided to a doctor her suspicions that murders were taking place in the hospital. For several months, Ferrada had watched patients being 'calmed' with the tranquillizer Rohypnol, and dying shortly afterwards. She noticed that quantities of Valium mysteriously vanished from the medicine store, and overheard staff discussing rumours that the death rate in Ward D was higher than average. Wagner's name was mentioned. Shortly afterwards, Anna Urban died in Ward D and a blood test revealed traces of Rohypnol. The unit's medical chief, Franz X. Pesendorfer, contacted the police. A postmortem which found that Anna Urban had died of pulmonary embolism, and that no traces of Rohypnol were present, seemed to allay doubts; the police abandoned their investigation and Pesendorfer seemed satisfied that the rumours were groundless. But from that point on, unknown to the rest of the staff, the doctors initiated a tighter monitoring of Ward D by independently taking blood samples.

A year later, on 13 March 1989, a doctor discovered seventy-one-year-old Franz Frey in a coma, due to an overdose of insulin. The man, however, was not a diabetic, and Wagner later admitted to having administered the drug, describing him as a 'very awkward patient' whom she injected hoping that would necessitate his move to another ward.[2] Seventeen days later, Wagner and Mayer were working the night shift on Ward D. Once again, an elderly patient's insulin-induced coma was noticed, and Franz Kohout's life was saved. At the trial two years later, Kohout appeared as a witness to the fact that the killings were not directed only at terminally ill patients. In this case the women denied injecting insulin.

Soon afterwards, on 7 April 1989, all four women were arrested.

The police investigation followed standard procedure. Different teams questioned the suspects simultaneously, indirectly encouraging each to denounce the others by confronting them with confessions from the others. Three days later the women confessed to killing over fifty sick and elderly patients. Mayer admitted to drowning people by forcing water down their windpipes (a procedure euphemistically described as 'oral hygiene care'), both alone and with Wagner. Leidolf confessed to killing several people by deadly injections, as did Gruber. Wagner was immediately named as the main suspect and 'leader' of the group. When police showed her a book registering all the deaths which occurred between 1987 and 1989 she picked out thirty-nine names, admitted to involvement in their deaths, and even named the method of killing in each case.

Asked how she could still remember all these details, Wagner is reported to have looked up, winked, and said: 'You'd remember something like this!' She is later quoted as saying, 'I really wanted to release these poor people from suffering. I do admit that it became a kind of a habit later on, but the main reason still was to release from suffering. I have now made a kind of a life-confession. I deeply regret all my deeds.'[3]

The case was greeted in Austria with a mixture of fascination and horror. How did the murders go undetected for so long? The public was also shocked by the nurses' revelations about conditions at the hospital. It emerged that owing to a general shortage of staff, and what appeared to be mismanagement at the highest level, the assistant nurses at the hospital were overworked and did jobs for which they were not qualified. Statements and protests from nurses at other hospitals revealed that these problems were by no means confined to Lainz. It also came to light that the conservative opposition party in the City Council, ÖVP (Austrian People's Party) and the unions had been highlighting these shortcomings in the Vienna health system for years. The Vienna health authorities came under attack and the opposition called for the resignation of Dr Alois Stacher, head of the Vienna hospital system. He refused.

Two separate investigations into the situation in Vienna's hospitals were initiated by the Vienna City Council, one carried out by a Local Council Commission and one by an independent international group. The police and Pesendorfer, head of Pavilion V, also faced growing criticism by the Lord Mayor for their mismanagement, and for abandoning the 1988 investigations. Shortly after the women had been remanded, Pesendorfer said: 'Wagner seems to be a dehumanized personality. These four women must have been lunatic singular culprits.'[4] Vienna's police chief Günter Bögl called the cases 'the biggest series of murders ever committed in Europe',[5] and Lord Mayor Helmut Zilk compared the killings to the Nazi murders in Auschwitz: 'The death angels of Lainz remind me of the death angels of Auschwitz'.[6] With these exaggerated statements, all the people who might themselves have shared responsibility for creating the conditions in which the murders happened passed the buck. Meanwhile, the tabloid press joined the chorus of outrage, pointing to the women's 'cold-bloodedness' and 'lack of emotion'.

The vehemence with which press and officialdom denounced the women focused on a single factor: their transgression of their role as nurses. They had perverted the image of the female nurse as the ever-patient preserver of life. It was suggested that the women had seized power and cruelly abused it. They had betrayed society. The conservative paper *Die Presse* reported rumours that the women had 'suffocated patients with cushions' and 'beaten them to death'.[7] A leader in the same edition spoke of 'the raging of the she-devils'. This, together with images like 'witches' and 'death-angels', evoked archaic fears. One article in the tabloid *Kronenzeitung* alleged that Wagner had worked as a hostess in a Vienna night club and called her a 'secret prostitute', explicitly linking female sexuality with corruption and power.[8]

Austrian journalist Tessa Prager, who covered the case for various papers, explained the public outrage in terms of a collective guilty conscience: 'We keep our guilty conscience in the face of inhumane death locked away, until it can burst out with even more power . . . the guilty conscience that we do not look after these people ourselves. So when there is murder, our outrage knows no bounds.'[9]

Sociology professor Leopold Rosenmayr saw a connection between the shortcomings of social policy and the background to the murders. He criticized Austria as a typical modern industrialized society where the number of old people grows continually, but the health system provides insufficient facilities and qualified staff to deal with them. The health system, he said, was 'a reflection of a society which is geared entirely towards feasibility', in which weakness and illness are met with contempt. The elderly are pushed aside into the dark corners of the health system.[10]

Women on the margins

Pavilion V is one of these dark corners. It was there that the four assistant nurses met. Stefaniya Mayer, born in Yugoslavia in 1939, joined the hospital as an assistant nurse in 1978. When she left her husband in 1967 and arrived in Austria with her two-year-old daughter, she could not speak a word of German. She worked in factories and as a nanny, finally qualifying as an assistant nurse through a short course.

A year later Irene Leidolf joined the department. The daughter of a teacher and a chemist, she had just failed a two-year diploma course in nursing. She was, however, still qualified to work as an assistant nurse. The previous year she had had an illegitimate child, but gave it up for adoption, fearing that she would be unable to cope. At home, she nursed her father, who suffered from cancer of the salivary gland and begged her to cut away the dead parts of his mouth. Although it sickened her, she did it. Later, when interrogated by the police, she said that this taught her 'to switch off'.[11] Irene became good friends with Waltraud Wagner, who came to the department in 1980. Like Leidolf, Wagner had nursed a member of her family, her grandmother, whose sores everybody else in the family found revolting; she too failed her exams.

Maria Gruber started in Pavilion V the same year. She had also given up nursing school because of 'learning difficulties'. Although she was already working at the hospital as an assistant nurse, she studied hard and completed a course which properly qualified her for the job. Like the other women, this policeman's daughter had always dreamed of becoming a nurse.

In Austria, assistant nurses, who usually qualify through a course of about 200 hours, are supposed merely to fulfil the tasks of an auxiliary: feeding, cleaning, making beds, etc. But in Pavilion V the assistant nurses gave intravenous injections, took blood samples and even put on intravenous catheters – tasks which were far beyond their authority and which contravened the nursing laws. In Vienna hospitals, an average of 13 per cent of the staff are assistant nurses; at Lainz hospital the figure is 39 per cent.

The general shortage of nurses in Austria can be traced back to an inflexible, fossilized health system which does not allow nurses to work part-time, but insists on physically and psychologically exhausting duty shifts, where the working hours can reach sixty a week. The chances of promotion and career advancement are slim.[12] The pressure on the assistant nurses at Lainz to breach the rules must have been particularly strong. In court, however, one nurse who worked in Pavilion V testified that she always refused to give injections, although she admitted that the unit would have had to close if the nurses had restricted themselves to the tasks they were qualified to carry out.[13]

At first Maria Gruber felt uneasy about performing tasks which were beyond her jurisdiction. Her colleagues laughed at her when she said: 'But we are not allowed to give injections!'[14] Later she began to accompany the doctor on his rounds, to administer drugs – and to give injections. There were the cleaning jobs, too: wiping the beds, bed frames and floors of excrement and vomit. Patients had to be washed; sometimes one nurse was responsible for forty patients and began washing them at 3 a.m., finishing at 6.30 a.m. when the next shift started. Everything had to go like clockwork, from morning to night, day in day out. Former ward sister Helene Speiser later stated in court: 'They were real good workers, otherwise they could not have worked in the medical ward. We always got rid of the bad ones quickly.'[15]

These women were at the lowest rung of a rigid hierarchy, but they worked the hardest. They were the least qualified, but they had the most difficult task: to deal with the dying. No one told them that there are illnesses which make people turn aggressive; nobody talked to them about death. They had no official supervision of their work to help them deal with their problems and fears. Everybody worked in their own sphere, without questioning the actions or efficiency of the rest. Communication between the different positions in the hierarchy was rare.

Described by the staff as both professionally competent and hard workers, the four women appear to have enjoyed the sense of power their work gave them. They established their own little hierarchy by accepting Wagner, who was always jolly, industrious and popular with the doctors, as their boss. Other colleagues interpreted her strong commitment as high-handedness. The four women protected their position by driving qualified nurses from their wards: ('At home they wouldn't have a qualified nurse either!'[16] or by mocking a young nurse who put an elderly woman's hair in curlers. They found it hard to understand why the doctors seemed to administer pain-relieving drugs at random.[17] When Franz X. Pesendorfer's brother was admitted to Pavilion V and Pesendorfer gave him a drug which can shorten life while soothing the pain, both Mayer and Wagner were convinced that Pesendorfer had killed him.[18]

The women, however, had long since started to make their own decisions about who should live and who should die.

In 1983, Wagner watched an elderly patient come close to death after being 'calmed' by the doctors with half a diluted ampoule of the tranquillizer Rohypnol. 'Calming' patients like this was a common practice in Pavilion V.[19] Soon afterwards she injected three undiluted ampoules of the same drug into an elderly woman's catheter. The woman died shortly afterwards. Wagner told both Leidolf and Gruber about Rohypnol and its effects. During the trial Irene Leidolf stated that her friend had shown her how to inject the drug. She pleaded guilty to having 'helped three suffering people to die a few hours earlier in 1983 and in 1988'. She spoke about her guilty conscience and admitted she had known it was illegal.[20]

Maria Gruber testified that she had injected Rohypnol into two patients because she could not bear to see them suffering any longer, but there are huge discrepancies between her statements then and during the first police interrogations. Interviewed by police, she claimed not to have known about the drug's lethal effects when she used it. She also said that she had withdrawn completely from the group once she did know.[21] Of the four women, she alone pleaded not guilty. Wagner in her turn said that Gruber had asked her to draw up the injections for her, and that she had told her about the effect beforehand.

The fatal injections were made all too easy in the chaos of Pavilion V, where overworked doctors on night duty often left orders not to be awakened except in extreme emergencies and frequently only arrived – be it day or night – hours after somebody had died. The records of time and cause of death were made by the nurses, and were often not even checked by the doctors.[22] Former ward sister Helene Speiser in court: 'Did we notice what was happening? Wagner was a good nurse. Besides, if a patient is bad today and dead tomorrow, what is there to notice? They would have died anyway.'[23]

The medicine cabinet was left unlocked, and the consumption of drugs was not registered. Once a month the head of department signed a computer list which showed the amount of drugs consumed in the whole department. Public prosecutor Karl Ernst Kloyber stated in his indictment that from 1983 to 1987 the first floor in Pavilion V, where Wagner and the others worked, used 2,495 ampoules of Rohypnol, while the second floor ordered just 285. The hospital pharmacists denied noticing anything suspicious.[24]

One of the illegal tasks carried out by some of the assistant nurses was the 'oral hygiene care', which involves moistening the mouths of comatose patients with water and disinfectant. Wagner used this as another method of killing. She poured water into the patient's mouth while blocking the gullet with the tongue, thus forcing the water into the lungs through the windpipe. The patients would drown internally in about twenty to sixty minutes. This means of killing went undetected because water in the lungs quite often accompanies a coma, especially in elderly patients.

By 1987 the relationship between the four women seems to have changed. Wagner and Mayer worked together in one shift cycle in Ward D, while Gruber worked in C and Leidolf in B, Pesendorfer's private ward. Mayer is described as a rough but committed person who had cried when patients were transferred to an old people's home. Unlike Wagner, Mayer refused to do main duty, which meant giving injections, doing the job of a graduate nurse, a ward nurse or even a doctor. As a result, the senior nursing officer threatened to dismiss her. Mayer later described how Wagner herself gave orders like a doctor, even advising patients against taking a prescribed drug.[25]

In court Mayer claimed that Wagner had asked her to assist with the 'oral hygiene care'. She stated that on one occasion, Wagner had said to her: 'Come on, help me' when she was going to see a patient. Then Wagner had done the 'oral hygiene care'; forty-five minutes later she had brought the temperature chart back to the staff room – the patient was dead. Later, she said, Wagner had asked her to help her change the wet bedclothes and to watch out in case somebody should come into the room.

Mayer denied killing anybody herself, despite admitting to it in the first interrogations. During the trial she painted a picture of Wagner as a dominant woman who 'used me, who was a favourite with everybody, always jolly, even in the face of death, a personality who through the killings wanted to prove how good she could be'.[26] Wagner, in her turn, claimed that Mayer was jealous of her.[27] When the judge asked Mayer why she thought Wagner was nicknamed 'the witch' among her colleagues in Ward D, she shouted: 'Because she *is* a witch!'

Leidolf and Gruber were allegedly not involved with what was called 'oral hygiene care', even though during the first interrogations Gruber had admitted assisting Wagner with it as early as 1983.

As rumours began to spread that more people died when Wagner was on duty, a doctor examined the register of deaths in Ward D and found that the number of deaths increased five to six times when Wagner was on duty, and dropped drastically when she was on leave. Wagner was reported as saying: 'I only have to stand beside somebody and he'll be dead.'[28] Other comments hint at the self-satisfaction and pride she felt: 'The dear lord has got a free room for him', 'I have sold this one' (about someone to whom she gave an insulin injection to cause him to be transferred to another department).[29]

'Killing became a kind of habit,' she said during the police interrogation, implying that for her, killing had become banal. Mayer's testimony – that she had been afraid she might be transferred to another ward if she had not 'assisted' Wagner with the killings – strengthens this impression: had killing become a lesser evil for Mayer too? To describe a method of killing as 'oral hygiene care' also indicates that somehow killing had become 'normal', part of the everyday routine.

When Leidolf read an article on the German nurse Michaela Roeder, who was charged with killing seventeen patients, she told Wagner that this would happen to her too some day. Wagner replied: 'It won't happen to me.'[30] Clearly, the nurses were aware of the condemnation they would face if ever they were found out.

In a context where death was part of daily routine and patients were allocated to the nurses like so much human debris, the moral threshold which makes killing unacceptable became lower and lower. Pavilion V was an isolated world with its own unwritten rules, its own jargon, a world in which generally accepted ethical and moral values inevitably had to be qualified in order to get the job done. But neither this nor the women's defence of compassion explains their motives. Wagner admitted that at first she had tried to get rid of patients who 'bothered her too much'.[31] Aggression played its part too. As an Austrian nurse interviewed in the Austrian magazine *Profil* pointed out: 'Compassion is none too significant an emotion for people who work in the nursing profession. The more awkward a person is, the more tiresome he/she becomes . . . Work has to function, everything is organized through routine jobs and timing. Patients who claim time will be disciplined.'[32]

Assistant nurse Dorah Ferrada Avendano, whose suspicions helped to bring the killings to light, told in court how Wagner had asked her to inject a yellow liquid which looked like Valium. Ferrada refused. For several years she did not dare confess her suspicions for fear of losing her job. Gruber stated that Ferrada had warned her that 'Waltraud should be watched as she was doing "wrong things".'[33] The other women seem to have been intimidated by Wagner, who appears to have initiated a process which developed a momentum of its own, and took hold of the other three women. Perversely, killing seems to have been one way four women who had failed to climb the career ladder could assert their authority, feel a sense of power.

The caring profession

In its 1989 report on the conditions in Vienna's hospitals and homes for the elderly, the International Commission stated:

> The Commission, however, is of the opinion that the special structures and forms of organization in Vienna cannot be regarded as cause for those offences as similar incidents can occur and have occurred in completely different structures. Factors arising from this kind of situation can at the most have an encouraging effect.[34]

In other words, many nurses work under similar grim conditions as the nurses in Pavilion V, yet do not kill.

Studies on the physical and psychological strain experienced by nurses cite certain stress factors affecting them. Dr Peter Herschbach of the Munich University Institute for Psychosomatic Medicine, Psychotherapy and Medical Psychology lists those high-risk groups which may suffer acute psychological strain – nurses who:

- work in large hospitals;
- are young and professionally inexperienced;
- often do overtime and have few weekends off;
- have very little time for breaks;

- care for a high number of terminally ill, long-term patients.[35]

Nearly all these factors applied to Waltraud Wagner, Irene Leidolf, Stefaniya Mayer and Maria Gruber.

These ideas are borne out by the work of intensive-care nurses Heidrun Hirsch and Jürgen Zander, whose degree dissertation examines 'Strains in Nursing'. Caring for a high number of terminally ill patients and patients in continuous need of care, they say, results in acute psychological and emotional strain and distress. The nurses' hard work reaps little benefit, and in many cases their care accompanies a patient's death, rather than a process of healing. This stress is often reinforced through inflexible time schedules and a lack of staff, which means that a nurse cannot devote as much time and personal care as she or he might like. 'Continual inner tension and irritability are the consequence of the lack of omnipotence, the fact that the nurses cannot be everywhere at the same time, and the permanent feeling that yet another task should have been accomplished long ago.'[36]

In a series of articles on the causes of aggression among nurses who care for elderly people, internist and psychotherapist Dr Erich Grond wrote:

The permanent sense of frustration among nurses [who care for the elderly] contributes to feelings of aggression. Those with perfectionist personalities especially . . . are in danger of becoming angry with themselves because they cannot attain their ideal of . . . perfect care. Their own powerlessness and feelings of hopelessness about the fact that the patient gets worse in spite of their efforts produces helpless rage.[37]

Grond goes on to argue that even when aggression is expressed, it rarely frees the aggressor from feelings of anger or rage; instead, it reinforces them. Nurses who become violent, he says, affirm their behaviour through exerting power and asserting themselves.[38]

Referring directly to the Lainz case, the report of the International Commission stresses the danger of aggression among staff who are not specifically trained to deal with elderly, long-term patients:

> Nurses who are not psycho-gerontologically trained
> have to put up with aggression from mentally disturbed
> people. They are in danger of blaming themselves, and
> feeling guilty; they often subconsciously answer with
> aggression, too. If this hatred builds up, it can lead
> to revenge and – if a person lacks moral barriers and
> shows weaknesses of personality – to extremely sadistic
> reactions.[39]

Interviewed about the events in Lainz hospital, sociology professor Leopold Rosenmayr said: 'These women are overburdened, they have to deal with depressed people and they do not really feel appreciated. These factors lead to intolerable strains. They are heroines and heroes who do their work, which society does not want to see, in an environment which is cut off from the world.' He concluded that official supervision, during which the nurses could talk about their working conditions, should be compulsory: 'It is incredible that those people are left alone – with their disgust, their hatred, with their sadistic feelings, and that nobody helps them to find a way out.'[40]

At Pavilion V, four women's need to gain power and authority, their feelings of aggression due to overwork, frustration and lack of proper training, proved a fatal combination.

During the nineteenth century, nursing, which until then had been an occupation shared equally between women and men, was restructured. While medicine became a technically orientated male-dominated science, nursing became a profession dominated by women. In her book

Frauen in der Krankenpflege ('Women in Nursing') Claudia Bischoff describes how various factors in the then developing health systems brought about such a change. She examines the establishment of the modern hospital system, the development of medicine into a science, the consequences of industrialization which called for medical treatment on a broader scale, and the numerous wars throughout the nineteenth century.[41] Serious shortcomings in the existing health systems called for a new influx of well-trained staff. In the context of the then prevalent ideologies of femininity, middle-class women were thought to be ideally suited for this profession. The ideal nurse was supposed to be patient, loving and, above all, self-sacrificing – qualities which were seen as originating in femininity itself:

> Woman's fulfillment is based on the balance of all
> energies . . . This is of benefit to nursing because illness
> seizes the whole person. This means that nursing . . .
> must be done with a fullness of respect for humanity
> . . . Perseverance and understanding of this wholeness
> is part of the female disposition. Consequently, all
> indicators of nature and the profession point to the
> female soul as the born hospital worker.[42]

Bischoff points to the contradictions inherent in the popular image which has since developed: 'The nurse should be a truly supernatural being. On the one hand an ascetic, self-denying personality is expected which implies hardness towards oneself and must lead to coldness; on the other she is expected to show love towards the patients.'[43] The attempt to fulfil this ideal results in a constant feeling of personal failure.

Within today's specialized, scientific medicine, she argues, little room is set aside for issues of old age and death. Human beings have become objects of medical study; it is left to the nursing profession to provide warmth, sympathy and personal care. Nursing compensates for the deficiencies of a rationalized medicine – a hopeless task so long as the inhumane structures prevail.[44]

Nurses on trial

The dramatically dubbed 'biggest murder trial of the second Austrian Republic' lasted just eighteen days. Those who expected answers to the numerous questions raised by the case quickly learned that there was only one question to which the trial would address itself: Who is guilty, and of how many murders? Numbers were trotted out, along with the implicit assumption that the only guilty and responsible persons were Waltraud Wagner, Stefaniya Mayer, Irene Leidolf and Maria Gruber. As *Profil* magazine put it: 'The . . . murders and attempted murders are answered by the four women in the dock. The circumstances as they were described during the trial and in which the murders . . . were committed are not answered for by anyone in court.'[45] No doctor was asked: 'Is it true that you appeared only three hours after somebody had died?' No member of the Health Department of the Vienna City Council was called upon to explain why, for several years, nurses in Pavilion V left their jobs shortly after they had started.

The one morning which was reserved for the interrogation of Franz Pesendorfer and Wendelin Wanka, leader of the Local Council investigation commission and spokesman for the health authority, passed with each engaged in eloquent attempts to blame the other. Wanka, while denying any flaws in the Vienna hospital system, described a 'silent agreement between doctors and nurses' as the most serious shortcoming. Pesendorfer, he said, could have changed the conditions in Pavilion V. In his defence, Pesendorfer responded that his requests to the City Council for more staff had gone unanswered.[46]

The eighty-eight-page indictment by prosecutor Karl Ernst Kloyber painted a gloomy picture of the shortcomings of the

Lainz hospital, calling them the 'nutrient ingredients for the seeds of violence to grow . . . None the less, all that does not begin to make these offences comprehensible.'[47] The women faced forty-two charges of murder, including aiding and abetting murder – a number which Kloyber believed to be only the 'tip of the iceberg'.

Traces of lethal drugs could be discovered in only four corpses, while 'oral hygiene' had been proven in just one case. In the absence of forensic evidence, the charges were almost exclusively based upon earlier confessions. The women did not plead guilty to all the charges. Gruber claimed total innocence, stating that she had not known about the drugs' lethal effect beforehand.

Throughout the weeks preceding the trial, the women had begun to contradict their initial confessions. In court they tried to explain this by saying that they did not care at the time and that nobody would have believed them anyway. Wagner (referring to the thirty-nine names she had chosen from the death register) stated: 'I did not know anything then, but nobody would have believed me anyway – just like now.'[48]

The proceedings consisted mainly of the prosecution, the judges and members of the jury citing earlier confession and the defendants answering in a monotone, often crying. They hardly looked up.

Wagner: I have done everything out of compassion. It never became a habit . . . I wanted to help, compassion, really.
Judge Peter Straub: To relieve pain? After the water the patients did not moan, but worse, they choked. Could you explain the 'helping' to me, Ms Wagner? Do you understand me? Ms Wagner![49]

There were few signs of the 'mistress over life and death', the woman who had 'reigned more high-handedly than the Gods in white',[50] as Kloyber's indictment had described

Wagner. Tense, hands twisted, hunched over and most of the time inert, she remained on the verge of tears.

Confronted with the eloquence of the middle-aged university graduates who cross-examined them, the women were helpless and stammering. Even their own lawyers seemed to push them further into a corner. Leidolf's defence counsel called her 'this pretty, dainty woman', and appealed to the jury: 'Please do not destroy the life of this woman, who was only a twenty-two-year-old idiot when she committed the offences'; Gruber's lawyer pointed out her 'primitivity'.[51] Wagner's lawyer, however, who on her arrest had remarked that 'she is just like an angel',[52] now stressed her deep compassion while trying to prove that she could not have committed the killings because she lacked the time. Continually protesting that they had acted out of compassion, the women contradicted themselves and did little to answer the most pressing questions: Where did the idea of the killings originate? How could it become part of a routine?

'The accountancy of horror', as the press called the trial, did not extend further than a speedy haggle over more than forty death cases. As a result the women's personal backgrounds and the circumstances of their individual lives, were hardly taken into account. Even the certificates of two psychiatrists and one psychologist revealed little about the defendants' personalities. In less than two hours they read out their certificates in court, concluding that all the women were sound of mind and fully responsible for their actions. Wagner was being described as of modest intelligence and slightly depressive; Leidolf as easily influenced, intellectually talented, emotionally balanced, purposeful and bright. Gruber, according to the expert, was easily influenced, slightly immature, dutiful and thorough.[53]

The superficial statements of the experts contrasted sharply with the proceedings in a similar case in West Germany. In 1989 graduate nurse Michaela Roeder, charged with killing seventeen patients in intensive care by means of deadly injections, was convicted of manslaughter in five cases and sentenced to eleven years' imprisonment. Over seven months, twenty-three psychological examinations of the thirty-one-year-old woman, and even of her parents, resulted in a 200-page document which provided some context for the killings. It helped to explain how the particular working environment Roeder had found herself in had made her fail, how she had hidden her strain behind a veneer of industriousness.[54] Under Austrian law, psychiatric experts are not permitted to speculate on the overall context of a crime, and perhaps lend some psychological logic to it. Their job is merely to state whether or not the defendants are responsible for their actions.

Waltraud Wagner remained the final scapegoat. The other women blamed her. The more 'evil' Wagner appeared, the better they appeared. Wagner, wearily, tried to fight back. To demonstrate Mayer's own cruelty, Wagner described a scene where Mayer allegedly pushed a dying woman's head down several times and killed her. Wagner commented: 'Not even *I* would have done that!' While Wagner tried to show that she was 'better' than Mayer, at the same time she accepted the role in which the public had cast her: as the 'worst' woman of the four.

The verdict, which found each woman guilty of murder or attempted murder, concluded the trial on Good Friday 1991. The lawyer for Mayer, Herbert Eichenseder, said: 'I am more interested in the truth behind the truth of the events than in this accountancy of horror. Especially as we are not dealing with an isolated case but with a phenomenon which is increasing internationally. Nobody cared about the individual human beings in these women. We have missed the central theme of the trial: humanity.'[55]

On 15 May 1992, the final decision in the women's appeal against their sentences was announced by the Supreme Court in Vienna. Wagner's and Leidolf's life sentences and Mayer's twenty-year sentence were confirmed. Gruber's sentence was reduced by three years to twelve years on the grounds that she was under twenty-one when she committed the crimes and that she withdrew from Wagner's influence in 1983, while the others continued to kill – or attempt to kill – until 1988.

A deep fascination with the murders at Lainz hospital remains to this day. This, the most extreme example of the phenomenon of hospital killing to date, has brought murder frighteningly close to our own experience, to a public institution and to its employees – all of whom appeared to be as sane as you or I. The public reaction to the killings, the attempts to blame someone else, something else, for what happened, is, I believe, an expression of a deep-rooted fear of linking one's own life with murder, with the unknown.

This fear showed itself in the demonizing of the women by the media, and in the sometimes patronizing treatment they received in court. Yet another question remains: How could their colleagues, the doctors, the hospital pharmacists, all claim not to have realized that for a period of seven years, patients were killed right under their noses? Was it just for these four women that murder had become 'normal' in this atmosphere of death and suffering – and ignorance?

Waltraud Wagner, Irene Leidolf, Stefaniya Mayer and Maria Gruber will remain in prison for many years. But the shortcomings of our treatment of the elderly, of the hospital system, and the responsibility of those with the power to change them, cannot be locked away.

The female serial killer

*An evolving
criminality*

Candice Skrapec

His name was Richard Mallory. The middle-aged divorcee
picked up the thirty-three-year-old blonde on his way
from Tampa to Daytona Beach, Florida. On 13 December
1989 his decomposed body was found in Volusia County.
According to the medical examiner's report, Mallory had
been shot four times with a .22-calibre gun; his 35 mm
camera and the radar detector from his car were linked
to a pawnshop in Daytona Beach. As required by Florida
law, the broker's receipt included the right thumbprint of
the person leaving the goods, which was then matched
to 'Lori Grody', who was being sought by police for a
1986 concealed-firearms charge. Grody's prints were also
found to match the bloody palm print recovered on an
abandoned car on 4 July 1990. The owner of that car,
Peter Siems, is still missing. The gold and diamond ring
of sixty-year-old Walter Antonio, found dead in Dixie
County on 19 November 1990, was located in the same
pawnshop. 'Cammie Greene' was noted on the receipt.

Lee Wuornos, as she was known to her friends, was
a hitchhiking prostitute who claimed to have worked
the highways for seventeen years. Her father committed
suicide in prison following his conviction for kidnapping
and sodomizing a child, and her grandparents raised her
after her mother handed her (at six months of age) and her
brother into their care. Early adolescence acquainted her
with drugs, alcohol and sex, and the child she gave birth to

241

at fifteen was given up for adoption. Before she was sixteen she herself would be a throwaway; there is little doubt that necessity made her streetwise. She apparently lived by panhandling and prostitution, although at twenty-five she was sentenced to three years for armed robbery.

Police investigation raised Wuornos and another woman as suspects in a series of killings of men whose bodies were found along north central Florida and southern Georgia highways. Aileen Carol Wuornos – a.k.a. Susan Lynn Blahovec, a.k.a. Lee Blahovec, a.k.a. Lori Kristine Grody, a.k.a. Cammie Marsh Greene – was arrested on 9 January 1991, on the outstanding weapons-violation charge. Shortly afterwards she confessed to the killing of Richard Mallory, claiming self-defence, and was charged with his murder. She insisted that the reason for her confession was to clear the name of her lesbian lover, Tyria Moore, who had been identified as her travelling companion and implicated in the killing.

The two-week trial in January 1992 saw only Wuornos herself testify as witness for the defence. She asserted that Mallory had raped, tortured, and threatened to kill her, and that she had used the handgun in her purse, which she carried for protection, to save her life. During her confession to police, Wuornos explained that after the first shot, she realized she had a decision to make: to continue shooting or to stop and help her assailant. But who would believe a prostitute claiming that she had been raped and feared that she had either to kill or be killed? She continued to shoot. By her own account, Aileen Wuornos killed a total of seven men, under similar circumstances, in self-defence.

The female as multiple murderer

Violent criminality has been marked out as an essentially male province by the criminal justice system, criminological researchers, and the media. Homicide, in particular, is viewed as a predominantly male crime, female offenders tending to be relegated to an 'exceptional case' status that rests upon some exceptional or untoward, compelling circumstance: the battered wife who kills her abusive husband; the postpartum psychotic mother who kills her newborn infant. The motif of a threatened Medea killing those in her charge surfaces repeatedly. Murders are the solution to real or imagined tensions.

Despite recent sensational portrayals of women murderers in Hollywood cinema,[1] they still do not figure regularly as killers in fact[2] or fiction. Women hold even smaller claim to our perception of multiple murderers (the image of a woman killing a number of people, over a period of time or upon a single occasion, is not familiar). As one who has delivered many presentations on the subject of serial and mass murder to a wide range of audiences, I frequently encounter amazement at the revelation that women have long been, and continue to be, multiple murderers. The notion so violates the idea of femaleness, tied to her traditional nurturing role, that a woman is denied her identity as a multiple murderer. Indeed, an FBI spokesperson distinguished Wuornos as 'the first female text-book case of a serial killer', contributing to this prevailing misconception.[3]

Serial murder is typically presented as a male phenomenon, but the reality does not support this. Women do kill. Moreover, American society's experience with female serial killers is consistent with its experience with female murderers in general. If we look at rates of homicides committed by each gender in the United States over time, females account for roughly 12 to 15 per cent of all murderers. Intriguingly, women represent the same proportion of serial murderers. In criminologist Eric Hickey's research on serial murderers and their victims, 17 per cent of the 203 offenders he studied were females.[4]

Typically presented as case studies and summarily typecast as 'black widows' (women who kill a series of husbands, their children and other relatives), 'angels of death' or 'mercy killers' (women who kill patients in their care), and the like, female multiple murderers have not been examined as a group, apart from the 'celebrity' and inherent sensationalism of individual cases. This case-by-case, largely biographical approach certainly owes part of its currency to the relatively small number of cases, but case studies, while they are valuable in and of themselves, so dominate the literature on female multiple murder that the larger picture is obscured. Scant attempt has been made to see how the women who kill repeatedly are like one another, or to see how they compare, as a group, with their male counterparts. Do these women come from similar places, psychologically and socially? What are the methods and motives of their crimes? Is there a discrete social phenomenon of female serial murder? The answers require a systematic look at the women and their crimes. I wish, however, to caution against viewing male and female serial killers as different 'breeds'. Indeed, it is a main point of this chapter that while it is tempting to focus on the readily apparent differences between the two, it is misguided to do so. I believe that these differences serve to mask more substantive, underlying similarities between male and female serial murderers.

The key distinction between male and female serial murderers is at the level of *modus operandi*, not of underlying motive: the how, not the why. The motive in each instance is a need for a sense of self as actor; a need for power that has generally arisen out of a formative history in which the individual as a child experienced him- or herself as powerless. This experience – as Alice Miller[5] and others point out – can lead to a simmering yet pervasive rage which, if it is not resolved in a healthy manner, will result in violence. A critical element in determining how such children develop, and in particular how they express their rage, is their sense of entitlement. It has been more socially acceptable for men, who are more likely to feel entitled by virtue of their gender, to express this rage outwardly.

Women have, until recently, been accorded less entitlement and have been more likely to turn their anger inward and to become self-destructive.

Serial and sexual and male?

Disagreement prevails among academics, law enforcement agents and journalists on what constitutes serial murder. While most definitions specify a minimum number of victims killed over time as the principal distinction, some are quite vague. Attorney Donald Sears[6], for example, speaks of 'many' killings. The relationship between murderer and victim has also been held to be a defining characteristic. Criminologist Steven Egger[7] includes only strangers in his definition of serial murder. My own research suggests that serial murderers, both male and female, share varying degrees of closeness in their relationships with their victims. While most serial murderers do not know their victims, an impressive number do. Some even know them intimately; some are relatives.

Early press accounts of serial murders typified them as random and motiveless. It is my sense that, by and large, they are neither random nor lacking in discernible motive. The killings tend to be selectively targeted and appear to be committed in the service of some inextinguishable personal need. Rather than using factors such as relationship to victims or motive to *define* serial murder, they are more meaningfully viewed as ways in which serial murderers can *differ* from one another. After studying the literature and interviewing male serial and mass murderers, I am comfortable with the basic definition of a serial killer as one who kills a number of people, at least three, over a period of time.[8]

The inclusion of a sexual component as part of the definition of serial murder is particularly problematic – so much so that when some people think of serial killers they can conceive only of the 'lust' killer, such as Ted Bundy.

Bundy was convicted of the serial murders of two women and a girl and, within forty-eight hours of his execution in 1989, admitted to killing twenty-five other women across six US states in the 1970s. He often used a ruse to lure victims into a vulnerable position, and then bludgeoned, raped and strangled them. While it does not appear that he was a sexual sadist who drew erotic pleasure from the actual suffering of his victims, Bundy sexually violated them when they were unconscious and dying, or dead. This is the image of serial murder that a number of people hold: a series of victims are stalked by a predator who kills them as part of a scene of perverse sexual frenzy. While this is not an uncommon scenario, neither is it the only one.

Serial murder includes – but is in no way limited to – sexual murders that are perpetrated by both men and women. There are serial killers who do not violate their victims sexually. And while many offenders do not engage in any kind of overt sexual behaviour during the commission of their crimes, the killing scenarios may none the less be highly sexually charged for them. Memories and 'souvenirs' of the murders in the form of personal items or body parts from the victims become stimuli for later masturbatory fantasies, enabling the offender to relive the crimes.

Most of the serial murderers familiar to the public did violate their victims sexually. Sexual or lust murder, in which the act of killing is itself eroticized, as feminist writers Deborah Cameron and Elizabeth Frazer view it,[9] is held by them to be an exclusively male phenomenon. They consider Myra Hindley, convicted in 1966 with her lover Ian Brady of murdering two children and being an accessory to the murder of a third, a lone exception in the 'tradition of sadistic sexual murder . . . [in which] . . . women are virtually non-existent',[10] but their dismissal does not appear to be adequately informed by empirical study of other cases. Tom Kuncl and Paul Einstein,[11] for example, cite the Georgia case of Janice Buttram, who, with her husband, killed a teenage acquaintance in 1980. The victim was stabbed ninety-seven times in her face, neck, breasts, abdomen, legs and vaginal areas. There were also wounds on her hands which showed that she had tried to defend herself. The dying victim had apparently been raped and sodomized by Danny Buttram, and afterwards by Janice, who penetrated her rectally and then vaginally with the base of an electric toothbrush. Her husband told prosecutors that when he finished and went to wash blood from his hands, he saw Janice continue to stab the victim's breasts while performing oral sex on her. Psychologist Henry Adams described Janice Buttram as 'a genuine sexual sadist . . . obtaining sexual gratification [through] acts of perversion committed on an unwilling female victim'.[12] Although not all the experts called into the case agreed with this depiction, they all believed that 'had [she] not been apprehended so swiftly, there was an almost certain chance she would have killed again in a sexually sadistic assault'.[13]

Nor is sexual serial murder by women a recent phenomenon. After the death of her husband in 1600, forty-year-old Hungarian Countess Elisabeth Bathory was compelled by the delusion that her complexion would retain its youthfulness if bathed in youthful human blood. She was tried and convicted of some eighty murders, based on the number of cadavers of girls and young women found at the remote Csejth Castle, Bathory's home. She and her sisters in crime, all practitioners in black magic, were allegedly responsible for the deaths of 300 to 650 victims. Bathory's own ledger tallied the number killed at 610. When her cousin, the Prime Minister, finally agreed to an investigation after years of rumours of torture and murder, and numerous reported kidnappings, the castle was raided. Bathory and her servants were discovered immersed in a mêlée of lesbian sex, marked by its extraordinary depravity. Found in the dungeon were a number of girls and women, many of whom had already been bled repeatedly; others had apparently been kept and fed to good health in preparation for slaughter. Bathory's servants were executed for their crimes, but Bathory herself was spared capital punishment by virtue of her nobility. Instead, she was held in solitary confinement in a walled-off room of the castle, where she died three years later in 1614.

Writers on crime have devoted far more attention to the case of Bathory's contemporary, French Baron Gilles de Rais, officer and confidant of Joan of Arc, who was allegedly responsible for murdering scores, or possibly hundreds, of children. R.E.L. Masters and Eduard Lea write:

> For the most part, *and curiously*, she has escaped the attention of English-language authors. Both are eternally infamous less for the formidable numbers of their victims – about which estimates vary – than for the sexual pleasure they derived from the slaughter of their helpless victims.[14] (emphasis added)

Yet it is de Rais who gets the press. Returning to the present century, Charlene Williams and her 'husband',[15] Gerald Gallego, were responsible for the sexual murders of ten people in Oregon, California and Nevada from 1978 to 1980. She pleaded guilty to second-degree murder in Nevada as the basis of a plea-bargain arrangement. Her primary role was to lure victims to Gerald, who wanted them as sex slaves. Eric Van Hoffmann[16] presents information that clearly implicates Charlene in the crimes. For example, bite wounds around the anus and nipples of different victims were from different sets of teeth, presumably Gerald's and Charlene's. It appears that Charlene actively participated both in abduction and sexual violation of victims. While there was no evidence that she killed any of their victims, Charlene testified that she did nothing to stop Gerald from doing so. There are also numerous reports of male and female workers in child daycare centres who sexually violate the children in their care. In 1987, for example, a twenty-three-year-old New Jersey woman, Margaret Michaels, was sentenced to forty-seven years in prison on 115 counts of sexual abuse against pre-school children in the day nursery in which she worked. Clearly, women are not immune from sexual perversions.[17] A number of documented cases, then, involve women operating alone or as accomplices to sexual murders with their male partners. The extent of their involvement varies from awareness of the crimes to active participation.

The sexual nature of crimes such as those committed by the Gallegos tends to render them more reprehensible in the eyes of the media and the public than they would be had there been no sexual assault. Perpetrators like these are often given monikers such as 'monster' or 'sex fiend' to reflect their heightened depravity. Even so, to focus on the sexual component of lust killings, as do Cameron and Fraser, is at the expense of a deeper understanding of the murders themselves. If one considers by analogy a sexual fetish, and focuses on the sexual behaviours involved, the underlying anxiety that is believed to drive the fetish will probably be neglected. Why does the fetishist need the red patent leather high-heeled shoe to reach sexual orgasm? Why do so many (male) serial murderers appear to need a suffering, dying, and/or dead victim to be sexually gratified? This is not to say that the link between sexual gratification and aggression among serial murderers is without meaning, but it may not represent the primary underlying motivation. While the gratification that accompanies sexual violation in a series of murders may be one reason why a killer repeats his or her crimes, it is, none the less, only part of the picture that is serial murder.

The ostensible motive for serial murder is sometimes monetary. While there are cases of 'black widowers',[18] they appear to represent a much smaller proportion of male serial killers than 'black widows' do of female serial killers.

Nevertheless, serial poisoners killing for money have long been a part of the criminal profile of women. Louis Charles Douthwaite[19] cites many examples of serial killing by arsenic poisoning in sixteenth- to eighteenth-century Europe, particularly by women seeking to gain fortune and/or status. Among the most prodigious black widows in American history was Belle Gunness of Indiana, who may have begun her criminal career by killing husbands for insurance, and then changed her mode of operating to advertising in newspapers for suitors with dowries and killing them once she got access to their money. In 1908, the charred remains of her three children were found alongside the headless, burnt corpse of a woman thought at the time to be Gunness. In a search for the missing head, the authorities unearthed the bones of one to two dozen bodies on her property. The handyman, who was found guilty of arson, confessed to disposing of the bodies of some forty men who had been drugged, bludgeoned, and then dismembered by Gunness over five years. She was also linked to the death of her adopted daughter and, possibly, her two husbands. If, indeed, Gunness escaped, as the handyman contended, she may have got away with as much as $100,000 from her victims.

In 1986, forty-four-year-old Stella Nickell of Seattle, Washington, killed her husband using cyanide-laced Extra-Strength Tylenol capsules in a plan to collect on a $176,000 life insurance policy. To divert suspicion from herself she placed poisoned capsules on local store shelves, killing a woman. While two victims does not meet the criterion for serial murder, certainly this was not by design. Margie Velma Barfield of North Carolina confessed to and was convicted of killing her fiancé by putting poison in his beer. She also confessed to killing her mother, her second husband, an employer, and two elderly people for whom she had been hired to care. There remain suspicions that she was also responsible for the death of her first husband, the alcoholic father of her two children, who burned to death while in bed. At the time, the fire was officially attributed to careless smoking. Barfield was apparently addicted to prescription drugs; bills were piling up, and her need for tranquillizers, barbiturates, hypnotics, mood elevators, amphetamines, and narcotic painkillers persisted. Barfield claims that out of panic and desperation she engaged in a series of frauds and forgeries. She forged her mother's signature as collateral for two bank loans, then poisoned her with an insecticide. This was her pattern: committing forgeries, then poisoning the person she had defrauded, presumably to avoid being confronted with her original crimes. Barfield claimed that while she intended to poison her victims, she had not meant them to die. She was, she said, buying time in the hope of getting a job so that she could pay back the money. In 1984, she became the first woman to be executed in the United States in twenty-two years. While in prison awaiting execution, Barfield wrote a book about 'her story',[20] in which she both claimed responsibility for her crimes and attributed them to her addiction.

There have also been instances in which women team up with men in a scheme of serial murder as a means to profit. During the 1940s in the states of New York and Michigan, Martha Beck and Raymond Fernandez, the 'Lonely Hearts Killers', murdered a number of women (and the baby of one of the victims) in a scam whereby Fernandez would promise marriage, secure the fiancée's funds, and then kill her. Beck and Fernandez were convicted of three such cases but were strong suspects in seventeen others.

The history of female serial killers, recent and remote, is littered with examples of women who have killed relatives and/or non-relatives whom they get to know and with whom they secure a position of trust for personal gain. While some appear to have had some measure of conscience about their deeds, others were decidedly more calculating. In 1989, for example, fifty-two-year-old Geraldine Parrish of Baltimore was indicted and jailed for killing four people for insurance money and making three attempts at killing a fifth person. This prompted an investigation into the death of her husband, who had died fifteen days after they were married in 1988, leaving her his social security benefits, his house, and a small inheritance. When police searched Parrish's house they found forty-five policies locked in closets and safes insuring the lives of various people. Fifty-nine-year-old Dorothea Montalvo Puente murdered tenants in California and collected their pension and disability benefits. The nine known victims, residents of her boarding-house, were between fifty-two and eighty years old. Before the series of murders, Puente had spent a decade in jails and prisons for drugging victims, stealing from them, and forging cheques in their names. While she was on parole for drugging and robbing ill and elderly people, she approached a local social worker offering to provide lodging for people on fixed incomes. In 1988, she was convicted of poisoning nine of them.

Other women have profited from murders, but by means other than poisoning. Some have killed as part of a more formal criminal enterprise. One of these was Griselda Blanco, who owned ranches in South America on which cocaine was grown and processed. Blanco also oversaw the concealment of the drugs as they were sewn into brassieres and girdles and put into the heels of women's high-heeled shoes before their transport to the United States. Over ten years Blanco established herself first in New York and then in Florida. Known as 'The Godmother', she paid lovers to assassinate those who betrayed her or threatened her vast cocaine empire. She then had her own hitmen murdered. One of these men was the father of one of her four sons. Rival drug dealers came to know her as 'the Black Widow'. The infamous Bonnie Parker and Clyde Barrow murdered at least thirteen people as a matter of course while travelling about the Midwest and Southwest in the early 1930s, committing a series of armed robberies. Although their killings generally occurred during robbery sprees and many of the victims were police officers, it is perhaps telling that the pistol found in Bonnie's hand when she and Clyde were killed by a police ambush in 1934, allegedly her favourite weapon, bore three notches on the grip.

The means in cases like these are extreme, but the ostensible motive is comprehensible: personal gain. How, then, are we to understand women who kill those entrusted to their care, for no apparent financial gain? So-called 'angels of death' have claimed to kill terminally ill or suffering patients in their charge as a humane gesture. But many cases suggest perversity of purpose, where people in little immediate health risk or discomfort are killed by their care-takers. A remarkable example, discussed in this volume, comes from Austria and involves four nurse's aides (aged twenty-eight to fifty-one) who were convicted of killing twenty patients since 1983 with lethal injections in a Vienna hospital. The women alleged that they were 'mercy killings to end suffering of terminal patients'. Further police investigation revealed that while all the deceased patients were feeble (they were between seventy-five and eighty years of age), not all were terminal. It is alleged that some were deemed 'bothersome' or too demanding.[21] The nurse's aides used overdoses of – for example – insulin or a tranquillizer, or forced infusions of water into lungs. Remarkably, each nurse knew the others were killing patients: in some cases, two acted together to administer lethal injections.

Of all serial murderers, none are held to be so reprehensible as the baby-killers. Nurse Genene Jones was found guilty of the murder of a fifteen-month-old child following lethal injections of the muscle relaxant succinylcholine, which is extremely difficult to trace. Indeed, in earlier criminal cases, forensic medicine identified succinylcholine as the perfect murder weapon. Jones was also convicted of injecting heparin, an anticoagulant, into a four-week-old infant who survived. How many babies

Jones actually killed will probably never be known. It has been estimated by experts from the Center for Disease Control in Georgia, who investigated a series of questionable deaths, that one paediatric intensive care unit alone where Jones had worked may have been the site of as many as fifteen murders by lethal doses of digoxin. Investigators also determined that forty-seven babies died 'suspicious' deaths during Jones's four-year nursing tenure at another facility. At her murder trial the prosecution alleged that the divorced mother of two had sought to become a heroine by causing a life-threatening condition from which she would then try to save the child. This kind of motivation is also seen in the arsonist who sets fires and then proceeds to be the hero who saves everyone. If this was true for Genene Jones, however, it would seem that she construed such self-importance differently. The indications are that rather than attempting to save the babies, her role was to ensure that they died. Possibly she was responding to what she believed were goals of a higher-order, albeit a deluded mission. Serial murderers in care-taking roles have been known to claim that they killed to prevent further or anticipated suffering by the people in their charge.

Among cases apparently devoid of any possible monetary or 'humanitarian' motive are those in which mothers kill their own children. Much infanticide goes unrecognized. In part this is because suffocation, the method used most frequently, is very difficult to distinguish from natural death and perhaps even more difficult to imagine. In the United States, cases often tend to be prosecuted only when they are sufficiently unusual or repeated often enough that they signal foul play. Mary Beth Tinning was convicted in 1987 of smothering her three-month-old daughter. Astoundingly, no one, not even her husband, disputed the explanations that her seven other babies (plus an eighth child she was caring for and planned to adopt) died of natural causes – possibly a genetic condition, or sudden infant death syndrome. Not until the death of the ninth child was it acknowledged that all the deaths but the first, which had definitely resulted from meningitis, were consistent with suffocation. A similar hindsight suggested that Tinning may have suffered from postpartum psychosis, or some other form of serious mental disorder. Certainly, rational motive for a series of killings like this is elusive.

Sometimes history has provided the context in which the female serial killer finds her niche. Irma Grese took up her role as supervisor of Nazi concentration camps for female prisoners and children with a fanatic enthusiasm. She apparently took great pleasure and no conscience in her sadistic and brutal deeds, kicking, whipping, and shooting helpless inmates to death, and was hanged as a war criminal in Germany in 1945. One of her Nazi cohorts, Ilse Koch, was found guilty of the murders of forty-five prisoners (shooting many of them herself 'for sport') and being an accomplice to 135 other concentration camp deaths. The mark of her depravity was evidenced by her fancy for human trophies, which included lampshades she had made from the skins of selected prisoners.

Examples like these illustrate how different female serial murderers can be. Not unlike their male counterparts, female serial murderers are diverse in their backgrounds. Some have been impoverished individuals without status in their community; others come from the privileged classes or the nobility. They are single, married, living in common-law relationships, or divorced. Many are mothers. About a third of the female serial killers in Hickey's study were housewives and a fifth were employed in health-care positions. Fifteen per cent were 'career criminals', deriving their primary source of income from criminal activities. Another 15 per cent were housekeepers, waitresses, and the like. Twenty per cent of the sample were transient or living with relatives, and declared no occupation. There is, therefore, no one profile of the kind of woman who commits serial murder.

Yet for every serial killer, what begins as unthinkable fantasy evolves into action. Serial murderers have been known to recall, in connection with their first killing, the realization that the act was, indeed, do-able: that they *could* do it. With this confidence and increasing experience, subsequent murders evoke less fear of discovery. As they continue to go undetected, both male and female serial killers tend to become increasingly sophisticated in the commission of their crimes. For some, however, it is as if they reach a point where they perceive themselves to be invincible, and they begin to leave incriminating clues at their crime scenes, or make errors of judgement, such as responding to media hype about their case by throwing the police a few 'crumbs', flaunting their 'wins' in a game of one-up-man-ship. This appears to be more of a masculine trait, however; perhaps owing to a greater sense of competitiveness than his female counterpart. It may be her greater need for security (rather than competitiveness) that cautions her against undue risk and allows her to elude detection longer, or sometimes altogether.

Modus operandi: the means to an end

Modus operandi, the method or means employed in accomplishing a task, is different from motive. It is the way in which a person goes about committing a crime: what he/she does and – just as significantly – does not do. In the case of homicide, *modus operandi* is the means by which one person kills another; literally, the means to an end. Beyond its importance to nuts-and-bolts police investigations, *modus operandi* helps to inform us about underlying motive. Elements of rage, disdain, greed, sadism, and the like can be inferred from what the perpetrator does. Are the victims subjected to 'overkill', a degree of violence that exceeds that necessary to kill the victim? Are corpses treated with any degree of respect, or are they humiliated in some way? For example, are the bodies found off the beaten track, fully clothed and perhaps even cleansed, or are they left nude along a well-travelled roadside, with the legs spread apart? Does a period of sadistic torture, psychological or physical, precede death? The emotional underpinnings of the acts of murder are often evidenced through *modus operandi* and, as such, provide clues about motive.

Generally, the victims of women are conned or overtaken while naturally in – or rendered into – a vulnerable state. They are killed by various means, including poisoning, smothering, stabbing and shooting. We should not be surprised that women tend not to kill by means that require overpowering physical force unless the physical strength of their victims – as children, or frail and elderly – makes this possible. A killer chooses his or her method according to what it takes to do the job and how familiar (and confident) he or she is with those means. It is unusual for a murderer to choose means that are outside her realm of life experience. Most female serial killers we know about, as the 'black widow' and 'angel of death' motifs indicate, killed people by poisoning or asphyxiating them: both means which are likely to be closer to their life experience than, say, shooting. They do not usually use a weapon like a gun or knife in confrontation.

Paradoxically, the fact that male *modi operandi* are more likely to involve sexual activity is an illustration of the *similarity* of basic motive for male and female serial killers, all of whom, regardless of their gender, seek a very specific end. Both will seek this through what we can call empowerment.

Men are traditionally expected to seek domination, particularly in sexual relations. Psychological and cultural evidence suggests that men experience feelings of power through sex, and since serial murder is essentially about power, we would expect those murders committed by men to be sexually charged. Men are expected to direct their anger at its source. In cases of sexual murder, perhaps the clearest example of this, the source of anger is the object that has power over him, the object he needs. He may fear the power of the need he has for the sexual object, feeling that it threatens his sense of control. Taken to its extreme, this fear, coupled with an underlying feeling of entitlement, may result in a need to exert absolute life-and-death control over the object of his desires. Women do not generally experience sex in the same way. They are not socialized to experience power directly through the sex act,[22] and may even feel diminished by the way some men view them as sex objects. It is not surprising, then, that female serial killers do not tend to sexualize their killings.

Serial murderers first present themselves to us via their *modus operandi*. So struck are we by the terrifying image of the intensive-care nurse overdosing her infant patients, or the greed of the landlady who subjects her ageing tenants to the agonizing effects of poison in a scheme to collect their social security money, that typologies have been created based upon *modus operandi*. In terms of gender, differences manifest themselves through such aspects as physical strength, the male serial murderer being generally more able and more inclined to use physical force in the commission of his murders and his means more visceral (e.g. strangulation rather than suffocation).

Murderous comfort zones

We have yet to see a significant increase in the proportion of women who kill, but we are witnessing changes in the methods women use in killing. Perhaps the most useful concept to understand these changes is that of 'comfort zones', a term used by the law enforcement community. Generally speaking, people choose to behave in ways that do not arouse discomfort. While comfort zones are often physical places, they also include psychological environments that do not evoke undue anxiety. From our real and imagined experience we develop a repertoire of behaviour. We learn that there are a number of ways to deal with a situation to get what we want and to act in ways that generate the least unease. Criminals tend to behave in ways that at once maximize their sense of mastery and minimize any anxiety. They experience confidence and a sense of security when they operate in particular ways, under known conditions. This familiar arena or comfort zone may in large part account for the differences in *modus operandi* between men and women. Like men, women choose means that are accessible to them in terms of their familiarity and availability. It is more likely, for example, that a man will be exposed to and (in the USA at least) socialized in the use of weaponry during his life than it is for a woman; therefore a man will use a gun when he commits a crime, while a woman, who experiences guns as more foreign, is less likely to do so. None the less, in the United States, we are beginning to see cases of women who, like Aileen Wuornos, take up arms and commit serial or mass murder.

In 1988 Laurie Wasserman Dann went on a nine-hour rampage in an affluent Chicago suburb. Like her (mass murderer) male counterparts, Dann, who had a history of making harassing telephone calls, had recently learned that her employer planned to leave the state, which would have left her jobless. She began by setting fire to the house where she worked as a babysitter. From there she went on to an elementary school where she shot six children, killing one and critically wounding five others. Leaving the school, she went to a nearby house, wounded a twenty-year-old man there and then barricaded herself inside before shooting herself. The car she had driven was found; it contained incendiary devices and ammunition. Just before the rampage, Dann had posted and delivered packages of food and juice poisoned with arsenic to as many as two dozen friends and acquaintances. She is also suspected in the ice-pick stabbing of her former husband two years earlier. In a similar case, thirty-year-old Elizabeth Teague, a Vermont industrial engineer, shot her male supervisor in the head and wounded three co-workers whom she encountered in the hallway. Before she left, she set a fire with a home-made explosive.

As rather 'typical' examples of mass murder, these two women perceived their lives as a progressive series of failures, to a final point beyond which they could not tolerate any additional demands, be they socially or self-imposed. Unsurprisingly, female mass murderers use the same means to kill their victims as male mass murderers, largely because of the neccessity of using a weapon capable of killing a number of people at once. However, cases of female mass murderers appear to be so rare that, until very recently, they were virtually unheard of.

Another point of departure between male and female serial murderers is that women are more apt to kill in or close to their home or workplace, presumably where they feel most secure. Male serial killers often travel hundreds, or even thousands of miles during the course of their crimes. The greater geographic mobility of male serial murderers is consistent with the idea of broader zones of comfort for men in general. The Wuornos case, like that of Dann and Teague, among others, is evidence of a broadening of women's comfort zones, paralleling women's increasing integration into society. We may find that, increasingly, female serial murderers will kill in ways that have historically been the province of the male.

From prey to predator

It is important to distinguish killings that are essentially crimes of opportunity from those in which the murderer deliberates on and carefully executes his or her plan. Opportunists take advantage of situations in which they happen to find themselves. Their crimes lack premeditation. Predatory criminals operate according to a preconceived cognitive map that will guide them to their prey; they purposely seek out those they can violate in the service of some rational or irrational need. Perhaps the key distinction, though, is that the opportunist is reactive, responding to a particular situation with a criminal act. By contrast, while the predator may capitalize on any opportunity that presents itself, he or she will also, with single-minded determination, create opportunities.

Predation has been more characteristic of male criminals – although, as a long history of 'black widows' attests, it is by no means unheard of among women. As she moves further out into the world, through work or travel or social mobility, today's woman will acquire a broader base of competence and confidence. Her comfort zones of psychological tolerance and physical location expand. She moves from reactive object to proactive agent. Increasingly, over time, the prey becomes predator.

The vulnerablity of victims of female serial killers tends to be inherent in their condition (as children, elderly or ill) or circumstance (the offender is in a position of trust, or manipulates this). Moreover, the female killer has the advantage of not being considered capable of or inclined to murder. For the multiple killer, the chosen victims will be those who can serve a vehicle for the experience the killer is seeking. At the same time, she must be able to overtake the victim by virtue of her greater size, strength, or cunning. In most cases, the female serial murderer kills by her wits.

Sociologist Gwynn Nettler argues that 'culture and opportunity expand or contract the exercise of biological differentials. This is particularly apparent with changes in the social roles of women'.[23] Changing social factors affect women in ways that result in changes in their behaviour. One of these – and one where we may see further developments – is in the *modus operandi* of the female serial killer. Largely owing to the feminist movement, increased social awareness of women's growing sense of entitlement has begun to legitimize the outward expression of tensions that arise out of unmet needs. For the female killer, this can mean that the opportunist may become a predator. For Aileen Wuornos, early experience of herself as powerless, particularly at the hands of men, may have produced an underlying vulnerability, coupled with anger, on which a growing sense of entitlement fed. Then as an adult prostitute, possibly feeling subjugated by her male clients, she may have felt disdain for those who (ab)used her. The targets of this hatred may be specific men who press to go beyond a line she found unacceptable (e.g. demanding a sexual service she does not wish to provide), or the rage may become generalized to all men who, in her mind, want to (ab)use her and therefore deserve to be punished. Some media accounts suggest that because of her lesbian relationship with Tyria Moore and her choice of male victims, Wuornos was a man-hater. While man-hating, or 'misandropy' as I call it, *might* describe Wuornos, more needs to be learned about her, particularly how she experienced herself with others both male and female, before her killings could simply be attributed to man-hating.

It is one thing to kill once, in the heat of passion or in response to a threat to life. It is another to kill repeatedly. Or is it? What frees us to cross the line to kill?

The very notion of a line to be crossed, on the other side of which we can kill, presupposes a moral prohibition against killing that controls otherwise murderous impulses but can be overriden in extreme circumstances. We feel entitled to kill when our lives are threatened, and even repeated killings can be understood as acts of self-preservation. If a person experiences particular types of people or circumstances as exceptionally threatening or enraging, he or she may feel fear or rage that can be dispatched only by the killing or deaths of people to whom it is instrumentally or symbolically linked. A single murder will not protect the perpetrator from others who pose a similar threat. This is how the serial murderer comes into being, and how we can begin to understand serial murder and what – if any – differences there are between male and female serial killers.

Cameron and Frazer understand murder as an act that liberates the murderer from social constraints. It is this that perhaps most engages the public imagination. How is it that people can be so lacking in moral faculty that they are not bound by the most basic tenet of human decency? The public is at once fearful of and fascinated by the individual who lives by his or her own rules. Yet, as Cameron and Frazer argue, sexual murder is merely an extension of 'normal' male behaviour. Male desires are largely socially constructed in terms that depict women as objects for their sexual pleasure, and in this context masculine sexuality demands conquest and penetration. As the ultimate affirmation of his masculine identity, a man may kill the object of his sexual desires. The crucial issue here is not masculinity *per se*, but identity.

All people need a sense of self, of being, although we may not always be conscious of it. For serial murderers, whose sense of self is fragile or diffuse, killing becomes a way of actively experiencing a vital sense of self – their very being, in the face of some perceived threat to their existence. The act of killing gives their life meaning. Almost incidentally, largely because the killer feels empowered by it, he or she can come to enjoy killing and develop a 'taste' for it. The notion that Janice Buttram, for example, would almost certainly have killed again seems relevant here. Others thrive on the hunt, experiencing the actual act of killing as anticlimactic. One key to understanding a woman who kills repeatedly, especially when the crimes seem unrelated to practical considerations such as monetary gain, may be the recognition that by killing, she experiences herself as someone who matters, as the agent of some substantial happening and, by inference, as powerful. Feminism may have provided some women with justifications for taking a more active role (against the world) than their traditional reactive posture (against themselves) had previously allowed.

While *modus operandi* reflects the idiosyncratic ways in which the offender commits her crimes, motive speaks to specific needs shared by those who kill – what the murders mean to the killer. Motives for killing can have a primarily emotive current – fear, rage, jealousy, hatred, revenge – or a rational, instrumental basis, such as monetary gain.

Traditional theories of human development largely build upon stages of the individual's separation from the mother, or what psychoanalysts call individuation. We mature towards autonomy through a process of becoming separate from others. For females, however, relationships with others seem to be a continuing and central organizing principle in their self-development, to the point where they may define themselves or be defined in those terms – as wife or mother, for example. Individual growth is a process of interaction at the expense of separation, and a woman may develop a unique sense of herself as the product of interaction with others: indeed, it may be only through her connection with significant others that she experiences a sense of being.

Gender differences in *modus operandi* turn on differences in the social construction of masculinity and femininity, on individual psychological make-up, as well as on physical constraints. Women, for example, are more prone to turning their rage inward, becoming depressed or self-destructive – victims rather than victimizers. Men are generally encouraged and rewarded for expressing their anger outwardly, and will do so to the extent to which they feel entitled.

If certain preconditions are in place, the individual feels powerless and either lacks a sense of self or may develop a distorted self. If that fragile self is threatened, the individual may become fearful. To protect himself, a man will tend to try to control the threat. Paradoxically, in order to defeat his powerlessness he must control the source of power that threatens his own. When rage is coupled with powerlessness, and the individual feels entitled to express this state as intolerable and unacceptable, then he or she must have access to the means of disposing of the source of these feelings. For each individual, there are temperamental differences – to some degree biologically based – as well as differences that result from social conditioning, that help to determine how this release will occur. In the past, gender has exerted its main effect as an additional level of restraint on women's behaviour.

Conclusion

Serial and mass murder is but one colour in a disturbing portrait of society. We respond by filtering out the blinding spectrum of violence before us. Our collective sense of security is particularly threatened by the notion of female serial murderers. In the matter of women who kill, we have been fatally complacent. We seem to need to look at the women who are agents of multiple murder as aberrations rather than as symptoms of a phenomenon. I believe that many homicide cases remain unsolved, without viable suspects, because the offender was falsely assumed to be male. Current statistics indicate that the prevalence of female serial murder – as a phenomenon in its own right and as a phenomenon relative to male serial murder – is exceedingly small. But the Wuornos case should give us pause to reflect on our state of knowledge: it may be that women are becoming increasingly comfortable in those realms of human experience that have been traditional male preserves. It is probable that the number of female serial killers will increase as more law enforcement agents consider women as viable suspects.

As women become more a part of the workings of society, we will, I expect, increasingly observe predatory kinds of serial murders perpetrated by women. By virtue of her femaleness, a woman lacks exposure to many of the means that are more readily accessible to males. But feminism has arguably given women a greater sense of entitlement, facilitating the outward expression of emotion, and in practical terms, women's comfort zones have expanded. They are now more likely than ever to come into contact with a wider array of means to gratify their needs in general (and express their fears and rage in particular). In this way, feminism is serving a catalytic role in the evolution of the female serial killer, although the basis for the behaviour remains the same – a need for a sense of being and vitality that is experienced through empowerment. In certain cases her anger and need for empowerment will be directed at the power-brokers, those she has experienced as victimizing her. More specific than misanthropy, this emerging female is 'misandropic', decidedly hateful of men. She will seek to punish them for being men, the symbol of her oppressed sense of self. The victim becomes the victimizer. Murder is, in its most elemental aspect, an act of self-preservation. I believe that how it is committed is largely a function of gender; why it is committed is a function of the human condition.

In 1991 Jeffrey Lionel Dahmer went on trial for killing seventeen young men in Milwaukee, Wisconsin. Just as the seventeenth-century Bathory case has received little public attention, Dahmer's female contemporary, Aileen Carol Wuornos, tried for the murders of seven men in two states, it was much less notorious. Certainly Wuornos's more masculine style – using guns and travelling around – distinguishes her among her female serial murderer peers. Yet it was the Dahmer case which got the most 'air' time. Wuornos was presented in the press as a hitchhiking prostitute, and the discourse surrounding her in large part followed from this image. The media quote law enforcement sources which contend that Wuornos is 'America's first female serial killer'. While this is patently false, unless one uses a definition of a female serial killer as a female who kills a number of people over time using 'male' methods of killing, it highlights our reluctance to view women as murderous agents. We expect and tolerate women killing by methods that women typically use, and for the reasons that women typically kill: in self-defence for example.[24] We seem to have little to say about predatory violence by women. In the end, what appears outwardly to be offensive behaviour may essentially be defensive.

Many of the judicial proceedings around the Wuornos case, for the prosecution and defence, referred to her prostitution, although she had never been arrested for a prostitution offence. Is it that we need to see her as a prostitute and not a woman – the Madonna or whore dichotomy – in order to give meaning to what otherwise might appear as a series of murders committed by a man? What is it that resists this image? Since we do not expect society's care-takers to engage in predatory acts of violence, when they do our collective sense of order and security in the world is threatened. Whatever the rationale, the cultural construction of females as passive has impeded our understanding of serial murder by both men and women.

Aileen Carol Wuornos had sought to live, as she would say, 'to the max'. A product of her limited opportunities, her vision of the ultimate appears to have been a shallow one: her life a day-by-day contract, getting the money to keep herself – and, for a time, her lover – in a lifestyle they both enjoyed: being able to afford good meals and nights in bars, taking little stock of the future. At some point, however, prospects of the future would be increasingly difficult to ignore. She was drinking heavily and her body was ageing; both would work against her in her trade, and possibly have a negative effect on her *quid quo pro* means of doing business. On some level, it may also have served to diminish her sense of security as a prostitute, allegedly the only thing she knew how to do.

Wuornos confessed to killing six men, in addition to

Richard Mallory, over a thirteen-month period. All were white men, forty-one to sixty years of age, who had picked her up and, according to Wuornos, at some point negotiated to have sex for money with her. All were shot several times with a .22-calibre handgun. Of the bodies recovered, some were nude and robbed of possessions. Local police described her as 'a killer who robs – not a robber who kills', but Wuornos rejects the depiction, asserting self-defence in all cases. Yet as one corrections officer assigned to observe her noted, Wuornos, by her own account, distinguished 'a normal day', when she would have sex for money with up to a dozen men, usually at a roadside or behind a building, from 'a killing day', when the customer wanted to go deep into the woods, presumably with intent to harm her.[24]

A jury of five men and seven women took less than two hours to deliberate their guilty verdict in the Mallory case. Did they think of her as a victim of life? Did they, in their deliberations, view her as the opportunist she undoubtedly was? Finally, did they see her as a predator? The death penalty they imposed upon her for premeditated murder suggests that they did.

Notes

Introduction: Helen Birch

1. Twenty-six of the fifty-one cases in which women were convicted of homicide in 1989, for example, were 'domestic homicides': 'Homicides Committed by Women', a breakdown of the homicide statistics by gender compiled for the author by the Home Office.
2. The *Sun*, 30 July 1991.
3. In November 1992 the Northern Ireland Appeal Court increased Christie's sentence by four years on the grounds that she had 'considerable mental responsibility' for the killing.
4. Frances Heidensohn, *Women and Crime* (London: Macmillan, 1985).

An eye for an eye: Nicole Ward Jouve

1. Simone de Beauvoir, *La Force de l'âge* (Paris: Gallimard, 1960), pp. 136–7: my translation. All further translations in this chapter are mine.
2. 'Motifs du Crime paranoïaque', *Le Minotaure* no. 3/4, 1933.
3. Jérôme et Jean Tharaud, *Paris-Soir*, 30 September 1933.
4. *Le Surréalisme au service de la révolution* no. 6, 1933, p. 28.
5. *Le Mur* (Paris: Gallimard, 1947).
6. Paris, Editions Lefrançois, 1933.
7. I shall be examining the whole case in greater detail in a forthcoming book.
8. J.-P. Sartre, *Saint Genet, comédien et martyr* (Paris: Gallimard, 1952), pp. 361–2.
9. J. Genet, *Les Bonnes* and 'Comment jouer les bonnes', *Oeuvres complètes*, vol. IV (Paris: Gallimard, 1968), p. 269.
10. Isak Dinesen, *Out of Africa*, (New York: Vintage, 1985), p. 271.

If looks could kill: Helen Birch

1. Allison Morris and Ania Wilczynski, 'Rocking the Cradle: Mothers Who Kill Their Children' (see, p.198).
2. Between 1975 and 1980, Peter Sutcliffe sexually assaulted and murdered thirteen women. He was sentenced to life

imprisonment in 1981 with a recommendation that he serve a minimum of thirty years. In 1983, Dennis Nilsen confessed to the murders of fifteen men and the attempted murder of seven others. He was found guilty of six murders and two attempted murders. He too was sentenced to life imprisonment.

3. Jonathan Goodman, *The Moors Murders: The Trial of Myra Hindley and Ian Brady* (London: David Charles, 1973). Many accounts of these events have been the subject of speculation and conjecture; as such they have become coloured and distorted. This, an edited transcript of the trial, is the most accurate account of evidence given. All subsequent references to the trial are taken from Goodman's book.

4. Elizabeth Wilson, *Only Halfway to Paradise: Women in Postwar Britain 1945–1968* (London: Tavistock, 1980).

5. ibid., p.3.

6. Jeffrey Weeks, *Sex, Politics and Society* (London: Longman, 1981).

7. She said, for example, that she had been in the kitchen when Evans was being killed; that she knew nothing of the killing of John Kilbride; and that although she was present while Brady took photographs of Lesley Ann Downey, the girl had left the house alive.

8. Ann Barr Snitow, 'Mass Market Romance: Pornography for Women is Different', in *Desire: The Politics of Sexuality* (London: Virago, 1984). Many other feminists have analysed the power of romantic fantasy as 'written out' in popular fiction. See Jean Radford (ed.), *The Progress of Romance* (London: Routledge & Kegan Paul, 1986); Susannah Radstone (ed.), *Sweet Dreams: Sexuality, Gender and Popular Fiction* (London: Lawrence & Wishart, 1988).

9. Keith Soothill and Sylvia Walby, *Sex Crime in the News* (Oxford: Polity, 1991).

10. Pamela Hansford Johnson, *On Iniquity* (London: Macmillan, 1967).

11. *Guardian*, 6 January 1973.

12. The Home Office can initiate parole proceedings after seven years, but this does not imply that the Home Secretary will authorize a prisoner's release. At this time, Myra Hindley had served six years and five months. A local committee reviews each case and makes its recommendations to the Parole Board, which is chaired by a High Court judge. The Home Secretary has the right of veto.

13. *Guardian* leader, 16 September 1972.

14. Following the controversy over publication of his book, Peter Topping stated that he 'may' donate some of the proceeds of his book to charity.

15. *The Times* published a full transcript in April 1966; the *Daily Mirror*, citing its working-class readership as a reason, declined to do so. See Tony Geraghty, *Guardian*, 17 April 1966.

16. Jonathan Dollimore, 'The Challenge of Sexuality' in Alan Sinfield (ed.), *Society and Literature 1945–1970* (London: Methuen, 1983), p. 54. See also Elizabeth Wilson, *Only Halfway to Paradise*, p. 136.

17. Pamela Hansford Johnson, *On Iniquity*, p. 33.

18. ibid., p. 136.

19. See David Marchbanks, *The Moors Murders* (London: Leslie Frewin, 1966); Emlyn Williams, *Beyond Belief* (London: Hamish Hamilton, 1967).

20. *Daily Telegraph*, 2 April 1974.

21. Jean Ritchie, *Myra Hindley: Inside the Mind of a Murderess* (London: Angus & Robertson, 1988).

22. In a two-part article in *The Sunday Times* in April 1982, for example, Linda Melvern and Peter Gilman talk of 'her extraordinary ability to engage the emotions of those who encounter her and win them to her point of view . . . she displays the personality that would win the approval of those she met . . . [she] repeatedly ensnared and manipulated her partner's [*sic*] emotions, inducing them to do her will'.

23. Olga Lengyel, *Five Chimneys* (London: Panther, 1959).

24. See Robert Hancock, *Ruth Ellis: The Last Woman to be Hanged* (London: Weidenfeld & Nicolson, 1963). Mike Newell's 1985 film *Dance with a Stranger* presents a more sympathetic view of Ellis.

25. Hansford Johnson, p. 23.

26. Richard Dyer, 'Resistance through Charisma: Rita Hayworth and *Gilda*', in E. Ann Kaplan (ed.), *Women in Film Noir* (London: British Film Institute, 1980).

27. Julia Kristeva, *Powers of Horror* (New York: Columbia University Press, 1982). See also Elizabeth Gross, 'The Body of Signification', in John Fletcher and Andrew Benjamin (eds), *Abjection, Melancholia and Love: The Work of Julia Kristeva* (London: Routledge, 1990).

28. Ann West, *For the Love of Lesley* (London: W.H. Allen, 1989).

29. Interview with Timms by the author, June 1992.

30. Fred Harrison, *Brady and Hindley: Genesis of the Moors Murders* (London: Ashgrove Press, 1986).

31. Interview with Timms by the author.

32. In those days, prisoners were allowed to write only to close friends and family unless they had permission from the Home Office.

33. *Sun*, 26 October 1989.

34. Home Office Prison Statistics 1990 show that of 2,795 life

prisoners, only 118 had served more than twenty years, and
14 more than thirty. These figures do not specify how many of
these prisoners are held in psychiatric hospitals.
35. *Guardian*, 2 January 1989.

The trials of motherhood: Briar Wood

1. A. Delbridge (ed.), *The Penguin Tasman Dictionary* (New South Wales: Penguin, 1986).
2. Ken Crispin, *The Crown Versus Chamberlain 1980–1987* (Sutherland: Albatross, 1987), p. 168.
3. John Bryson, *Evil Angels* (Victoria: Viking, 1985), p. 432.
4. For a discussion of the case that focuses closely on the significance of the Chamberlains' religious beliefs in an Australian context, see Stuart Piggin's paper 'Witchhunting in the Secular Society', which was read to the British Australian Studies Association Biennial Conference, June 1988.
5. Jennifer Craik, 'The Azaria Chamberlain Case and Questions of Infanticide', *Australian Journal of Cultural Studies* vol. 4, no.2, 1987, p. 125.
6. Julia Kristeva, 'Motherhood According to Giovanni Bellini', in Leon Roudiez (ed.), *Desire in Language: A Semiotic Approach to Literature and Art* (Oxford, 1980), p. 237.
7. Mary Jacobus, '*Dora* and the Pregnant Madonna', in *Reading Woman: Essays in Feminist Criticism* (London: 1986), p. 147.
8. Sneja Gunew discusses 'The Lacanian Other (Phallus/God)' as 'the site of truth and the fantasy of attainable satisfaction' in 'Home and Away: Nostalgia in Australian (Migrant) Writing', in Paul Foss (ed.), *Islands in the Stream* (New South Wales: Pluto Press, 1988), p. 218.
9. Jacqueline Rose, 'Introduction – I', in Juliet Mitchell and Jacqueline Rose (eds), *Feminine Sexuality: Jacques Lacan and the Ecole Freudienne* (London: 1982), p. 50.
10. Publicity on *A Cry in the Dark* from Cannon Entertainment Inc., 640 San Vicente Boulevard, Los Angeles, California 90048.
11. For an involved discussion of motherhood and abjection, see Julia Kristeva, *Powers of Horror: An Essay on Abjection*, transl. Leon Roudiez (New York: 1982).
12. Crispin, *The Crown Versus Chamberlain*, p. 174.
13. The idea of the 'limp' dingo can be linked to Freudian Oedipal metaphors in which Oedipus' 'limp' is also a signifier of castration.
14. Sneja Gunew 'Home and Away', p. 40.
15. Meaghan Morris, 'Panorama: The Live, the Dead and the Living', in Foss (ed.), *Islands in the Stream*, pp. 161, 162.

16. ibid., p. 40.
17. ibid, p. 40.
18. Gunew moves carefully between gendered definitions of various psychoanalytic categories such as the Lacanian Imaginary and Kristeva's discussions of the pre-Symbolic. There is no simple equating of maternity and paternity with one country rather than another in nationalistic terms because fantasies of national identity involve shifting terms and definitions.
19. Crispin, *The Crown Versus Chamberlain*, p. 11.
20. Craik, 'The Azaria Chamberlain Case', p. 138.
21. Crispin, *The Crown Versus Chamberlain*, p. 11.
22. Morris, 'Panorama', p. 165.
23. ibid., p. 165.
24. Crispin, *The Crown Versus Chamberlain*, p. 310.
25. Lindy Chamberlain, *Through My Eyes* (London: Heinemann, 1990), p. 181.
26. ibid. One way in which Lindy Chamberlain's dissatisfaction with the social and psychic construction of gendered roles emerges is in her articulated desire to erase the paternal function. In the autobiography she describes the establishment of a fantasy between mother and sons in which Azaria was Reagan's baby as Reagan had been Aidan's.
27. Morris, 'Panorama', p. 169.
28. Gunew, 'Home and Away', p. 38.
29. ibid., p. 39.
30. Crispin, *The Crown Versus Chamberlain*, p. 242.
31. René Girard, *Violence and the Sacred* (Baltimore, MD: Johns Hopkins University Press, 1972).
32. ibid., p. 12. Girard maintained that women are not usually chosen as sacrificial victims because they have links with two kinship groups – their husband's and their own. The risk of further violence erupting in order to secure revenge if a woman is sacrificed is therefore too powerful. However, women might often have been 'outsiders' in the group, lack strong family ties for various reasons, or, of course, be unmarried.
33. See Sarah Koffmann, *The Enigma of Woman: Woman in Freud's Writings*, transl. Catherine Porter (Ithaca, NY: Cornell University Press, 1985), pp. 59–65.
34. Gunew, 'Home and Away', p. 38.
35. Robyn Davidson, 'Rock of Ages', *Elle*, November, 1989.
36. See Jean-François Lyotard, *The Postmodern Condition: A Report on Knowledge*, transl. Geoff Bennington and Brian Masumi (Manchester; Manchester University Press, 1986) p. xxiv.
37. Davidson, 'Rock of Ages', p. 88.

38. Crispin, *The Crown Versus Chamberlain*, p. 100.
39. ibid. p. 16.
40. Girard, *Violence and the Sacred*, p. 6.
41. ibid. p. 49.
42. Crispin, *The Crown Versus Chamberlain*, p. 217.
43. Girard, *Violence and the Sacred*, p. 35.

References
Bryson, John, *Evil Angels* (Victoria: Viking Press, 1985)
Chamberlain, Lindy, *Through My Eyes* (London: Heinemann, 1990)
Craik, Jennifer, 'The Azaria Chamberlain Case and Questions of Infanticide', *Australian Journal of Cultural Studies* 4 (2) (1987)
Crispin, Ken, *The Crown Versus Chamberlain 1980–1987* (Sutherland: Albatross, 1987)
Girard, René, *Violence and the Sacred* (Baltimore, MD: Johns Hopkins University Press, 1972)
Gunew, Sneja, 'Home and Away: Nostalgia in Australian (Migrant) Writing', in Paul Foss (ed.) *Islands in the Stream*, (New South Wales: Pluto Press, 1988).
Johnson, Dianne, 'From Fairy to Witch: Imagery and Myth in the Azaria Case', *Australian Journal of Cultural Studies* 2 (2) (1984)
Lyotard, Jean-François, *The Postmodern Condition: A Report on Knowledge*, transl. Geoff Bennington and Brian Massumi (Manchester: Manchester University Press, 1986)
Morris, Meaghan, 'Panorama: The Live, The Dead and the Living', in Paul Foss (ed.), *Islands in the Stream* (New South Wales: Pluto Press, 1988)
Piggin, Stuart, 'Witchhunting in the Secular Society: Christianity's Australian Future'. Paper read to the British Australian Studies Biennial Conference, 'Australia Towards 2000', Lincoln Cathedral, June 1988
Reynolds, Paul, 'The Azaria Chamberlain Case: Reflections on Australian Identity'. Working Paper for the Sir Robert Menzies Centre For Australian Studies, Institute of Commonwealth Studies, University of London, 1989

Biting the hand that breeds: Deb Verhoeven

1. Luce Irigaray, *Speculum of the Other Woman* (New York: Cornell University Press, 1986), p. 126.
2. *Courier Mail*, 22 January 1991, p. 5.
3. Christopher Edwards, 'Accused "under vampire's spell",' *Sunday Age*, 10 February 1991, p. 5.
4. 'Teller' because it was this 'misplaced' card that revealed Wigginton's identity to the police.

5. *Murder Casebook: The 'Vampire' Killers* (Wiltshire: Marshall Cavendish), vol.6, no.3, 1991, p. 2957. Although this is a British publication, it is distributed throughout Australia and relies heavily on local journalism for its copy.
6. Jason Gagliardi, 'How Baldock met death', *The Courier Mail*, 16 February 1991, p.2.
7. These allegations of incest have been supported by close relatives and psychiatrists, but were never proven in court before George Wigginton's death.
8. 'Cruel childhood turns bright bubbly girl into evil killer', *Sunday Herald*, 17 February 1991, p.3.
9. Guy Kerr, 'Cradle of a demon: Hate-filled home bred a vampire', *Sunday Mail*, 17 February 1991, p.5.
10. ibid.
11. Stephen Lamble, 'Killer's mum tells: My Tracey wouldn't drink human blood', *Sunday Mail*, 17 February 1991, p.4; 'Four faces of Tracey', *Sunday Sun*, 17 February 1991, p.5.
12. 'Killer was a hurt child', *Sunday Sun*, 17 February 1991, p.4.
13. Peter Hansen, 'Vampire killer lost love child', *Sunday Mail*, 10 February 1991, p.3.
14. Bjelke-Petersen was Premier of Queensland from 1968 until December 1987. Despite his resignation the conservative National Party Government maintained power until the end of 1989 when it collapsed under the weight of legal investigations of massive corruption and misgovernment. A centre-left Labour Party which took power at this time continued to charge former ministers and government officials with legal offences resulting from the enquiries and some of these members are now serving prison sentences.
15. Psychoanalytic discourses on hysteria themselves have an archaeological relationship to the question of blood. The word is derived from the Greek for 'uterus', and its later usage in medical discourses retains the sense that women are at the mercy of their reproductive organs – literally driven by their biological proximity to blood or bleeding.
16. 'Killer was a hurt child', p.4.
17. Don Petersen and Jason Gagliardi, 'Lust for blood', *Courier Mail Weekend*, 16 February 1991, p.1.
18. Figures supplied by the Australian Institute of Criminology. Statistics accounting for the sex of offenders in murders involving complete strangers were not available, but according to the Institute's Executive Research Officer, Heather Strang, the number of women would be negligible, if not nil.
19. *Murder Casebook*, p.2968.
20. 'Frenzy of a deadly feed: Murderer was bride of the devil', *Herald Sun*, 16 February 1991, p.2.

21. *Murder Casebook*, p.2962.
22. ibid., pp. 2964–5.
23. Alan Baxter and a Brisbane correspondent, 'She planned her capture: Doc', *Weekend Truth*, 23 February 1991, p.9.
24. 'Frenzy of a deadly feed', p.2.
25. Stewart MacArthur, 'Killer was "devil's wife with power to control minds",' *The Australian*, 5 February 1991, p.5.
26. 'Jail for Vampire Trial Pair', *Herald Sun*, 16 February 1991, p.9.
27. 'Trial Woman Kill Target', *Herald Sun*, 13 February 1991, p.27.
28. 'Joke turned into nightmare – lawyer', *Herald Sun*, 12 February 1991, p.1.
29. 'Vampire murderer feared sun and mirrors, court told', *Courier Mail*, 7 February 1991, p.3.
30. Ben Robertson, 'Woman who plotted a blood-lust killing'. *Sunday Sun*, 3 February 1991, p.17.
31. 'My daughter, the vampire', *Sunday Herald*, 17 February 1991, p.1.
32. *Murder Casebook*, p.2960.
33. Alan Baxter and a Brisbane correspondent, 'Vampire's Sick Sex Secret', *Weekend Truth*, 23 February 1991, p.8.
34. *Murder Casebook*, p.2958.
35. Don Petersen and Jason Gagliardi, 'Lust for blood', p.1.
36. *Murder Casebook*, pp.2966–7.
37. ibid., p.2957.
38. 'Vampire murderer feared sun and mirrors, court told', p.3.
39. Petersen and Gagliardi, 'Lust for blood', p.1.
40. 'Vampire killer had Hitler-like influence, court told', *Courier Mail*, 13 February 1991, p.3.
41. Peter Hansen, 'Vampire killer lost love child', *Sunday Mail*, 10 February 1991, p.3.
42. Baxter and a Brisbane correspondent, 'Vampire's Sick Sex Secret', p.8.
43. Petersen and Gagliardi, 'Lust for blood', p.1.
44. 'Four faces of Tracey', *Sunday Sun*, 17 February 1991, p.5.
45. *Murder Casebook*, p.2957.
46. Petersen and Gagliardi, 'Lust for blood', p.1.
47. 'Vampire killer had Hitler-like influence, court told', p.3.
48. Gagliardi, 'How Baldock met death', p.2.
49. ibid.
50. ibid.
51. Mary Anne Doane has developed this line of thought in relation to the representations of gender in Hollywood films of the 1940s in 'The Clinical Eye: Medical Discourses in the "Woman's Film" of the 1940s', in Susan Rubin Suleiman (ed.), *The Female Body in Western Culture* (London: Harvard University Press, 1986), pp.152–74.

52. Petersen and Gagliardi, 'Lust for blood', p.1.
53. 'Vampire murderer feared sun and mirrors, court told', p.3.
54. 'Lover drank blood', *Herald Sun*, 7 February 1991, p.19.
55. Guy Kerr, 'Cradle of a demon', *Sunday Mail*, 17 February 1991, p.5.
56. Petersen and Gagliardi, 'Lust for blood', p.1.
57. 'Four faces of Tracey', p.5.
58. 'She planned her capture: Doc', *Weekend Truth*, 23 February 1991, pp.8–9.
59. 'High priestess to Satan', *New Idea*, 18 May 1991, p.29.
60. Petersen and Gagliardi, 'Lust for blood', p.1.
61. *Courier Mail*, 28 January 1991, p.1.
62. 'The murder no one could believe', *Sunday Age*, 10 February 1991, p.5.
63. Stephen Lamble, 'Killer's mum tells: My Tracey wouldn't drink human blood', p.4.

References

Dyer, R., 'Children of the Night: Vampirism as Homosexuality, Homosexuality as Vampirism', in S. Radstone (ed.), *Sweet Dreams: Sexuality, Gender and Popular Fiction* (London: Lawrence & Wishart, 1988): pp.47–72

Faith, K., 'Media Myths and Masculinisation: Images of Women in Prison', in E. Adelberg and C. Currie (eds), *Too Few to Count: Canadian Women in Conflict With the Law* (Press Gang, 1987): pp.181–219

Frayling, C., 'Haemosexuality', in *Vampyres: Lord Byron to Count Dracula* (London: Faber & Faber, 1991): pp.385–422

Jones, E., 'On the Nightmare of Bloodsucking', in R. Huss and T.J. Ross (eds), *Focus on the Horror Film* (Prentice Hall, 1972): pp.57–63

Silver, A. and Ursini, J., *The Vampire Film* (London: A.S. Barnes, 1975): pp.97–122

Twitchell, J.B., *Dreadful Pleasures: An Anatomy of Modern Horror* (Oxford: Oxford University Press, 1985): pp.105–59

Zimmerman, B., 'Daughters of Darkness: The Lesbian Vampire on Film', in B.K. Grant, (ed.), *Planks of Reason: Essays on the Horror Film* (Scarecrow Press, 1984): pp.153–63

A decade of deadly dolls: Christine Holmlund

1. *Agnes of God* (Norman Jewison: 1985), which deals with infanticide, is one of the few exceptions. Throughout the film, a psychiatrist (Jane Fonda) struggles to understand whether and why Sister Agnes (Meg Tilly) killed her baby, but in the

final analysis the issue of infanticide is safely contained by being literally cloistered.

2. Similarly, although the heroine (Natasha Richardson) of the feminist dystopia *The Handmaid's Tale* stabs the right-wing Commander (Robert Duvall) who raped her, the end of the film finds her sitting tranquilly in a trailer awaiting the birth of her baby, while her new boyfriend (Aidan Quinn) leads the rebel freedom fighters back in Gilead.

3. Figures generally include first- and second-degree murder and voluntary and involuntary manslaughter, though not killing in the line of duty. Hollywood films do not draw the same distinctions. As the discussion below of *Blue Steel* shows, movies find women cops as disturbing as women murderers.

4. See the 1989 study by Angela Browne and Kirk Williams discussed in Walker, 1989: 62. Drawing on figures compiled by the FBI, the 1990 *Sourcebook of Criminal Justice Statistics* also documents a decrease in the percentage of women killing, from 16.6 per cent in 1976 to 12.0 per cent in 1989. (US Department of Justice, 1990: 384.)

5. Jones, 1980. Elizabeth Pleck's comparisons between selected English counties from 1202 to 1276 and the US in 1984 also reveal surprisingly little variation in the percentage of husband – wife murders committed by husbands: 66 per cent to 62 per cent. Pleck does find, however, that the number of women killing men increased substantially by comparison with the Victorian era. See Pleck, 1987: 224.

   Interestingly, the United States is not the country with the highest proportion of intra-family violence: a 1960 study placed Denmark in the lead worldwide, with two of every three murders intra-familial. A 1977 Canadian study put intra-familial murders committed between 1961 and 1974 at 39 per cent, while 1960 research in Africa observed ranges of from 22 to 63 per cent in intra-family homicide (Straus, Gelles and Steinmetz, 1980: 16).

6. Similarly, Goetting reports in 'Homicidal Wives' that the majority of the 56 Detroit, Michigan, women she studied were 'disadvantaged along multiple dimensions, and, in many ways, isolated from mainstream culture . . . They are drastically limited in the educational and occupational resources and in the social skills required to maintain a life of comfort and dignity. Almost all of these women are obese and in other ways unattractive and unhealthy by media standards' (Goetting, 1987: 339–40). See further Walker's detailed and highly readable case studies (Walker, 1989).

7. See Blackman, 1989: 1–13 and Walker, 1989 for further

discussion of the shifts in how battered women have been perceived and treated.

8. Only Jews have a significantly lower incidence of family violence. See Blackman, 1989: 108 and Straus, Gelles and Steinmetz, 1980: 136.

9. Flowers writes: '[Freda Adler's 1975 *Sisters in Crime*] contended that "the black female's criminality exceeds that of the white female by a much greater margin than black males over white males." The *National Study of Women's Correctional Programs* in fourteen states recently found that although black women made up 10% of the adult female population in those states, they accounted for half of those incarcerated' (Flowers, 1987: 76).

Walker suggests that black women are convicted nearly twice as often as whites because '[t]he "angry Black woman" is a common stereotype in many white minds' (Walker, 1989: 206). The numbers she provides from the first 100 battered women defences she worked on are shocking: although 33 per cent of the accused were non-Caucasian, only 25 per cent were found not guilty. Of the 21 per cent who were black, only 10 per cent were acquitted. And the 25 per cent of the women who were poor and had no job skills fared even worse: only 5 per cent were found not guilty.

10. See, for example, Foster, Veale and Fogel, 1989: 276; Goetting, 1987: 333, 330; Straus, Gelles and Steinmetz, 1980: 135, 148–50.

11. In 1989, 61,407 women were arrested for violent crime (murder, forcible rape, robbery and aggravated assault); 433,525 were arrested for property crimes (burglary, larceny-theft, motor vehicle theft, and arson). The overwhelming majority of arrests were for other, less serious offences. Proportional comparisons with men by category are also instructive:

Offence charged	Per cent Men Arrested	Per cent Women Arrested
Murder and non-negligent manslaughter	88.1%	11.9%
Forcible rape	98.8%	1.2%
Robbery	91.4%	8.6%
Aggravated assault	86.6%	13.4%
Burglary	91.3%	8.7%
Larceny-theft	69.6%	30.4%
Motor vehicle theft	89.8%	10.2%
Arson	86.4%	13.6%

See US Department of Justice, 1990: 422.

12. Flowers explains: 'Women . . . tend to lack protection because they are less likely to have a lawyer, a preliminary hearing, or a

jury trial. Additionally, women spend more time in correctional facilities that are stricter and less adequate than those for men' (Flowers, 1987: 84).

13. Flowers also argues that the women's movement has nothing to do with female criminality and conviction, citing a 1977 study by Darrell Steffensmeir which found little change in female arrest patterns over a twelve-year period, and a 1976 study by Laura Crites. See ibid.: 102.

14. *Film noir* was similarly premissed on heterosexuality. See, for example, Harvey and Place in Kaplan, 1980.

   The fact that women worked on over half of these films – Callie Khouri wrote *Thelma and Louise*; Sherry Lansing produced *Fatal Attraction*; Demi Moore produced *Mortal Thoughts*; Kathryn Bigelow directed *Blue Steel* – does not significantly affect how female characters are portrayed and treated. To argue otherwise would be to overlook the force of conventions on Hollywood productions and spectators, as well as to deny the fact that the majority of those working on all these films were men.

15. For further discussion of the threat of female exchange and lesbianism in *Fatal Attraction*, see Holmlund, 1989.

16. In effect, *Fatal Attraction*'s acceptance of male violence echoes conventions popularized in 1940s Gothics. Although 1940s films often showed women being mistreated by their husbands or boyfriends, they usually excused this mistreatment as female paranoia or cordoned it off in a marginal masculine underworld. Both strategies effectively protected heterosexuality as healthy and the nuclear family as normal.

17. These films perpetuate many of the popular misconceptions about rape Flowers mentions, including the following: the majority of rapes are triggered by women being out alone at night; rape is a victim-precipitated crime; only attractive young women are raped; rape is motivated by the need for sexual gratification; most rapes are perpetrated by strangers; and rape is an impulsive act. (See Flowers, 1987: 34–6).

   In his discussion of 1970s–1990s rape revenge films, Peter Lehman argues that rapists are portrayed as 'excessively repulsive' in order to allow heterosexual male spectators to dissociate themselves from the extreme violence these characters commit, and thereby enjoy the horrible punishments they receive: see Lehman, 1992. While Lehman's argument would seem to contradict mine, I do not think they are mutually exclusive. Those differences which exist stem in large part from our choice of texts, and to a lesser degree from my focus here on femininity and female spectators rather than

on masculinity and male spectators. The discussion, below, of
the erotic aura which surrounds the murders in *Aliens* and *Blue
Steel* owes much to Lehman's analysis.

18. Embarrassingly, the woman critic for the feminist tabloid *New
    Directions for Women* seemed to find all darker-skinned people
    interchangeable, for she described Vasquez as black. (See
    Prigozy, 1986: 6).
19. See, however, Holmlund, 1990: 92–4.
20. See Daws, 1991: 92: 'Pic can't decide whether it's about
    abusive relationships or . . . the boundaries of femme
    friendship (it's not very strong in that department) or crafty
    police techniques.'
21. See also Mars, 1988: 31; Vincenzi, 1988: 114.
22. *Ms.*'s Ari Korpivaara, for example, hailed Ripley as 'a role
    model for all of us humans' (Korpivaara, 1986: 14); and
    Newsweek's David Ansen praised her for 'her wonderfully
    human macho' (Ansen, 1986: 64). For a comprehensive
    survey of reactions to the *Fatal Attraction* characters, see
    Holmlund, 1991a.
23. Many, like Kathleen Murphy, also mentioned how much
    they enjoyed Davis's and Sarandon's acting: 'What moves
    Thelma and Louise, and anyone watching the film, is the
    power of personality, of larger than life actresses like Davis
    and Sarandon playing joyously with and to each other
    until character and relationship are alchemically altered . . .'
    (Murphy, 1991: 29). According to *Variety*, the core audience
    for *Thelma and Louise* was quite atypical of summer movie
    audiences: 55–60 per cent women, aged twenty-five and over,
    'upscale'. (See Thompson, 1991).
24. Greenberg similarly described Ripley and Vasquez as
    characters 'compounded out of . . . bellicose phallocentricity'
    (171) and spoke of the film's 'doubtful "feminism"' (165) and
    'Neanderthal Politics' (170). (See Greenberg, 1988).
25. Geena Davis concurred: 'Let's get real here for a second.
    Ninety-nine per cent of all other movies are about women
    either having shallow, one-dimensional caricature parts or
    they're being mutilated, skinned, slaughtered, abused and
    exploited with their clothes off. Even if this film did convey
    some horrible man-bashing message – "Let's us gals all get
    guns and kill all the men" – it couldn't even begin to make up
    for all the anti-woman movies people don't even talk about'
    (Jerome, 1991: 90).
26. Geena Davis asked pointedly: 'Why, because [*Thelma and
    Louise*] stars women, is this suddenly a feminist treatise, given
    the burden of representing all women?' (Schickel, 1991: 56).
    Khouri likewise insisted that *Thelma and Louise* 'is not about

feminists, it's about outlaws' (Jerome, 1991: 94); while Terence
Rafferty felt that the film was 'less a feminist parable than an
airy, lyrical joke about a couple of women who go off in search
of a little personal space' (Rafferty, 1991: 87).

A few argued that *Blue Steel*, too, was neither a feminist
diatribe nor a Dirty Harry rip-off, but, as Jude Schwendenwien
wrote, a film which 'operates from a difficult position of
wanting to challenge a patriarchal society that denies the
power of women . . . [in a] society . . . not ready to see a
female terrorizing males' (Schwendenwien, 1990: 51). See also
Bronski: 'By letting Jamie Lee Curtis join the forces of men
who get satisfaction and emotional release from firing a gun,
Bigelow is questioning why men were doing it to begin with'
(Bronski, 1990: 82).

27. See further Case, 1991 and Sheldon, 1984 on lethal lesbians.
Another common narrative device used by *Maedchen in
Uniform* (Leontine Sagan: 1931), *The Children's Hour* (William
Wyler: 1962) and, yes, *Thelma and Louise* as well, is to have
lesbian characters direct their deadliness against themselves.

28. These films include *Personal Best* (Robert Towne: 1982), *Entre
Nous* (Diane Kurys: 1983), *Lianna* (John Sayles: 1983) and
Desert Hearts (Donna Deitch: 1986). (See Holmlund, 1991b;
Straayer, 1990).

References
Ainslee, Peter, 'Mortal Thoughts', *Rolling Stone* 603 (2 May 1991): 48
Alleva, Richard, 'Lethal Smoochies', *Commonweal* 118 (12) (14 June
1991): 407
Ansen, David, 'Terminating the Aliens', *Newsweek* 108 (3) (21 July
1986): 64–5
Ansen, David, 'Female Bonding: The Long Hello', *Newsweek* 109
(16 February 1987): 72
Beaulieu, Janick, '*Fatal Attraction*', *Sequences* (January 1988): 75–6
Billson, Anne, 'Women Drivers', *New Statesman and Society* 4 (12
July 1991): 32
Blackman, Julie, *Intimate Violence* (New York: Columbia University
Press, 1989)
Bronski, Michael, '*Blue Steel*', *Zeta Magazine* 3 (5) (May 1990):
78–82
Carlson, Margaret, 'Is This What Feminism Is All About?', *Time* 137
(24 June 1991): 57
Case, Sue-Ellen, 'Tracking the Vampire', *differences* 3 (2) (Summer
1991): 1–21
Dargis, Manohla, 'Roads to Freedom', *Sight and Sound* 1 (3) (July
1991): 15–18
Daws, '*Mortal Thoughts*', *Variety* 343 (3) (29 April 1991): 92

de Lauretis, Teresa, 'Guerrilla in the Midst: Women's Cinema in the 80s', *Screen* 31 (1) (Spring 1990): 6–25

Denby, David, 'Widow's Pique', *New York* 20 (7) (16 February 1987): 72–3

Durbin, Karen, 'The Cat's Meow', *Village Voice* (15 December 1987): 90

Flowers, Ronald Barri, *Women and Criminality* (New York: Greenwood Press, 1987)

Foster, Lynne, Veale, Christine and Fogel, Catherine, 'Factors Present When Battered Women Kill', *Issues in Mental Health Nursing* 10 (1989): 273–84

Goetting, Ann, 'Homicidal Wives', *Journal of Family Issues* 8 (3) (September 1987): 332–41

Greenberg, Harvey R., 'Fembo: *Aliens*' Intentions', *Journal of Popular Film and Television* 15 (4) (1988): 164–71

Harvey, Sylvia, 'Women's Place: The Absent Family of Film Noir', in E. Ann Kaplan. (ed.), *Women in Film Noir* (London: British Film Institute, 1980): 22–34

Heung, Marina, '*Black Widow*', *Film Quarterly* 41 (1) (Fall 1987): 54–8

Holmlund, Christine, 'I Love Luce: The Lesbian, Mimesis, and Masquerade in Irigaray, Freud and Mainstream Film', *New Formations* 9 (Winter 1989): 105–24

Holmlund, Christine, 'New Cold War Sequels and Remakes', *Jump Cut* 35 (April 1990): 85–96

Holmlund, Christine, 'Reading Character with a Vengeance: The *Fatal Attraction* Phenomenon', *Velvet Light Trap* 27 (Spring 1991 [a]): 25–36

Holmlund, Christine, 'When Is a Lesbian Not a Lesbian? The Lesbian Continuum and the Mainstream Femme Film', *Camera Obscura* 25–6 (January/May 1991 [b]): 145–80

Jerome, Jim, 'Riding Shotgun', *People Weekly* 35 (24) (24 June 1991): 90–94

Jones, Ann, *Women Who Kill* (New York: Holt, Rinehart & Winston, 1980)

Kael, Pauline, 'Virgins, Vamps and Floozies', *New Yorker* 63 (1) (23 February 1987): 110–13

Kaplan, E. Ann, *Women in Film Noir* (London: British Film Institute, 1980)

Kauffmann, Stanley, 'Women in Pairs', *New Republic* 196 (9) (2 March 1987): 24–5

Korpivaara, Ari, 'Roll Over, Rambo', *Ms.* 15 (3) (September 1986): 14

Lehman, Peter, '"Don't Blame This on a Girl": Female Rape Revenge Films', Steven Cohan and Ina Rae Hark (eds) *Screening the Male* (London: Routledge, 1992)

Leo, John, 'Toxic Feminism on the Big Screen', *U.S. News & World Report* (10 June 1991): 20

McBride, Stephanie, 'The Female Gaze', *Spare Rib* 44 (March/April 1989): 19–21

Mars, Roslyn, 'The Mirror Cracked: The Career Woman in a Trio of Lansing Films', *Film Criticism* 12 (2) (1988): 31–2

Murphy, Kathleen, 'Only Angels Have Wings', *Film Comment* 27 (4) (July/August 1991): 26–9

Novak, Ralph, 'Picks & Pans', *People Weekly* 35 (15) (22 April 1991): 13–14

Place, Janey, 'Women in Film Noir', in E. Ann Kaplan (ed.) *Women in Film Noir* (London: British Film Institute, 1980) 35–67

Pleck, Elizabeth, *Domestic Tyranny* (New York: Oxford University Press, 1987)

Prigozy, Ruth, '*Aliens* Alienates . . . Disaster for Women', *New Directions for Women* 15 (6) (November 1986): 6

Rafferty, Terence, 'Outlaw Princesses', *New Yorker* 67 (15) (3 June 1991): 86–8

Rapping, Elayne, 'Blood and Guts Feminists Can Enjoy', *Guardian* 48 (12) (20 August 1986): 24

Sargent, Lydia, 'Kill the Bitch!', *Zeta Magazine* 1 (1) (January 1988): 33–4

Sawyer, Charles, '*Black Widow*', *Films in Review* 384 (April 1987): 226–7

Schickel, Richard, 'Help!' They're Back!', *Time* 128(4) (28 July 1986): 54–8

Schickel, Richard, 'Gender Bender', *Time* 137(25) (24 June 1991): 52–6

Schwendenwien, Jude, '*Blue Steel*', *Cineaste* 18 (1) (1990): 51

Shapiro, Laura, 'Women Who Kill Too Much', *Newsweek* 17 (24) (17 June 1991): 63

Sheldon, Caroline, 'Lesbians and Film: Some Thoughts', in Richard Dyer (ed.), *Gays and Film* (New York: Zoetrope, 1984): 5–26

Sibley, Adrian, '*Black Widow*', *Films and Filming* 394 (July 1987): 32–3

Straayer, Chris, 'The Hypothetical Lesbian Heroine: *Voyage en Douce, Entre Nous*', *Jump Cut* 35 (April 1990): 50–58

Straus, Murray, Gelles, Richard and Steinmetz, Suzanne, *Behind Closed Doors* (Garden City, NY: Anchor, 1980)

Taubin, Amy, 'Road Work', *Sight and Sound* 1 (3) (July 1991): 18–19

Thompson, Anne, 'Can *Thelma and Louise* Continue to Defy Gravity?', *Variety* 343 (10) (17 June 1991): 9–10

US Department of Justice, *Sourcebook of Criminal Justice Statistics* (Washington, DC: US Government Printing Office, 1990)

Van Gelder, Lindsy, 'Attack of the "Killer Lesbians"', *Ms.* 2 (4) (January/February 1992): 80–82

Vincenzi, Lisa, 'Stanley R. Jaffe and Sherry Lansing', *Millimeter* (January 1988): 114
Walker, Leonore, *Terrifying Love* (New York: Harper & Row, 1989)

Body talk: Melissa Benn

1. Susan Edwards, *Women on Trial* (Manchester: Manchester University Press, 1984).
2. Katherina Dalton, '*The Menstrual Cycle*, London: Penguin, 1989. For example, research by O'Brien, Selby and Symonds in the *British Medical Journal* (May 1980) found that sufferers from PMT did not suffer progesterone deficiency. Other studies are quoted by Susan Edwards in *Women on Trial*.
3. Court of Appeal hearing R.v. Smith (Criminal Division), 27 April 1982.
4. Susan Edwards, *Sunday Times*, 27 January 1985.
5. Sophie Laws, 'The Sexual Politics of Pre-Menstrual Tension', *Women's Studies International Forum*, Vol. 6, No.1. pp. 19–31, 1983.
6. Hilary Allen, 'At the Mercy of Her Hormones', m/f, no.9, 1984.
7. This account of the Christine English trial is based on press reports of the time. Shorthand notes of the judgement were not available.
8. Sue Lees, 'Naggers, Whores and Women's Libbers' in Diana Russell and J. Radford (eds), *Femicide: The Politics of Women Killing*, (Oxford: OUP, 1992).
9. Simone de Beauvoir, *The Second Sex*, (Penguin, 1976), p.354.
10. Anna Reynolds, *Tightrope* (London: Sidgwick & Jackson, 1991).
11. *Woman's Own*, 23 July 1988.
12. Transcript of the shorthand notes of Martin, Walsh, Cherer Ltd of Court of Appeal hearing on Regina v. Anna Louise Reynolds, Royal Courts of Justice, Friday 22 April 1988.
13. Emily Martin, *The Woman in the Body*, (Oxford: Oxford University Press, 1989). In her chapter on PMT, 'Work, Discipline and Anger', Martin offers a convincing materialist and psychological account of PMT.

Pleading for time: Lorraine Radford

1. Section 1 Homicide Act 1957; R v. Maloney (1985) 1 *All England Law Reports* (*All ER*) 1025 HL; R v. Hancock and Shankland (1986) 1 *All ER* 641 HL; R v. Nedrick (1986) 3 *All ER* 1 CA.
2. Section 3 Homicide Act 1957; DPP v. Camplin (1978) 2 *All ER* 168 HL.
3. Section 2 Homicide Act 1957.
4. Section 4 Homicide Act 1957.

5. There are other exceptions to murder that are not relevant to the present discussion, as they are covered by the category 'involuntary manslaughter'. For further information on the law of homicide, see J. Smith and B. Hogan, *Criminal Law: Cases and Materials* (14th edn) (London: Butterworths, 1990).

6. Beckford v. R (1987) 3 *All ER* 425.

7. Smith and Hogan, *Criminal Law*.

8. ibid.

9. R v. Duffy (1949) 1 *All ER* 932.

10. ibid.

11. Victim precipitation, a term often employed by psychologists, basically means that the victim's actions trigger the aggressor's violent response.

12. In 1985, Nicholas Boyce strangled his pregnant wife, then dissected her corpse into over one hundred pieces which he placed in dustbin bags and disposed of in various parts of London. Boyce's defence to murder rested on the claim that he had been provoked into the crime by his wife's nagging him to get a job. Mrs Boyce, a social worker, had supported her husband for the past five years whilst he worked to finish a Ph.D thesis at the University of London. She feared that she might be unable to continue supporting him after the birth of their child. On searching Boyce's home the police found a text on crime and punishment with the key defences to murder charges underlined. The jury accepted Boyce's argument about the provocation, found him guilty of the lesser charge of manslaughter, and he was sentenced to four years' imprisonment. If we compare this case and the killing of Julie Stead, with Kiranjit's and Mrs Duffy's it is hard not to conclude that women are dealt with more harshly as victims and as offenders, whilst wife-killers are treated with relative leniency

13. R v. Duffy (1949).

14. R v. Ibrams and Gregory (1981) 74 *Cr. App. Rep* 154 CA.

15. Sandra McNeill, 'Change the Law', *Trouble & Strife*, no. 22, 1992, pp. 7–12.

16. Susan Edwards, *Women On Trial* (Manchester: Manchester University Press, 1984); *Policing Domestic Violence* (London: Sage, 1989).

17. Lee Ann Hoff, *Battered Women As Survivors* (London: Routledge, 1990).

18. For a thorough discussion of the life histories of battered women who kill, see Angela Browne, *When Battered Women Kill* (New York: Free Press, 1987).

19. Val Binney, Gina Harkell and Judy Nixon, *Leaving Violent Men* (Bristol: Women's Aid Federation, 1981); Jan Pahl (ed.),

Private Violence and Public Policy (London: Routledge & Kegan Paul, 1985).

20. ibid.
21. Angela Browne, *When Battered Women Kill*.
22. Marjorie Homer, D. Leonard and J. Taylor, *Private Violence: Public Shame* (Cleveland: Cleveland Refuge and Aid for Women and Children, 1984).
23. Jackie Barron, *Not Worth the Paper* (Bristol: Women's Aid Federation, 1990); Alan Bourlet, *Police Intervention into Marital Violence* (Milton Keynes: Open University Press (1990); Susan Edwards, *Women on Trial*; Amina Mama, *The Hidden Struggle* (London: London Race and Housing Research Unit, 1990); Kathryn McCann, 'Battered Women and the Law: The Limits of the Legislation', in Julia Brophy and Carol Smart (eds), *Women in Law* (London: Routledge & Kegan Paul, 1985); Jill Radford, Jalna Hanmer and Elizabeth Stanko, *International Perspectives on Women and Policing* (London: Routledge, 1990).
24. Pat Carlen, *Women's Imprisonment* (London: Routledge & Kegan Paul, 1983); R. Dobash and R. Dobash, *Women in Prison* (London: Routledge & Kegan Paul, 1988).
25. Ann Jones, *Women Who Kill* (London: Victor Gollancz, 1991); Angela Browne, *When Battered Women Kill* (London: Free Press/Macmillan, 1987); R. Dobash and R. Dobash, *Violence Against Wives* (Sussex: Open Books, 1980); Coramae Richey Mann, 'Black Female Homicide in the US', *Journal of Interpersonal Violence* vol. 15, No. 2, 1990.
26. Sandra McNeill, 'Change the Law'.
27. Martin Daly and Margo Wilson, *Homicide* (New York: Aldane de Gruyter, 1988).
28. R v. Davies (1975) 1 *All ER* 890; Val Binney, Gina Harkell and Judy Nixon, *Leaving Violent Men*.
29. Jill Radford, 'Womanslaughter and the Criminal Law', *Feminist Review*, Summer 1982.
30. Hansard Written Answer 361 to John Patten, 19 October 1991, Home Office, 'Domestic Homicide Statistics'.
31. *Criminal Statistics 1989* (London: HMSO).
32. *England and Wales: Prison Statistics 1990* (London: HMSO).
33. *Criminal Statistics 1989*.
34. Hansard Written Answer 361.
35. John Carvel, *Guardian*, 11 November 1991.
36. The ranges were 11 manslaughter findings out of 18 murder and manslaughter charges for women in 1987 to 14 manslaughter findings out of 15 murder and manslaughter trials in 1986; for men, 47 manslaughter findings out of 93 murder and manslaughter trials in 1985.
37. Hansard Written Answer 361.

38. Susan Edwards, *Women On Trial*; Sandra McNeill, 'Change the Law'.
39. Hansard Written Answer 361.
40. ibid.
41. Ann Jones, *Women Who Kill*.
42. ibid.
43. Angela Browne, *When Battered Women Kill*.
44. L. Walker, *The Battered Woman* (New York: Springer, 1985).
45. Vermont v. Grace (1992) Independent Television, April.
46. See Ginny McCarthy, *Talking It Out: A Guide to Groups for Abused Women* (Seattle, WA: Seal Press, 1984).
47. E. Pizzey and J. Shapiro, *Prone to Violence* (Feltham: Hamlyn, 1982).
48. L. Walker, *The Battered Woman*.
49. This point is also made by Rebecca Emerson-Dobash and Russell Dobash, *Women, Violence and Social Change* (London: Routledge, 1992).
50. Ann Jones, *Women Who Kill*.
51. Joyce Johnson, *What Lisa Knew* (London: Bloomsbury, 1991).
52. R v. Davies (1975) 1 *All ER* 890.
53. See Smith and Hogan, *Criminal Law*.
54. Rights of Women, *Submission to the Royal Commission on Criminal Justice* (Rights of Women: London, 1991).
55. Anne Worrall, *Offending Women* (London: Routledge, 1991).
56. Lorraine Radford, 'Legal-ising Woman Abuse' in M. Maynard and J. Hanmer (eds), *Women, Violence and Social Control* (London: Macmillan, 1987).
57. *England and Wales: Prison Statistics 1990*.

Rocking the cradle: Allison Morris and Ania Wilczynski

1. Some of the material used in this chapter is drawn from Wilczynski (1989, 1991a).
2. The nanny secretly breastfeeds the new baby so that he rejects his mother's milk, becomes the older daughter's protector, friend and confidante, and makes superb chocolate soufflés for dinner while at the same time systematically undermining the mother's confidence and competence.
3. Patriarchy has two main elements: structural and ideological. By structural, we mean those social institutions which shape and maintain women's sudordination to men; by ideological, we mean those processes which ensure women's acceptance of that subordination.

4. Pat Mayhew and her colleagues (1989) found this in the British Crime Survey.
5. For an account see *Guardian*, 29 February 1992; *Daily Mirror*, 29 February, 2 March 1992.
6. The Statistical Branch of the Home Office prepared for us a special analysis of the information currently published under the guise of 'parents'. We are grateful to Chris Lewis and William Burns for this.
7. See the Domestic Homicide Statistics released by the Home Office on 17 October 1991.
8. In 1986 Ann Jones published an article based on several case histories of mothers who had killed their children. All were serving prison sentences despite histories of abuse, socioeconomic deprivation and a lack of social support. Jones questions the value of imprisoning them on the grounds that they were not a danger to anyone but themselves, their imprisonment was unlikely to deter others, and such women rarely reoffend.
9. Homicide Act 1957, s.2.
10. Infanticide Act 1938, s.1.
11. See, for example, Otto Pollak (1950), Nigel Walker (1965), Herbert Mannheim (1965).
12. See generally, for example, Susan Edwards (1984, 1986), Ann Worrall (1981) and Pat Carlen (1983).
13. For a discussion, see Platz and Kendell (1988); Meltzer and Kumar (1985).
14. See d'Orban (1979), Cheung (1986) and Lansdowne (1990) respectively.
15. See d'Orban (1979); Cheung (1986).
16. For more information, see Wilczynski (1991b).
17. Cited in (1989) 11 *Criminal Appeal Reports (Sentencing)* 532 at 534; emphasis added.
18. R. v. Scott (1973) *Criminal Law Review* 708.
19. *The Times*, 9 January 1988.
20. The information on this case is taken from Yvonne Roberts (1989).
21. R v. Poole and Scott (1990) *Criminal Law Review* 67.
22. *Guardian*, 23 January 1992.
23. Psychiatric dispositions are not always 'lenient'. Occasionally restriction orders are attached to hospital orders; this usually occurs when the judge believes that the offender is likely to commit further offences. A restriction order means detention in a psychiatric hospital without limit of time, and release must be approved by the Home Secretary, as in the case of life imprisonment. See, for example, the case of Leonora Taylor referred to in the *Guardian*, 25 March 1992.

References

Allen, H., *Justice Unbalanced* (Oxford: Open University Press, 1987)

Carlen, P., *Women's Imprisonment: A Study in Social Control* (London: Routledge & Kegan Paul, 1983)

Cheung, P.T.K., 'Maternal Filicide in Hong Kong, 1971–1985', *Medicine, Science, and the Law*, 26 (3,) (1986): 185–92

D'Orban, P.T., 'Women Who Kill Their Children', *British Journal of Psychiatry* 134 (1979): 560–71

Edwards, S., *Women on Trial* (Manchester: Manchester University Press, 1984

Edwards, S., 'Neither Mad Nor Bad: The Female Violent Offender Reassessed', *Women's Studies International Forum* (9) 1 (1986): 79–87

Home Office, *Criminal Statistics England and Wales 1989* (London: HMSO, 1990)

Home Office, *Domestic Homicide Statistics*, News Release, 17 October (London: Home Office, 1991)

Jones, A., *Women Who Kill* (New York: Fawcett Columbine, 1981)

Jones, A., 'Mothers Who Kill', *Newsday*, 19 October 1986

Kumar, R., *'General Overview – What is Postnatal Mental Illness?* Paper presented at the Post-Natal Depression conference 'More than Just the Blues for One in Ten', Royal College of Obstetricians and Gynaecologists, London, 28 February 1989

Lansdowne, R., 'Infanticide: Psychiatrists and the Plea-Bargaining Process', *Monash University Law Review* 16 (1) (1990): 41–63

Mannheim, H., *Comparative Criminology* (London: Routledge & Kegan Paul, 1965)

Mayhew, P., Elliott, D. and Dowds, L., *The 1988 British Crime Survey*, Home Office Research Study 111 (London: HMSO, 1989)

Meltzer, E.S. and Kumar, R., 'Puerperal Mental Illness, Clinical Features and Classification: A Study of 142 Mother-and-Baby Admissions', *British Journal of Psychiatry* 147 (1985): 647–54

Oakley, A., *From Here to Maternity: Becoming a Mother* (Harmondsworth: Penguin, 1986)

O'Donovan, K., 'The Medicalisation of Infanticide', *Criminal Law Review* no.5 (1984): 259–64

Pearson, R., 'Women Defendants in Magistrates' Courts', *British Journal of Law and Society* 3, (1976): 265–73

Phillips, A., 'The Abuse That Paralyses', *Guardian*, 28 January 1992

Platz, C. and Kendell, R.E., 'A Matched-Control Follow-up and Family Study of "Puerperal Psychoses"', *British Journal of Psychiatry* 153 (1988): 90–94

Pollak, O., *The Criminality of Women* (Philadelphia: University of Pennsylvania Press, 1950)

Roberts, Y., 'A Bad Mother', *New Statesman and Society*, 23 March 1989: 10–11

Scutt, J., 'Sexism in Criminal Law', in S. Mukherjee, and J. Scutt, (eds) *Women and Crime* (Sydney: Institute of Criminology/George Allen & Unwin, 1981)

Walker, N., *Crime and Punishment in Britain* (Edinburgh: Edinburgh University Press, 1965)

Wilczynski, A., 'Women Who Kill Their Infants: Debunking the Myth of the "Mad" and the "Bad" Offender'. Thesis submitted for the M.Phil. in Criminology, Institute of Criminology, University of Cambridge, June 1989

Wilczynski, A., 'Images of Women Who Kill Their Infants: The Mad and the Bad', *Women and Criminal Justice* 2 (1991[a]): 71–88

Wilczynski, A., 'Neonaticide'. Paper presented at 'Perspectives on Female Violence: A Multidisciplinary National Conference', St George's Hospital Medical School, London, 7–8 March 1991[b]

Worrall, A. 'Out of Place: Female Offenders in Court', *Probation Journal* 28 (3) (1981): 90–93

'Angels of death': Bettina Heidkamp

1. This list of other cases is probably incomplete, as it is assumed that most hospital killings remain undetected. Others are: In 1987 a male nurse in Cincinnati confessed to killing twenty-four patients through cyanide, oxygen injections and suffocating. He received three life sentences. In 1989 Michaela Roeder, a West German graduate nurse, charged with killing seventeen patients in intensive care by means of deadly injections, was convicted of manslaughter in five cases and sentenced to eleven years' imprisonment.

2. Kurt Langbein and Paul Yvon, *Profil* no. 9, 25 February 1991, p. 91.

3. Langbein, *Profil* no. 9, p. 93.

4. *Der Spiegel* no. 16, 1989, p. 175.

5. *Guardian*, 12 April 1989.

6. Gisela Friedrichsen, *Der Spiegel* no. 11, 1991, p. 206.

7. *Die Presse*, 10 April 1989.

8. *Kronenzeitung* 25 April 1989.

9. Tessa Prager, *Die Zeit* no. 12, 15 March 1991.

10. Leopold Rosenmayr in *Profil* no. 13, 25 March 1991, p. 80; and *Salzburger Nachrichten*, 19 February 1991. According to Rosenmayr, there are organizational problems in the Austrian health system. He criticizes the tendency to establish large projects instead of small-scale solutions. There are not enough specially trained staff; he would like to see concepts which link institutional care with care at home ('partly institutional care').

11. Gisela Friedrichsen, *Der Spiegel* no. 11, p. 208.

12. Report of the International Commission, Vienna, June 1989, pp. 21–7; and *Wochenpresse* no. 10, 7 March 1991. The staff shortage in nursing in Austria is severe in terms of international standards. This fact is being attributed to circumstances which have not changed since the 1970s (according to studies): unfavourable working conditions, few possibilities for further qualification, slim chances for career advancement, inadequate employment, low image of nursing profession, curriculum not up to date, no supervision, inadequate pay and high number of working hours. The report goes on to say that there is not enough co-operation between nurses and doctors, and hardly any part-time nursing. It calls for a more efficient health system, particularly the participation of more staff members at all levels of decision-making and the improvement of training.
13. Paul Yvon, *Profil* no. 12, 18 March 1991, p. 75.
14. Friedrichsen, *Der Spiegel* no. 11, p. 211.
15. Yvon, *Profil* no. 12, p. 74.
16. Gisela Friedrichsen, *Der Spiegel* no. 14, 1991, p. 191.
17. Langbein and Yvon, *Profil* no. 7, 11 February, 1991, p. 64.
18. ibid., p. 66.
19. ibid., p. 65.
20. *Salzburger Nachrichten*, 5 March 1991.
21. ibid., 6 March 1991.
22. *Profil* no. 12, pp. 74, 75: former ward sister Helene Speiser in court: 'The nurses entered time and origin of death in the death register . . . It did happen that the doctors arrived only hours after somebody had died during the night.' Another nurse from Pavilion V: 'During the day the doctor was called immediately if somebody had died. But sometimes he came later. And I have heard that during the night he often came at 5 o'clock in the morning even though the patient had died hours before.' *Profil* no. 8, p. 75: Wagner said that in cases where the doctors expected a death they merely shone a torch in the eyes of the dead person to confirm it.
23. *Der Standard*, 10 March 1991.
24. Langbein and Yvon, *Profil* no. 7, p. 65.
25. Langbein and Yvon, *Profil* no. 8, 18 February 1991, p. 75.
26. *Der Standard*, 7 March 1991.
27. *Die Presse*, 22 March 1991.
28. ibid.
29. Yvon, *Profil* no. 11, 14 February 1991, p. 74.
30. Langbein, *Profil* no. 9, p. 90.
31. Langbein and Yvon, *Profil* no. 9, p. 91.
32. Yvon, *Profil* no. 13, 25 March 1991, p. 81.
33. Yvon, *Profil* no. 10, 4 March 1991

34. Report of the International Commission, p. 3.
35. Peter Herschbach, 'Eine Untersuchung zur psychischen Belastung von Krankenschwestern und Krankenpflegern', *Deutsche Krankenpflege-Zeitschrift* no.6, 1991, pp. 434–8 (p. 438).
36. Heidrun Hirsch and Jürgen Zander, 'Belastungen in der Krankenpflege (2.Teil)', *Die Schwester, Der Pfleger* no.5, 1991, pp. 446–50 (p. 447).
37. Erich Grond, 'Aggressionen des Pflegepersonals gegenüber den Alten. (Teil 2)', *Altenpflege*, no.8, 1991, pp. 467–8 (p. 468).
38. ibid., p. 471.
39. Report of the International Commission: Supplement by Renate Reimann and Leopold Rosenmayr, 'Die Betreuungssituation alter Menschen', p. 7.
40. Rosenmayr, in *Salzburger Nachrichten*, 19 March 1991.
41. Claudia Bischoff, *Frauen in der Krankenpflege. Zur Entwicklung von Frauenrolle und Frauenberufstätigkeit im 19. und 20. Jhd.* (Frankfurt/Main/New York 1984), pp. 66 ff.
42. ibid., p. 78.
43. ibid., p. 83.
44. ibid., pp. 89 ff.
45. *Profil* no. 12, p. 75.
46. *Salzburger Nachrichten*, 19 March 1991.
47. *Die Presse*, 28 February 1991; and in Friedrichsen, *Der Spiegel* no. 11, p. 212.
48. Yvon, *Profil* no. 10, 4 March 1991, p. 77.
49. *Die Presse*, 2–3 March 1991.
50. *Süddeutsche Zeitung*, 28 February 1991.
51. *Der Standard*, 1 March 1991; *Salzburger Nachrichten*, 27 March 1991.
52. *Guardian*, 16 April 1989.
53. *Salzburger Nachrichten*, 19 March 1991.
54. Yvon, *Profil* no. 13, p. 82.
55. Yvon, *Profil* no. 14, p. 68.

The female serial killer: Candice Skrapec

1. A recent *Vanity Fair* (Karen Durbin, June 1992) article observes that there has been a spate of recent movies in which a female character murders one or more people. Many of these so-called 'psychofemmes' are aberrations held to be suffering from some pronounced psychiatric disorder (*history*, anyone?), and seen as dangerously plausible. While some of the screenplays are based on true-life incidents, most are fiction and cater to popular notions of women who kill. (See Holmlund above.)
2. A notable exception has recently been reported by Margo

Wilson and Martin Daly, 1992, 'Who Kills Whom in Spouse
Killings? On the Exceptional Sex Ratio of Spousal Homicides
in the United States', *Criminology*, 30 (2), 1992, pp. 189–215.
They found that in contrast with women in other nations
(including Canada, Great Britain and Australia), women in the
United States commit a larger proportion of spousal homicides.
Their data showed that women kill their husbands almost
as often as husbands kill their wives. American women do
not, however, perpetrate a disproportionately higher number
of non-spousal murders. A large proportion of the spousal
killings committed by wives are acts of self-defence, unlike
those perpetrated by husbands. According to Wilson and Daly,
males tend to adopt a 'proprietariness about their wives of a
quality and vehemence rarely seen in women' (p. 207). This
point speaks to the role of entitlement that may underlie much
of the violence against women by men. It certainly suggests
objectification of women by men.

3. This quotation appears in investigative reporter Michael
Reynolds' book on the Wournos case, *Dead Ends* (New York:
Warner Books, Inc., 1992), p. 238.
4. Eric W. Hickey, *Serial Murderers and Their Victims* (Pacific
Grove. CA: Brooks/Cole, 1991).
5. Alice Miller, *For Your Own Good: Hidden Cruelty in Child-
Rearing and the Roots of Violence* (transl. H. and H. Hannum),
(New York: Farrar, Straus & Giroux, 1983).
6. Donald J. Sears, *To Kill Again: The Motivation and Development
of Serial Murder* (Wilmington, DE: Scholarly Resources
Books, 1991).
7. Steven A. Egger, *Serial Murder: An Elusive Phenomenon* (New
York: Praeger, 1990).
8. Spree killings should be mentioned and distinguished here for
purposes of clarification. The spree killer murders a number
of people within a time-limited interval. The period of the
killings is generally not sustained over time, often a few hours
or days. This chapter will consider spree murderers as serial
killers.
9. Deborah Cameron and Frazer, Elizabeth, *The Lust to Kill:
A Feminist Investigation of Sexual Murder*. (New York: New
York University Press, 1987). Cameron and Frazer examine
sexual murder from a feminist perspective. They argue that
some men derive erotic pleasure from the act of killing, while
women virtually never do. They explain this as a function of
a patriarchal culture which institutionalizes violence against
women and expresses itself in terms of a continuum of
behaviour, from stealing underwear, to rape, to its ultimate
expression as sexual murder. The perpetrators of these crimes,

Cameron and Frazer maintain, are virtually always males, seeking to dominate and humiliate their victims. The reality, however, is that women have been identified as experiencing the same kind of lust to kill. The Cameron and Frazer argument is, I believe, an important one. It falls, however – not on its own merits – but in its failure to recognize what can be called a lust to kill, including sexual murder, on the part of females.

10. ibid., p. 24.
11. Tom Kuncl and Paul Einstein, *Ladies Who Kill* (New York: Pinnacle, 1985).
12. ibid., p. 18.
13. ibid., p. 20.
14. R.E.L. Masters and Eduard Lea. *Perverse Crimes in History: Evolving Concepts of Sadism, Lust-Murder, and Necrophilia – from Ancient to Modern Times* (New York: The Julian Press, 1963), p. 9.
15. The marriage between Charlene Williams and Gerald Gallego was apparently illegal, as he had not divorced his fifth wife.
16. Eric Van Hoffmann, *A Venom in the Blood* (New York: Kensington Publishing Corp., 1990).
17. Recent research on sexual fantasies has suggested that women are as inclined to engage in perverse fantasies as are men (e.g., Louise Kaplan, *Female Perversions* [New York: Doubleday, 1991]). This is important to the present discussion in so far as sexual fantasies have a germinal role in the development and expression of sexual behaviour.
18. The cases of William Palmer and George Smith are illustrative of 'black widower' murders. Palmer, in fact, has come to be known as the 'Prince of Poisoners'. He may have been the first serial poisoner to use strychnine. Although he was hanged for killing a male friend for money in 1855, the English physician is suspected of having murdered fifteen others. Among his victims were a wife and her relatives, and his own legitimate and illegitimate children. He apparently killed for money, often to settle his gambling debts, or for the convenience of getting someone out of the way. George Smith profited by his bigamous marriages to three women whom he drowned over a three-year period from 1912. The Englishman proved a skilful womanizer, very adept at the con. He 'married' other women, whom he did not kill, but whom he abandoned after they served his purposes.
19. L.C. Douthwaite, *Mass Murder* (New York: Holt, 1929).
20. Velma Barfield, *Woman on Death Row* (Minneapolis, MN: World View Publications, 1985).

21. Ferdinand Protzman, 'Killing of 49 patients by 4 nurses stuns the Austrians', *New York Times*, 18 April 1989.
22. This is not to say that women do not experience power through sex. For some women, a woman-as-seductress role may provide a sense of empowerment derived from their ability to secure the attention and compliance of a potential partner. For other women, to deny sex might be similarly experienced as a way of feeling powerful. Women seem generally not to be socialized, however, in such a way that they experience power directly through the sex act itself.
23. Gwynn Nettler, *Killing One Another* (Cincinnati, OH: Anderson Publishing Co., 1983), p. 20.
24. Dolores Kennedy, *On a Killing Day* (Chicago: Bonus Books, 1992).

Notes on contributors

MELISSA BENN is a writer and journalist based in London. Some of her previous essays have appeared in *Feminist Review, Women: a cultural review*, and *Storia*.

HELEN BIRCH is a former literary editor and editor of *City Limits* magazine and currently works as a freelance journalist, writer and editor for many different publications, including the *Guardian, Independent* and *New Statesman & Society*.

BETTINA HEIDKAMP lives in Berlin and is currently completing a master's degree in Modern History, English and Media Studies. She contributed to a book, *German Reunification and Irish Partition* (1991) and has written articles for the *Guardian, Der Tagespiegel, Die Tagezeitung* and *Fortnight Magazine*.

CHRISTINE HOLMLUND is assistant professor of French at the University of Tennessee, where she teaches regularly in the Cinema Studies and Women's Studies programmes. She has written several articles on lesbian and feminist theory and French and Hollywood film. The most recent of these, 'Masculinity as Multiple Masquerade: "Mature" Stallone and the Stallone Clone', is published in *Screening the Male*, edited by Steven Cohan and Ina Rae Hark (Routledge 1992).

NICOLE WARD JOUVE is Professor of English and Related Literature at the University of York. She is author of *Baudelaire: A Fire to Conquer Darkness* (1980), *Shades of Grey* (1981), *The Street-Cleaner: The Yorkshire Ripper Case on Trial* (1986), *Colette* (1987) and *White Woman Speaks With Forked Tongue* (1991).

ALLISON MORRIS is a lecturer in Criminology at the Institute of Criminology, Cambridge. She is co-editor of *Women and Crime* (1981), *Women and the Penal System* (1988), *Feminist Perspectives in Criminology* (1990) and author of *Women, Crime and Criminal Justice*

(1987). Her current research interest is female prison officers' experience of men's prisons.

LORRAINE RADFORD is Senior Lecturer in Social Administration and Women's Studies at the Roehampton Institute in London. She is an experienced researcher of the law, social policy and violence against women and has published a number of articles in this area. She has been an active member of a women's refuge support group for the past twelve years.

CANDICE SKRAPEC is a Canadian psychologist who has researched serial murder since 1984, when she moved to New York City. She lectures at John Jay College of Criminal Justice, New York and has worked extensively with police departments in Canada and the United States, where she is consulted by journalists, authors and police forces about specific cases, as well as on the subject of serial murder more generally.

DEB VERHOEVEN is a lecturer in film at the Victoria College of the Arts, in the Film and TV School, and a broadcaster on Australian community radio. She is currently researching the representation of sheep in Australian cinema, and is a regular contributor to the blood bank.

ANIA WILCZYNSKI is a graduate in arts and law from the University of New South Wales, Australia and in criminology from the Institute of Criminology, Cambridge. She is currently completing a PhD in Criminology at Cambridge on parents who kill their children and has presented conference papers and published in the journal *Women and Criminal Justice* on that subject.

BRIAR WOOD was born in New Zealand. She is a lecturer in New Literatures at the University of North London and a poet. She was poetry editor of *City Limits* magazine and her poems have been published in *New Women Poets* (Bloodaxe, 1990).

INDEX